Lycidas and the Italian Critics

LYCIDAS

AND THE ITALIAN CRITICS

Clay Hunt

with a preface by Irene Samuel

New Haven and London   Yale University Press

1979

Designed by John O. C. McCrillis
and set in IBM Press Roman type.
Printed in the United States of America by
Vail-Ballou Press, Inc., Binghamton, N.Y.

Published in Great Britain, Europe, Africa, and
Asia (except Japan) by Yale University Press,
Ltd., London. Distributed in Australia and
New Zealand by Book & Film Services, Artarmon,
N.S.W., Australia; and in Japan by Harper & Row,
Publishers, Tokyo Office.

Library of Congress Cataloging in Publication Data

Hunt, Clay.
  Lycidas and the Italian critics.

  Includes bibliographical references and index.
  1. Milton, John, 1608–1674. Lycidas. I. Title.
PR3558.H8   821'.4   78-15344
ISBN 0-300-02269-7

Contents

Preface

After the comprehensive work by A. S. P. Woodhouse and Douglas Bush in *A Variorum Commentary on the Poems of John Milton* it seemed unlikely, almost impossible, that anyone could suggest a new way of regarding *Lycidas,* much less provide a fresh and compelling reading of the poem. Yet that is what Clay Hunt has achieved in *"Lycidas" and the Italian Critics.* Following the clues of Milton's avowed agreement with the rhetorical theory of stylistic levels and with the Renaissance enthusiasm for defining poetic genres at least partly in terms of their appropriate level of style, Hunt finds in *Lycidas* a new poetic form, evolved from the fusion of pastoral and high lyric. For while Milton clearly marked his poem as a pastoral through his many echoes of earlier poetry in that kind, he just as clearly marked it as considerably more.

Hunt discovers in the Italian critics, especially those of the cinquecento, a wealth of material with unmistakable bearing on Milton's poem. Step by step he takes us to the conviction that Milton intentionally refashioned the pastoral genre to produce effects traditionally associated with epic and tragedy. From a survey of the theory and practice of pastoral—Greco-Sicilian, Roman, and Renaissance—Hunt turns to the theory and practice of the canzone elaborated by Dante, Minturno, and Tasso. And here he uncovers a major development as the Italian vernacular tradition merged with the characteristic Renaissance attempt at reviving classical models to produce a new literary kind: from the native Italian canzone assimilated to the Pindaric ode—as well as to what were taken to be lyrical poems interspersed in the Old Testament—the "high lyric" emerged with its own decorum of matter and style.

By the time Hunt offers his definition of the form of *Lycidas* he has led us to see with refreshed vision features of the poem that we had no doubt in some sense always known to be there but had missed the broad significance of. He has also led us to understand something of the liveliness and precision with which cinquecento critics tackled their favored questions about poetry, not least by his own liveliness and precision in rehearsing their arguments. Their favored questions were unlike those of critics in our time, and therefore need all the more to be recalled to our attention if we aim to comprehend the literature of the era. Out of his expert knowledge of Italian critical thought, and not only on poetry but on music as well, Clay Hunt has provided us with the materials that establish the context in which Milton's intentions in *Lycidas* grew. No one who rereads the poem with Hunt's guidance is likely to put aside a major author's purposes as irrelevant to the major work he produced, whoever may belabor us with cries about the intentional fallacy. In short, Clay Hunt's quest for the genre of *Lycidas* leads him to a far-ranging historico-critical investigation that sheds light not on one poem alone but on the continuities and discontinuities of literary history and on the procedures and assumptions of literary theorists.

Starting from the marked tonal shifts that the poet himself called attention to in *Lycidas,* the "higher mood" of Apollo's speech on fame and the "dread voice" of St. Peter on the corrupt clergy, Hunt determines that the poem could not have been intended simply as a pastoral elegy on the model of classical eclogues; for while antiquity developed no theory of pastoral, its practice warranted attributing to the genre the decorum of the humble style. True, pastoral had evolved considerably by the time it reached Milton from its Greek Sicilian antecedents and its Latin developments: Sannazarro's *Arcadia* had notably raised the genre from the humble level theorists had assigned it, and Tasso's *Aminta* had further enlarged its stylistic reach. But *Arcadia, Aminta,* and the works they gave rise to were in the narrative and dramatic genres, not the lyrical, so that we must look elsewhere to find the precedents for *Lycidas.*

Hunt turns to the theory of the lyric as it evolved out of Horace's casual assignment in his *Ars Poetica* of various subject matters to various forms. Dante's *De Vulgari Eloquentia* proves a landmark with its definition of poetry as "a metrical composition set to music" and its concern to make Tuscan a language worthy of a poetry that would meet classical standards. For Dante in working out his conception of the canzone explained its structure as determined by an imagined musical setting with a mixture of two contrasting melodies, and assigned to it a division into stanzas in a pattern of irregular rhymes—recognizable features of Milton's *Lycidas.* Minturno, taking off from

Dante's discussion and practice, equated the canzone with the Pindaric ode, and in his concern to allow the vernacular form a wide range of new possibilities, argued for variety in its subjects, with digressions to give it a heroic tone, and even assigned it a heroic matter—again recognizable features of *Lycidas*. Tasso, in turn, whose critical thought was of great importance to Milton, propounded in his *Discorsi* a theory of the high lyric, its appropriate subjects and style, that, while placing it chiefly at the level of the middle or graceful, allowed it to borrow attributes of the heroic or *magnifico*. And in *La Cavaletta*, questioning parts of Dante's prescription for the canzone, Tasso arrived at a notion of the tragic as a mode that may be found not only in tragedy and epic but in the lyric as well. The canzone as a high lyrical form thus comes to be seen as rightly having its share in the highest poetic matter and the most magnificent stylistic effects. And again we recognize critical pronouncements that have large bearing on *Lycidas*.

In Hunt's exposition of the thought of Dante and Minturno on the canzone and of Tasso on the high lyric, we observe time after time how their ways of thinking about poetry bear points of relation with Milton's whole poetic habit. And similarly when Hunt expounds the theory of the cinquecento musical humanists to account for the sense of a musical accompaniment that *Lycidas* evokes we again recognize not only important aspects of Milton's poem but ways of thinking about the relations of poetry and music remarkably close to Milton's. As Hunt traces the varying tonal effects both explicit and implicit in *Lycidas* he provides an analysis that warrants his calling it a transmutation of eclogue into the grand lyric, in the free style of the canzone stanza, its norm the middle style but with digressions in the manner of the Pindaric ode, reaching to the level of heroic-tragic magnificence, constructed according to a continuous musical pattern, designed to produce a harmonized state of mind by a purging of pity and fear comparable to the effect of tragedy, and properly subtitled a monody. —Every phrase in that description summarizes reaches of exploration and discovery that the bald summary phrases inevitably belie.

Clay Hunt died on December 1, 1977, shortly after submitting the manuscript of *"Lycidas" and the Italian Critics* to the Yale University

Press. The publishing agreement was therefore worked out with the consent of his heirs and with the cooperation of his colleagues at Williams College, particulary John F. Reichert, the chairman of the English department there. Having read the manuscript for the Press and urged its publication, I agreed to the Press editor's request that I oversee the editorial process; but since I had had no acquaintance with the author, I could not know what suggestions he might have accepted—say, for an additional footnote here and there or for an occasional modification of phrase. In the circumstances it seemed best to restrict editorial interference to a minimum. Except for the rare obvious slip, the book has been kept as Clay Hunt sent it to the Press. It has been exhilarating to follow his large-minded pursuit of the questions *Lycidas* raises and to arrive with him at his conclusions. His book demonstrates what the combination of critical acumen and historical scholarship can still accomplish to shed new light on a literary masterpiece.

Irene Samuel

1

The Poem and the Problem

It behooves any critic who, at this latter point of time, asks his reader to undertake a careful reexamination of *Lycidas* to make clear at the start just what he intends to do with the poem, and what might come out of it all. I intend to attack one problem about *Lycidas*—its literary form—and to arrive, finally, at a new analysis of the poem. I point at the start to one fact about *Lycidas* which seems to ask that we read the poem with a more wary scrutiny of all its literary details than we need give to many of Milton's other poems, both earlier and later, and also that we define for ourselves more precisely, as critical decisions which have been analytically formulated by the author, its technical methods and its principles of formal structure. What I have in mind is the fact that the poem spends so much time discussing itself with the reader. I am thinking not so much of the biographical passages which tell us about Milton's preparations and plans for his future literary career as of the considerable part of this short poem which Milton allots to wondering aloud about whether he is yet up to the demands of the kind of poem he is trying to write, and then to asking us to notice exactly what he is doing as he goes ahead and writes it.

After the opening lines, which give us to understand that all his earlier poems have shown a talent that is still immature—lines which probably make a glancing reference ("Yet once more . . .") to the publication of *Comus*, which had appeared a few months before—Milton then reflects on his unreadiness to execute this poem, one he is "forced" to write: he wonders if he dares, and goes on to tell us why he must. Having devoted fourteen lines to this difficulty, he at last firmly banishes his timidities (though not without further remarks on why he should write the poem), calls upon the Muses to begin the lament for Lycidas, and tells them exactly how they should begin. The Muses thereupon perform as requested,

1

but after some thirty lines they start to exceed their initial instructions, and the poem seems to get a little out of hand. Milton assures us that he has noticed this fact, tells us what has gone wrong, and takes it in hand again.

Things then proceed as expected for some time, until the poem takes off on another artistic swerve. Milton again points out that he is aware this has happened, suggests specifically what ought to be the style for a poem of this kind, and writes a passage on funeral flowers to get the poem back on course. He explains why he has put that passage into the poem, defines for us the artistic effect he wants it to have, and suggests why such an effect might be needed just at this point. The poem then resumes the lament for Lycidas, which is carried to a normal and satisfying conclusion. And it ends with an octave that discusses Milton's writing of the poem and also gives us a clear hint as to the stylistic methods by which it has been constructed. We are once more reminded that Milton is a young and unfinished artist, told that with "eager thought" he has spent a whole day, from dawn to dusk, in writing this poem, and given to understand that, now that he has finished this one, he will go on in the future to other works of a new kind.

There is nothing like this in *Comus*, which was written more than three years before. And *Comus* is not only Milton's first major poetic undertaking and major success; it is also in many ways a more ambitious work than *Lycidas*, one that is broader in its philosophic reach and, in its elaborate structure of interrelated poetic and stage symbols, poetically more intricate. But *Comus*, although it also presents itself to us as the work of a "shepherd Lad" (line 619), spends no time either in explaining itself to the audience or in apologizing for the uncouthness of the shepherd-author. It is sustained by a powerful poetic assurance from start to finish; and though we are told that the shepherd lad is, at this date, "of small regard to see to" (and, in this sense of the term, "uncouth"), we are immediately reassured that he is "well skilled," nevertheless, in all the arts of his craft and, in fact, that he knows a good many of its ancient secrets which his own countrymen have yet to discover. At the one point where Milton pauses, for only seven lines (513–19), to consider that any of his contemporaries might have difficulty in understanding the artistic techniques of his poem— techniques which are, after all, simply those used "of old" by "the sage Poets, taught by the heav'nly Muse" in writing their "high immortal verse"—he lightly dismisses the blindness of these poetic illiterates as "shallow ignorance."

To juxtapose the two works in this way brings out the somewhat surprising fact that it is in the later rather than the earlier poem that Milton seems to feel tentative and unusually self-conscious over what he is attempting; and it also dramatizes a distinctive quality of the artistic character of *Lycidas*. This quality, as a basic organizing principle in a work of art, has been neatly defined by some remarks of Igor Stravinsky on the difference between the music of Webern and Beethoven:

> To begin with, can we be certain that the scope we are looking for is really Webern's and not your Beethovenesque idea of what it should be . . . ? There is simply no movement from simple to complex, no development of subsidiary parts or integration of counter-themes, second subjects, fugal episodes, and the like. *The listener is definitely not invited to participate in the argument of the creation* as he is in the symphonies of Beethoven. On the contrary, each opus offers itself only as a whole, a unity to be contemplated.[1] [My italics.]

While I would not push Milton's artistic practice to the point of any close analogy to Webern's—who, as Stravinsky says, "often seems to have put a low premium on his listener's sense of involvement" and is "wholly unrhetorical"—I would say that his normal procedure in most of his best poems, from "On the Morning of Christ's Nativity" to *Samson Agonistes,* is the latter of these two kinds. In his prose works, when he undertakes, usually in one of those digressions to which he is addicted, to talk about his poetry, he will tell us quite freely about his literary principles and tastes, and the artistic plans and choices that he is making for his poetic work. But when he addresses us in the role of the English Poet, his habit is to let each opus offer itself to us only as a whole, a unity to be contemplated. *Paradise Lost* alone resembles *Lycidas* in inviting the reader, at some points, "to participate in the argument of the creation." But in the great expanse of *Paradise Lost* this occurs infrequently, and at wide intervals, for the most part in the personal Inductions to four of the twelve books, and even there we are told only a few things about the poetic decisions the author has made, or the technical methods he is using as he constructs the poem.

Only *Lycidas* follows the artistic strategy of repeatedly inviting the listener to participate in the argument of the creation throughout the poem: it calls his attention to movements from simple to complex and asks him to be aware that the poem contains subsidiary parts, second subjects, and episodes, and that it is introducing counterthemes, which need somehow to be integrated with the primary themes. And *Lycidas* describes the process of creation, moreover, as though it were in fact something like an actual argument Milton is having with himself as he writes the poem. In this respect *Lycidas* is unique in Milton's poetic work.[2]

I conclude that in writing the poem Milton thought he was undertaking something different from the kind of poetry he had written before in *Comus,* as well as in such other early successes as the Nativity Ode, "L'Allegro" and "Il Penseroso," and "At a Solemn Music," and something for which the particular skills he had mastered in writing those works did not fully prepare him. At first glance, it seems a little hard to see why poetic powers that were already considerable should be taxed by the writing of a mere pastoral. But perhaps it is partly this fact—that he is now undertaking his first eclogue—which sends through *Lycidas* the slight tremor that *Comus* is untouched by.

For so had Virgil begun. And so, following consciously in Virgil's footsteps, had Spenser, whom Milton acknowledged as his "original" among the English poets. The fact is that in the eclogues Virgil had turned to after his experimental early verse and later compiled as his first significant work, he not only made clear at several points his plans for writing future poems of a more ambitious kind, but also, in his Fourth Eclogue, made his first, tentative experiment with both the style and some of the subject matter of his *Aeneid*. Virgil thus established, for after ages, an archetypal dramatic pattern for the career of a master poet which caught the imagination of many humanist poets of the Renaissance and continued to cast its spell over English poetry up to the time of Alexander Pope. The significance of this pattern would hardly have escaped the imagination of the young Milton, who not only had an intensely theatricalized conception of the role played by the poet in the dramatic pattern of history, but who was always concerned, even in his undergraduate days at Cambridge, to create a public drama out of his personal career.

In this traditional Virgilian drama, the protagonist's enactment of an eclogue had a two-sided symbolic significance. Because of Virgil's imaginative maneuver of making the actual shepherd-singer of Theocritus into a poetic symbol for the apprentice poet, naturally talented and spontaneously creative but not yet adept in the civilized skills required for the major literary forms, this action signified, on the one hand, that the young poet was—as E. K. explained when introducing the "New Poet" of *The Shepheardes Calender*—"following the example of the best and most ancient poets, which devised this kind of writing, being both so base for the matter, and homely for the manner, at the first to try their abilities; and as young birds, that be newly crept out of the nest, by little first to prove their tender wings, before they make a greater flight."

On the other hand, if pastoral singing required only humble talents and made only modest poetic pretensions, the assumption of the shepherd's role implied also that the new poet was setting in action the plot which, if the drama were played out to its proper end, would show him rising to the enactment of a heroic poem. That Spenser had seen this double symbolic implication in his act of finally undertaking a set of eclogues after the eclectic experimentation of his earliest verse is clear from his October Eclogue, in which he first announced his ambition to write an epic poem, attempted a few stanzas in the heroic style, and, following the precedent of Virgil's proto-epic Fourth Eclogue, sketched, in a tentative form, the subject which later grew into the central plot of *The Faerie Queene.*

Milton's plans for a major poem at the time he wrote *Lycidas* were inclining toward the form of epic, but he was also interested in the form of tragedy. In the neo-Aristotelian criticism of Renaissance Italy, however, it was a widely held view that epic and tragedy not only were the two magisterial literary forms but were also closely analogous, or actually ·interlocking literary genres. Aristotle's opinion

that the Homeric epics showed many of the essential characteristics of tragedies and Dante's conclusion—arrived at without
benefit of Aristotle—that Virgil had conceived his *Aeneid* as an
"alta tragedia" were frequently cited, and approved, by many of
the humanist critics of the Italian Renaissance.[3] That these two
literary forms, and the analogies between them, were upper-
most in Milton's mind as he meditated the choices for his major
poem in the years just before and after he wrote *Lycidas* is fairly
certain. From the evidence of poems written within the next two
or three years, it seems likely that at this time his plans were inclining less toward a tragedy than toward a nationalistic epic about
legendary British heroes; but we can be pretty sure, at least, that if
he had felt emboldened to undertake his projected "graver subject"
immediately after *Lycidas,* the poem would have been in the form of
either an epic or a tragedy or, most probably, of an epic which had
assimilated the essential elements of the tragic genre.

   There is, however, more than the presumptive evidence of Milton's
acceptance of Virgil's eclogue-to-epic pattern to indicate that when
he wrote *Lycidas* he felt he was at the point of a decisive step
forward in his preplanned literary career. There are suggestions both
in the poem itself and in the letter to Diodati, written about the
same time, that he was feeling almost ready to put his apprenticeship
behind him and to venture his wings, at last, for the greater flight.
The personal passage in the poem which reflects apprehensively on
the threat of early death, striking abruptly to snatch from a man
who had dedicated his youth to retired study the earthly fame he
had expected as the reward for these self-denying labors, shows
Milton thinking of his attainment of that reward as both imminent
and dramatically sudden:

> But the fair guerdon when we hope to find,
> And think to burst out into sudden blaze,
> Comes the blind Fury with th' abhorrèd shears,
> And slits the thin-spun life.*

And the parallel passage in the letter to Diodati, written, probably, a
few weeks before *Lycidas,* provides further evidence that just at this
time Milton was beginning to feel, with a sort of shaky excitement,

---

*Lines from *Lycidas* conform to the Douglas Bush edition of *The Complete
Poetical Works of John Milton* (Boston: Houghton Mifflin, 1965).

that he was now ready to burst forth with a work which would dazzle by the revelation of poetic powers his earlier poems had given no hint of—and that he was still doubting whether he was up to it:

> Now I must satisfy your curiosity. You ask many questions, even about what I am thinking of. I will tell you, but let me whisper it in your ear (to spare my blushes!); and you must allow me for a moment to boast. What am I thinking of? So help me God, of immortality. What am I doing? Growing wings and learning to fly. My Pegasus can only rise on tender wings as yet, however, so let my new wisdom be humble.[4]

If this was Milton's state of mind shortly before he wrote the poem, I suggest that the fact of Edward King's sudden death, and the request that he contribute an elegy to the memorial volume, made him decide to take the leap he was dreaming of. Brought face to face with the possibility that he himself might be cut off just when he was almost ready to burst out into sudden blaze in a major poem—a possibility inescapably actual to a man making plans for an overseas voyage in the Renaissance—Milton might well have decided to go ahead and make his gamble, that is, to present in *Lycidas* (after all, an eclogue, recognized as the form in which a young poet might try his wings and take the chance of his mistakes) the first evidence of the greater poetry he now felt capable of.[5] Whether or not this speculation about his motives is correct, I expect to show, at any rate, that he undertook *Lycidas* with the conscious purpose of refashioning the humble genre of the pastoral elegy in order to make it produce poetic effects traditionally reserved to poems in the major literary forms.

This much, so far, is conjecture—however plausible—about Milton's intentions in writing the poem, and it remains to be seen whether these conjectures have support in the poem itself. But I close this proem to my inquiry by pointing out that it comes to a conclusion about *Lycidas* closely parallel to the one arrived at, from entirely different evidence, by F. T. Prince, in his book, *The Italian Element in Milton's Verse.* This book, to which I will be indebted at several points, is a conclusive demonstration of Prince's central thesis: that the characteristics, both of style and of prosody, which distinguish Milton's mature poetry as we see it fully developed in the sonnets of the 1640s and 1650s, the two epics, and *Samson Agonistes,* were

derived from Milton's close technical study of the poetry of
sixteenth-century Italy, and chiefly of the epic style of Tasso, who
had built his style on the technical innovations of Giovanni della
Casa. Prince's book is also the most sure and subtle study yet made
of the graduate stages of technical experiment, and of the adaptation
of a variety of literary influences, through which Milton's verse
developed as it evolved the fully achieved style, modeled on "the
idea of the 'magnificent' style in Italian," which characterizes all the
poetry he wrote after his return from Italy. On the basis of his
analysis of Milton's early poetry, Prince concludes that *Lycidas* has a
particular "formal significance" in Milton's poetic development:

> After its composition Milton abandons the study and assimila-
> tion of English poetry which he undertook, among many other
> labours, in the Horton period. Henceforth his poetry is to be
> planned entirely under the influence of the two Classical
> literatures and Italian, the authority of which he considers equal
> to theirs.

Prince argues, I think correctly, that the literary influences behind
Comus are still those of English Renaissance poetry, and that though
we can see Milton beginning to experiment with the stanza forms of
Italian verse as early as the Nativity Ode, and carrying those experiments further in "On Time," "Upon the Circumcision," and "At a
Solemn Music," his use of Italian techniques in these poems does not
extend beyond the stanzaic patterns of his verse. It is not until
Lycidas, Prince finds, that Milton first attempts the further technical
innovation which was decisive in the formation of his mature style:

> In all the early poems, except the early sonnets, the following of
> Italian verse affects the prosody rather than the diction. Indeed,
> Milton's adaptation of devices of Italian diction, which is
> all-important to the understanding of his mature verse, does not
> begin until *Lycidas*, the last poem of his youth.

Of this poem in which poetic youth sees its end, and which shows
Milton "more conscious than ever before of the possibilities of
moulding English verse by Italian methods," Prince concludes,
"*Lycidas* cannot be dissected without a knowledge of the Italian
poetry of the sixteenth century."[6]

The purpose of my own dissection is to determine the literary genus of the poem as Milton himself conceived it. Prince's analysis of the "specific means Milton employed to 'build the lofty rime' " seems to me impeccable, so far as it goes, and his findings will have a part in my final conclusion. But his analysis is limited, by his choice, almost solely to explaining the scheme of verse structure on which the poem is built. He concludes that the discipline which guides *Lycidas* "is the discipline of the *canzone,* as it was modified and adapted in lyrics and eclogues of the Cinquecento"; and he demonstrates precisely the prosodic principles by which Milton makes patterns of rhetoric and meaning interact with those of rhyme, stanza, and verse movement so that verse patterns and rhetorical design coincide to create a poetic structure "built upon movements of thought and emotion."[7] This discipline, however, which Prince defines as a sort of "rhetoric of rhyme," is only one of a number of formal principles that shape the poem. The poem is clearly disciplined also by other controlling concepts about its genre, about style, and about the fitting of style to genre, which must enter into any comprehensive definition of the kind of poetic structure Milton was trying to build.

It is precisely these problems of style and form which Milton seems to be arguing out with himself in the writing of the poem, and which he invites his reader to notice and to raise questions about.[8] And when I accept his invitation to participate in the argument of the creation and ask, as I finish the poem, how that argument has been resolved and what literary form has emerged as the controlling design for the whole piece, I find some puzzles. To this question the perfectly obvious answer—that the poem is a pastoral elegy, modeled primarily on the classical eclogues—seems both undeniably right and somehow partly wrong. And I cannot dismiss as lightly as most critics have done the critical judgment on *Lycidas* roundly asserted by G. Wilson Knight:

> Exquisite Spenserian melodies and flowery description do not cohabit very happily with the thunderous St. Peter. . . . Exquisite in parts and most valuable as a whole, *Lycidas* reads rather as an effort to bind and clamp together a universe trying to fly off into separate bits; it is an accumulation of magnificent fragments.[9]

It is not only that this judgment (if I trim a bit off the last clause) corresponds to my own sense of conflicting tonal qualities in a poem which seems made up of separate, contrasting stylistic blocks: it corresponds also to what Milton seems to be plainly telling his reader in the text of the poem itself.

Let us look, first, at the way in which Milton handles the two digressions from his central subject (lines 64–84 and 112–31). It is no good for critics to shilly-shally by referring to these passages as "digressions" and then, putting that word in quotation marks, to imply that of course they are not really digressions if we can only somehow feel how marvelously they harmonize with the grand design of it all. Milton himself makes perfectly clear that this is exactly what they are. At the end of the first of these passages he points out that in these lines we have been listening to verse of a "higher mood," but that "now" he will "proceed" with the kind of poem he had begun to write. And later, after the voice of St. Peter is "past," he again calls on his poem to "return" to its proper business as a pastoral elegy. Further, if we have missed these indications in the text that Milton wants us to recognize these two passages as deliberate divagations from the central artistic direction of the poem, we find an additional reminder in the headnote he added when *Lycidas* was published in the 1645 edition of his early *Poems.* After defining the form and the subject of the poem by calling it a "monody," in which "the author bewails the death of a learned friend," he explains that St. Peter's prophecy of "the ruin of our corrupted clergy" has been introduced into the poem "by occasion."

I raise the question of why either of these passages should seem an extraneous intrusion in a pastoral poem of the Renaissance. They present no logical incongruity with either the subject matter of the rest of the poem or with the traditional symbolic meanings which, by this point in literary history, were inherent, or potential, in the pastoral fiction. Evidently the artistic problem they present is rather one of tone—of a change in style which intrudes a "higher mood." But even on these grounds one wonders why there should be any problem, either in terms of what is traditional in pastoral poetry or of what is poetically possible and manageable when one is writing an eclogue. When Virgil, at the start of his Fourth Eclogue, invoked the Sicilian Muses for a "somewhat grander" song, he began a tradition of attempts to broaden the range of bucolic poetry which had been followed—to mention only some of the modern poets whose practice in the pastoral Milton might have considered exemplary—by Petrarch, by Mantuan, by Sannazaro (in both his vernacular and Latin eclogues), by Tasso, and by Spenser. Nevertheless, though Milton is certainly following this tradition in *Lycidas,* he shows no inclination to seek support from these precedents in order to justify the passages in which he lifts his pastoral to higher seriousness. He seems, rather, to insist that what he is doing is neither the normal practice nor an accepted variation from that norm in the literary tradition of the eclogue.

If we look where he points us and scrutinize, for a moment, the stylistic qualities of the two digressions, it does seem that they present us with verse which is poetically more rugged going than any of the sterner stuff we can find in the eclogues of Milton's predecessors. The effects are most striking in St. Peter's speech, but they are anticipated by similar stylistic tricks in the earlier digression, not only in the digression proper ("Alas! what boots it with uncessant care . . ."), but also in the preceding lines on the death of Orpheus, with their heavy stresses and their back vowels and gutturals. And it is after this passage that Milton suggests his own view of the style which is proper to pastoral poetry, when he writes,

> O fountain Arethuse, and thou honored flood,
> Smooth-sliding Mincius, crowned with vocal reeds,
> That strain I heard was of a higher mood.

If we place only these lines alongside the verse of the later digression, it is startling to see how completely one of these elegantly lyrical decasyllabics can fracture when it is wielded by the heavy hand of St. Peter:

> What recks it them? What need they? They are sped.

This is stuff to splinter a syrinx. And against any critic who would suggest that, after all, the Master knows best, and that St. Peter's sulfurous fit of temper is essentially in keeping with the tones proper

to a pastoral poem, I point to Milton's explicit statement, in the
lines which follow, that it certainly is not:

> Return, Alphéus, the dread voice is past
> That shrunk thy streams; return, Sicilian Muse,
> And call the vales and bid them hither cast
> Their bells and flow'rets of a thousand hues.

These lines say beyond any question that St. Peter's speech is out of
place in Arcady; and they imply, further, that the violence of its
broken rhythms, the rasping ugliness of its verbal sound ("Grate on
their scrannel pipes of wretched straw"), and the emotional
vehemence of its concluding prophecy of the death-stroke from the
sword of God's Avenging Angel—

> But that two-handed engine at the door
> Stands ready to smite once, and smite no more—

are literary effects which belong to an order of artistic intensity that
destroys the mood proper to a pastoral elegy.

It appears, therefore, that it is not merely some modern critic but
Milton himself who has told us, and in almost the same terms, that
"exquisite Spenserian melodies and flowery description do not
cohabit very happily with the thunderous St. Peter," and who has
suggested that in introducing this passage into *Lycidas*—"by
occasion"—he is producing something like a fragmentation in the
artistic unity of the poem.

It seems a little curious that any competent poet should
deliberately do this; rather more curious that he should advertise the
fact in the poem itself; and more curious still that the poet who is
doing it should be John Milton. With the single exception of Ben
Jonson, no major writer of the English Renaissance approaches
Milton in the habitual scrupulousness with which he lays out in his
mind the character of the literary genre that he is employing in a
particular poem, and then devotes himself to observing the
requirements of "decorum" in that genre. The passage in *Of
Education* in which Milton asserts his views on poetic decorum, as
well as his views on the proper methods of instruction in writing,
concludes with a blanket condemnation of the generality of writers

in England because they fail to observe these "laws" governing the
categories of "true" literary forms:

> And now, lastly, will be the time to read with them those
> organic arts which enable men to discourse and write perspicu-
> ously, elegantly, and according to the fitted style of lofty, mean,
> or lowly. Logic, therefore, so much as is useful, is to be referred
> to this due place with all her well-couched heads and topics,
> until it be time to open her contracted palm into a graceful
> and ornate rhetoric, taught out of the rule of Plato, Aristotle,
> Phalareus, Cicero, Hermogenes, Longinus. To which poetry
> would be made subsequent, or indeed rather precedent, as
> being less subtle and fine, but more simple, sensuous, and
> passionate. I mean here not the prosody of a verse, which
> they could not but have hit on before among the rudiments
> of grammar; but that sublime art which in Aristotle's *Poetics,*
> in Horace, and the Italian commentaries of Castelvetro, Tasso,
> Mazzoni, and others, teaches what the laws are of a true epic
> poem, what of a dramatic, what of a lyric, what decorum is,
> which is the grand masterpiece to observe. This would make
> them soon perceive what despicable creatures our common
> rhymers and play-writers be, and show them what religious,
> what glorious, and magnificent use might be made of poetry,
> both in divine and human things.

I have quoted this passage in full, not just for Milton's well-known
statement of the doctrine of decorum, but because it gives us, in
short space, a detailed and specific summary of his ideas about the
art of writing and of his fundamental concepts of literary form and
style, together with a list of the rhetoricians and critics from whom
he has derived his principles and whose views he regards as
authoritative. *Of Education* was written, pretty surely, in 1642 or
1643, soon after Milton's return from Italy. But there is good reason
to believe that almost everything Milton says in this
passage—including at least his recommendations of the most reliable
Italian critics—represents what he had already studied and thought
out by the end of his apprenticeship, by the time, that is, when he
moved to Horton and, soon thereafter, wrote *Lycidas,* in November

1637. The passage is, in effect, a retrospective summary of the conclusions about the literary art which he had formulated during the period of his self-education.

Moreover, if *Lycidas* offers itself as still the work of an apprentice not yet admitted to mastership in his craft, that apprentice seems fully aware in the poem itself that if he is to produce the masterpiece by which he will qualify for that rank—and thus earn the right to pluck his crown of laurel leaves, and not merely of laurel berries—his poetry must meet the essential requirement of observing decorum in its literary kind. *Lycidas* is certainly overt and explicit in giving us notice that it is following the most ancient and honorable models for its genre. The repeated invocations—to the Muses, to the "Fountain Arethuse" and Mincius, and to Alpheus and the "Sicilian Muse"—have this clear implication. And they are probably intended to notify us also that we are faced with a pastoral in which the author is pointedly ignoring what English pastoral poetry had come to, after its grave and responsible beginnings in *The Shepheardes Calender,* as it had fallen into the despicable hands of "our common rhymers and play-writers," and to suggest that the decorum in its kind which *Lycidas* undertakes to observe is specifically that established by the eclogues of Theocritus and the other Sicilian pastoralists, and of Virgil.

It appears, then, that *Lycidas* challenges the lettered reader with the artistic paradox of asserting its adherence to tradition and decorum in its genre, while at the same time telling him it is doing things which are not proper at all for a poem of this kind.

Since Milton can hardly be intending to shrink the very streams that he seems to want to set flowing again in English poetry, I think the most likely solution to this paradox is that he has somehow squared out his apparent breach of decorum by devising for the poem a new or unusual literary form, one wide enough to embrace the novel stylistic effects in the two digressions but still closely enough related to the poetic forms traditional to the eclogue, for *Lycidas* to seem a new, but properly derived, development in the tradition of the classical pastoral. A literary maneuver of this kind would be—from the point of view of a poet, at least, if not of every critic—entirely decorous. And it would be fully in accord with

Milton's humanist literary principles, because it would demonstrate
that some ancient Mediterranean roots had still the vigor to put out
new growth in England's northern clime.

2

Italian Criticism

Milton, I think, did have a novel poetic form in mind as he worked out *Lycidas;* what it was we can discover if we ask the right questions about the poem. For this undertaking the passage in *Of Education* is handy. Since it defines the critical concepts and literary categories with which he worked as he was making the basic decisions for his literary career, it can give us guidelines for asking questions about the poem which are not just our own but correspond in kind to the questions Milton might have put to himself as he conceived it.

If, for a start, there is some problem about the stylistic contrasts in the poem, we might ask what Milton would have learned from his teachers about the style that was "fitted" to a pastoral poem—was it the "lofty, mean, or lowly?" The man who notified the reader of his epic, when he was still only halfway through his invoking of the Muse, that this poem would pursue "no middle flight," would probably have made a similar choice among the recognized grades of style before he started on *Lycidas.* If the "higher mood" was not quite the thing for a shepherd's pipe, was the style fitted to the eclogue the mean, or the lowly, or a combination of the two? And is the "higher mood" passage actually written in the lofty style, as Milton conceived it, or in the mean style, which is merely higher than the lowly?

The gradation of the various levels of style had been established by the classical writers on rhetoric whose "rule" Milton recommends in *Of Education,* and their classifications were generally adopted by the medieval rhetoricians and, later, by the Italian critics of the sixteenth century, who drew on a wider knowledge of classical texts and were concerned also with the further enterprise of correlating the rhetoricians' categories of the styles with the categories they were trying to establish for the various poetic genres. Whether the levels of style were three, as Cicero and Quintilian had maintained, of four (or whether these should be subdivided, since writing in one of these styles often required some mixture with another), had occasioned some difference of opinion; but there was a substantial agreement, over some twenty centuries, that if men wished to "discourse, or write perspicuously, elegantly," in either prose or verse, they would find it expedient to systematize their handling of language, and to make a conscious selection—when "fitting" their style not only in general to the chosen literary form but also, within that form, when fitting it particularly to the subject, the speaker, and the "end" or purpose of the discourse—from among some such categories as the high, middle, and low levels of expression.

On the precise technical characteristics of each of these graded styles, the same writers would have offered abundant and particularized information. Since the ancient writers on rhetoric looked on poetry as analogous to oratory, they often drew as freely from the poets as from the orators in citing examples to illustrate the technical devices that entered into the different styles. And this practice of citing and dissecting particular passages of poetry was widely followed by the humanist critics of the cinquecento, whose "commentaries" on Aristotle and Horace often combined the stylistic doctrines of the ancient rhetoricians with close technical analysis, not only of classical poetry, but also of the vernacular poetry of their own country. The works of these writers, therefore, would have offered to a young and learning poet a mass of concrete and businesslike "practical criticism," of the sort which common rhymers and playwriters tend to be impatient of, but which major poets, especially in the formative phases of their careers, are likely to take very seriously indeed. They offer precise analyses of such components of style as the effects of diction (both the levels of usage and the connotations and sounds of words); the varieties and uses of imagery, or figures of speech; the methods of disposing thought within a sentence, both grammatically and in terms of rhetorical periods; the effects of patterns of meter and sound on the movement of sentences; and the ways of fitting the rhetorical units of sentences into the prosodic units of the various verse lines and stanza forms. In addition, Tasso "and others" among the Italians would have given Milton some shrewd and practical advice, grounded in experience, about the problems of taking over these technical tricks of the classical poets into a modern vernacular language different in character from Greek or Latin, in order to discipline that vernacular so that it could operate for poetic purposes according to the fitted styles of lofty, mean, or lowly.

Finally, we should ask what Milton might have learned from his teachers in the art of writing about the "laws"—beyond the requirements for the fitted style—which define decorum for the genres, and particularly for the genre of the eclogue, or the pastoral elegy, or the monody. On this question, and the broader one of the nature and basis of the critical categories of the various literary kinds, we can expect no unanimity—nor even, on some issues, a clear majority opinion—from Milton's masters in Italy, but we can find some strongly argued views on this vigorously debated subject; and if we keep our eye on the problems we have encountered in the text of *Lycidas* and look for critical theories which seem to correspond to what Milton is actually doing in the poem, we can hold our course among the contestants.

As we can see from Milton's reference to the Italian critics in *Of Education,* the problem of classifying and defining the principal poetic genres was a central preoccupation for the new criticism of the latter cinquecento in Italy, a criticism which took its direction from the rediscovery of the text of Aristotle's *Poetics* and the later wide dissemination of Aristotle's literary ideas, beginning in the 1540s and extending until the end of the century.[1] In surveying a body of literary theory so intellectually vigorous, clear-minded, and contentious—as well as voluminous—it is hard to find many literary propositions that one can confidently describe as "generally accepted" in "Italian Renaissance criticism." We are dealing with a tradition of critical thinking, and a method of critical debate, rather than a body of critical dogma. But there are lines of continuity within it; and in the discussion of literary genres one can distinguish two different approaches to the problem, approaches which may stand as logically opposed but which can often jostle one another in the mind of a single critic—as they do in the critical thinking of Tasso, for instance, and of the young Milton.

On the one hand, there is the tendency derived from Aristotle's persuasive distinctions between the different artistic forms on the ground of their different modes of "imitation," and from the Italians' further critical effort to harmonize the *Poetics* with the practical and nonphilosophical comments on literary forms in Horace's *Ars Poetica*: it led critics to categorize the established literary forms, make firm demarcations between them, and after determining the laws of each (rules of old discovered, not devised), maintain that modern vernacular literature should adhere to the genres and the laws which had helped to build the glory that was Greece and the grandeur that was Rome. On the other hand, neither the Italian critics nor the youthful Milton could entirely close their eyes to the quite different glories of Tuscan poetry in the late thirteenth and fourteenth centuries—sonnets, *ballate, canzoni,* and *La Divina Commedia,* which had not been based on Aristotelian critical theory and for the most part conformed either imperfectly or not at all to the genres of classical poetry and ancient critical doctrine. And when Pietro Bembo, in his *Prose della Volgar Lingua,* published in 1525 but widely circulated before, gave a new direction to Italian literature in the sixteenth century by exalting, and concretely defining, the literary form of the Tuscan dialect as it had been used by Dante, Boccaccio, and especially Petrarch as the standard of literary usage in Italian, and by asserting the possibility of producing, in this language and its new verse forms, a literature closely modeled on that of Greece and Rome, he gave critical definition to a literary situation both critically ambiguous and artistically productive.

One effect of Bembo's criticism was to recall Italian writers from neo-Latin literature, which had been the prevailing mode for art-poetry in the fourteenth century, and encourage them to write in the vernacular; his critical principles for vernacular poetry made him generally accepted as the literary dictator of Italy for most of the remaining century. From the point of view of critics, the paradox of conjoining generic models from two bodies of literature as diverse as those of classical antiquity and trecento Tuscany created a situation that was extremely troublesome for the maintenance of rigidly neoclassical critical categories. From the point of view of writers, however, hopeful for a second flowering of Italian vernacular literature grounded in a knowledge of classical literature more complete than that available to the century of Dante and Petrarch, this critical paradox set up a literary dialectic that was highly propitious for the synthesis of new literary forms.

The verse form of the sonnet, for instance, was a native product of the new vernacular literature of Italy. It had originally been devised, with no thought of classical models, by the Italian poets of the Sicilian school in the early 1200s, who conceived the *sonnetto* as merely a single stanza of an Italian *canzone;* and soon afterward Dante had given the form critical definition in *De Vulgari Eloquentia.* Although his discussion of the sonnet was left unfinished, it is clear that Dante wished to assign to this native verse form some of the attributes of a poetic genre, and he seems to have regarded it as suited only to the low style, and as restricted to the subject of love. By the cinquecento, however, the text of *The Greek Anthology* had been recovered, and from the numerous epigrams about love in this collection Italian critics of the later century were quick to discover an ancient analogue to their vernacular sonnet in the classical genre of the epigram. From this conjunction of the two literatures, and from the acceptance of the Latin epigrams of Catullus and Martial as the classical examples for the new, hybrid genre, the sonnet of the Renaissance soon expanded its matter beyond the subject of love to include public life, mores, and even religion, in the *Sonnetti Spirituali* written by Varchi, Piccolomini, and Minturno.[2] Dante's critical attempt to restrict the sonnet to the low style was likewise soon discarded—it had not been followed, in fact, by Petrarch nor by Dante himself in the writing of his own sonnets. In its stylistic development, the sonnet of the cinquecento, as Tasso described the process, underwent a mutation like a specially cultivated plant; and after it acquired from Della Casa Virgilian qualities of diction, syntax, rhetoric, and sonority, it was then crossbred with the epic poem in Tasso's "Heroic Sonnets," which Milton was later to imitate in English.

The classical eclogue also played a vigorous part in this galloping and disordinate evolutionary biology. As a short poetic form, it draped the literary costume of Sicilian shepherds over Neapolitan fishermen in the *Piscatory Eclogues* written early in the century in Latin by Sannazaro and afterward, in the vernacular, by Bernardino

Rota; Tasso's father, Bernardo, and Benedetto Varchi made a further use of it to classicize the form of the sonnet by writing "Pastoral Sonnets." But the brief eclogue evolved also into a new dramatic form. Beginning, probably from models chiefly in Theocritus, as a short stage dialogue between shepherds, it developed into a five-act pastoral drama which had no real antecedent in the drama of antiquity. This dramatic form was then elevated to literary dignity in *Aminta* by Tasso, who gave to the pastoral play dramatic verse of pervasive and subtle lyricism and inserted formal choruses between the acts; and after Tasso, by Guarini—who then undertook the critical defense of his *Pastor Fido* as a work in the genuinely new dramatic genre of tragicomedy, a genre which deliberately combined the originally humble form of the dramatic eclogue not only with the grand genre of tragedy but, stranger still, with the low genre of comedy, to which tragedy had been sharply opposed in classical critical theory.

Dante's *Commedia* presented an especially troublesome problem to the neoclassic criticism of the Renaissance, on grounds of both its style and its genre; but after a protracted critical debate it came generally to be regarded, by the end of the century, as, in some sense of the term, a poem in the epic genre, comparable to the Homeric epics and the *Aeneid*.[3] But when the century placed alongside the *Commedia* two other magisterial heroic poems in the vernacular that were as different in form from Dante's and from one another, as *Orlando Furioso,* a romance epic built on the principle of "variety," and *Gerusalemme Liberata,* which combined the unified classical epic based on Aristotelian principles with elements of the romance epic of Ariosto, it was hard for humanist critics to hold a firm line on the principle that it was only by keeping inviolate the integrity of the classical literary forms that a modern vernacular could hope to rival the literatures of Greece and Rome.

Nevertheless, if the majority of writers of talent in this century, and a number of critics, looked with favor on the creation of innovative poetic forms in the Italian vernacular, they did not, like many of the later writers of the Romantic era, wish their novel poetic structures to appear as wholly new things under the sun. In their view, poetic form was still *genre,* and their critical term *genus* often carries connotative suggestions of its meaning as a term of natural philosophy. When they undertook the creation of "things unattempted yet in prose or rhyme" (the phrase Milton lifted from the *Orlando Furioso*) they were likely to produce new poetic structures which manifested some recognizable genetic connection with genres already established in past literary history, either in classical literature or in their own vernacular literature of the trecento. Consequently, in the late cinquecento at least, innovative literary forms are characteristically conceived by writer and critic alike as literally *genera mista,* new forms produced by the synthesis of preestablished genres that had been distinct in classical antiquity; or, most propitiously, by the synthesis of one or more ancient genres with some analogous literary form of Tuscan poetry of earlier centuries. In this way a novel literary form would preserve some of the metaphoric suggestion of the term *genus* in the Aristotelian universe: it had been generated according to the natural processes at work in the continuity of literary history, and had its recognizable roots in its preexisting, natural literary kinds.[4]

Milton's own critical statements about the desirability of observing decorum in the classical genres reflect the same doubleness of view that we find among the Italian critics of the late cinquecento. On the one hand, he can assert as firmly as he does in *Of Education* that in order to learn "the sublime art of poetry" one must master, and "observe," the "laws" of the "true" literary kinds as they are taught by Aristotle, Horace, and the Italian commentators; and he evidently does regard this teaching as a basic rational discipline for a writer, in which not only English schoolboys but also England's common rhymers need to be instructed. But when he speaks about the creative decisions that he is considering for his own poetry, in the second Book of *The Reason of Church Government,* written a year or two before *Of Education,* his mind is perfectly open to the two alternatives for the epic poem which Italian critics had debated in the controversy over the epics of Tasso and Ariosto: he is still undecided "whether the rules of Aristotle are herein strictly to be kept, or nature to be followed, which in them that know art and use judgment is no transgression, but an enriching of art."

Placing these two passages side by side shows us something else about the character of Milton's interest in critical theory. He is not concerned with working out a systematic poetics; instead, he is looking to criticism for schematic formal concepts which he can turn to use in writing his own poems. His mind can entertain at the same time ideas about a particular genre which theoretical critics had regarded as logically distinct, or even contradictory to one another, reconciling them with that judgment which derives from an understanding of the principles that enter into the actual production of works in this particular art.

In his list of the true literary kinds in *Of Education,* Milton mentions only the major, comprehensive categories of the poetic genres as they had been systematized in the neo-Aristotelian criticism of Scaliger, Minturno, Tasso, "and others." But the categories he lists do indicate his controlling concepts about the basic literary forms, which, in turn, form the foundation for his ideas about the essential laws of decorum in the literary genres. We should inquire, then, to which of these general classes—the epic, the dramatic, or the lyric poem—he would have assigned the pastoral eclogue.

It is highly unlikely that Milton, who had formulated at least as early as 1629 (in "At A Vacation Exercise") an extremely lofty conception of the epic as a form, and of the persons and actions appropriate to it, would have wished to take uncouth shepherds for heroes and thus to confound the laws of nature by the birth of a pastoral epic—even though Sannazaro had taken several steps in that direction, and Sidney, coming after him and aided by the recovery of the texts of the Greek romances and by his reading of *Amadis of Gaulle,* had devised a scheme for following that road fully to its end. We should ask, then, whether Milton would have regarded the eclogue as a subvariety of the dramatic or of the lyric poem.

On this question Italian critics of the cinquecento had held different views. Finding no guidance in either the *Poetics* or the *Ars Poetica,* neither of which dealt at all with pastoral poetry, some of them, influenced by the new forms which the pastoral had assumed in their own vernacular literature, had thought of the eclogue as essentially a form of the dramatic poem. Others, however, wishing for a return of the Sicilian Muse in the cadences of smooth-sliding Mincius, and attracted less by the dramatic idylls of Theocritus than by the language and music of Virgil, had regarded the pastoral poem as a subspecies of the lyric. But I think there is little doubt about the answer Milton would have given. Though some parts of *Lycidas*—the speech of St. Peter, for instance—might be described, in a looser critical terminology, as "dramatic," this description would not have been acceptable to a man whose literary thinking had been clarified by the analytical intelligence of Aristotle. In terms of its technique—or, to speak more strictly, of its mode of "imitation"—*Lycidas* is not an example of the literary type of the dramatic eclogue: that is, one in which the speakers are two or more shepherds who appear as dramatic characters engaged in some kind of contention or discussion. Instead, it is a pastoral like the Fourth, Sixth, and Tenth Eclogues of Virgil, in which the poetic voice is that of the poet himself, metaphorically disguised as a shepherd but speaking in propria persona, in a mode of discourse alternately narrative and reflective, throughout the poem. In terms of Milton's three categories of the true poetic kinds, therefore, *Lycidas,* though it adheres in large part to the form of the pastoral elegy, would be a subspecies of the genus lyric.

It seems, then, that we might find help toward a solution to the artistic paradox of *Lycidas* if we investigate the ideas of Milton and his critical masters not only about the pastoral but also about the lyric as a literary form.[5] Those irruptions which temporarily banish the Sicilian Muse from the poem may prove to be artistically proper undertakings for a poet who is writing a certain kind of lyric poem and is following the laws which have been found to operate in the creation of works in that literary kind. And if, through a combination of some of the laws governing the subspecies of the pastoral with the laws governing its genus, the lyric, a new poetic form should be created, this would be no transgression but an enriching of art, since that form would have been generated judiciously in accordance with the principles that governed the development of poetry as one of the "organic arts."[6] Furthermore, to create a new poetic form in the vernacular out of the established genres of ancient literature by combining one of its forms with another to which it was genetically related would be to emulate a common practice of the poets who had produced in Italy the only modern vernacular literature Milton genuinely admired.

3

The Pastoral

Our inquiry narrows to what Milton may have learned from his early masters, both in critical theory and in poetry, about the forms and stylistic effects suitable first for the pastoral and then for the lyric—what they could have afforded him in the way of examples or suggestions for what he seems to be doing in *Lycidas*.

Critical theory about the pastoral need not detain us long. Despite the wide appeal which literary forms directly imitated or derived from the classical eclogue had for Italian writers of both neo-Latin and vernacular poetry in the late fifteenth and early sixteenth centuries, Italian critics of the late cinquecento seem to have rather lost interest in the pastoral as a poetic form and frequently ignored it entirely in their critical works. They were much more occupied either with trying to classicize the various lyric forms of trecento Tuscan verse, or with following the new light of the *Poetics*—which said not a word about pastoral poetry for the reason that Greek literature at the time of Aristotle had not yet produced this form—to an analysis of the great genres of epic and tragedy.

Not even Tasso, although his first major poetic achievement and greatest popular success had been the pastoral play *Aminta,* gives any serious attention to pastoral poetry in the considerable body of his critical writings.[1] Critics like Scaliger and Minturno, who wrote comprehensive treatises on poetics, and therefore had to give systematic coverage to all the ackowledged literary forms, dealt with pastorals in their due turn; and they generally restated, with little essential modification, the commonplaces about the form we have already encountered in E. K.'s introduction to Spenser's *Shepheardes Calender.* These commonplaces derive from the schematic design, known as "the Wheel of Virgil," which medieval rhetoricians, following Donatus and Servius's Commentary, had imposed on Virgil's work.

25

According to this design—visually represented by a wheel figured as a trisected circle with concentric internal rings—the Eclogues were the lowest step in the graded progression of literary styles (lowly, mean, and lofty), as well as their corresponding actions, persons, animals, plants, and poetic forms, by which Virgil had advanced from the humble *Bucolics,* through the ampler *Georgics,* to the culminating achievement of the *Aeneid.*[2] The same critical commonplaces persist in English criticism of the Elizabethan Renaissance. In Sidney, in Puttenham, and in E. K.'s introductory letter to the *Shepheardes Calender,* we see little variation from the traditional doctrine: the eclogue is a form "base for the matter and homely for the manner." Since it deals, normally, with persons of low birth and no education, it adheres to the low, or humble, style—colloquial in syntax, diction, and verse rhythms, devoid of poetic ornament, rhetorical effects, or sententiae, and inclining on occasion, to jokes and other comic effects. And if this homely manner should mask, at times, subjects and persons of greater worth, the poet, in consequence, may follow the example of Virgil's Fourth Eclogue and raise his voice to what Puttenham describes as "a somewhat swelling style."[3] Some critics, like Scaliger, who could find little fault in anything that had been done by "the Divine Poet," admired these occasional swells from Virgil's shepherd pipe;[4] others ignored them as nonessential deviations from the basic type for pastoral poetry; and some, like Minturno, disapproved of them as dubious or absurd violations of the laws of decorum in this genre.[5]

Clearly this critical theory can be of little use to us for defining the form of the pastoral that Milton had in mind for *Lycidas,* which shows only a handful of scattered lines in which the syntax, diction, rhetorical patterns, or cadences of verse music ever descend to anything approaching the lowly style. But accepted poetic theory is not always poetic practice, and if we look to the writers of pastoral in the vernacular, to Spenser, and to some Italians whom Milton might have followed "in the modelling of this poem, . . . with good reason," because of their "authority and fame,"[6] we immediately discover that when the mantle of Virgil descended on vernacular poets who were swelling with the spirit of Renaissance, both their styles and their poetic forms had a way of swelling rather more than the "somewhat" authorized by the plain words of Virgil, and by critical doctrine.

Spenser, by sprinkling his diction with Chaucerisms and other archaic usages that had survived in English country dialects, had made one of the most ingenious of the Renaissance experiments in creating a new style for pastoral verse in the vernacular. It was a style that would satisfy the neoclassical critical requirement of maintaining the lowly style fitted to the genre, one that could look like an imitation of the speech of country people, but which, at the same time, would achieve Spenser's high artistic aim of carrying on what Chaucer had begun by creating from the vernacular a new, and distinctively English, poetic diction, set apart from actual colloquial speech by those archaisms which, as E. K. explained, would produce an effect of strangeness and bring "great grace and, as one would say, authority to the verse." Spenser's persona, Colin Clout, repeatedly reminds us that he is observing the traditional view of stylistic decorum in the genre, as he does, for instance, in the June Eclogue:

> Of Muses Hobbinol, I conne no skill:
> For they bene daughters of the highest Ioue,
> And holden scorne of homely shepheardes quill,
> For sith I heard, that *Pan* with *Phoebus* stroue
> Which him to much rebuke and daunger droue:
> I never lyst presume to Parnasse hyll,
> But pyping lowe in shade of lowly groue,
> I play to please my selfe, all be it ill.

But Spenser nevertheless avails himself of the Virgilian option of singing *paolo maiora* in two experiments in poetic form which could have given Milton some hints for what he does in *Lycidas*. The Muses from Parnassus are certainly called upon in the dirge for Dido in "November," which opens with an invocation to Melpomene, employs a style continuously heightened by formal rhetoric, mythological decoration, and Senecan tragic machinery, and makes use of an elaborate new stanza form derived from the Italian canzone.[7] The other formal experiment, which certainly has its parallel in *Lycidas,* is the trick of mingling two levels of style—the lowly and the lofty—in the structure of a single eclogue. This is done in one way in the April Eclogue, and in another in "August."

For the blazon of Elizabeth in "April," the Parnassian Muses are also invoked, and clearly manifest their presence; and Spenser devises for the poem another formal lyric stanza, modeled on the canzone, in place of the simpler, native English verse forms which are the norm for the other Eclogues. Still, we are reminded at several points that the singer of this formal laud is, after all, no one but the rustic poet Colin Clout, who has been temporarily rapt beyond himself, it would seem, by the glory of Eliza. This reminder is given, first, in the seventh stanza, where the ornate style and lyric flight of the poem are cut sharply back to the rude diction, gawky rhythms, and local-color realism of English country speech, and where we find Colin thinking not of the Parnassian Muses but rather of Pan, who is the Sicilian Muse of the style of rustic pastoral. A second descent to the low style occurs in the three concluding stanzas, which modulate gradually from the Muses' high-literary speech to the life and language of the English countryside, concluding with five bumpy lines in which an awkward and unpoetical "Southerne Shepheardes boy" gulps out his leave-taking with comic bathos.

In the August Eclogue, Spenser devises a different formal pattern for the same effect of combining in a single poetic structure two contrasting poetic styles, one of them homely, and English, and the other a strain of a higher mood, either Italian or classical-Italianate in origin. Here the structural scheme combines two love poems paired into a "L'Allegro"–"Il Penseroso" sort of diptych, on the joy and the sorrow of love-longing. The first is a virtuoso performance in which Spenser mixes country dialect with just a touch of the language of the Muses in order to raise to literary status the lowly English folk-song form of the roundelay—much as the Provençal and Italian poets had developed a new form for art poetry out of the folk-dance form of the *ballata*. And this piece in a humble style and verse form is set off against a courtly love-complaint, written, we are told, by the poet Colin Clout, in the Provençal-Italian verse form of the sestina, which Italian critics regarded as a specialized type of the dignified canzone stanza.

The formal dirge of the November Eclogue, according to our officious adviser E. K., was made in imitation of the pastoral elegy for Louise of Savoy written by Marot (of whom E. K. thinks poorly). But although this elegy is undoubtedly Spenser's most direct model for his poem, I think that both this eclogue and Spenser's other experiments in introducing a somewhat grander style into his pastorals have a less immediate but more significant source—one of greater authority and fame—in the *Arcadia* of Sannazaro, a work E. K. mentions, in his introductory letter to Gabriel Harvey, as one of Spenser's models for *The Shepheardes Calender.* This early work of Sannazaro's, written in the late 1480s, was first published, in a corrupt and unauthorized edition, in 1502 and then reissued in 1504, with the addition of two concluding chapters and an epilogue, in an edition evidently approved by the author. Although Sannazaro expected his fame to rest on his later Latin poems and seems to have maintained a rather apologetic attitude toward this youthful work in the vernacular, the *Arcadia* stands as one of the earliest and most widely popular of the works that marked the second birth of Italian vernacular literature around the beginning of the sixteenth century. And it certainly exerted an influence, not only in Italy but throughout Europe, on that process of imaginative transformation by which Renaissance writers discovered in Arcadia a region of the mind more spacious by far than it had seemed not only to earlier imitators of Virgil's pastorals but also to Virgil himself.

Time has faded the *Arcadia.* Modern scholarship, moreover, has demonstrated that the work is largely a pastiche not only of passages from ancient eclogues and many other classical sources, but also from Dante and Petrarch and from the romances of Boccaccio, especially his half-pastoral *Ameto,* a work Sannazaro often follows closely.[8] Deliberate eclecticism of this kind, amalgamating classical literature with the native tradition of the earlier Tuscan writers, was, to be sure, characteristic of the humanism of Sannazaro's time; and this amalgamation had a further literary attractiveness for the Italians of the early cinquecento who accepted the critical dictates of Pietro Bembo, since the *Arcadia* spoke for the emerging literature of Naples but spoke in the Tuscan dialect. But neither this immediate contemporary appeal, nor Sannazaro's technical innovation of introducing, in the eclogues dispersed through his prose narrative, experiments in a wide variety of lyrical verse forms, seems to account adequately for the continued republication of the *Arcadia* throughout the sixteenth century, or for the respect and even admiration the work gained for its author (sometimes as "*il divino Sannazaro*") among Italian critics of the latter part of the century.

Nor can it explain the attraction which the *Arcadia* held, in this century and even later, for new writers in Spain, Portugal, France, and England.

If one looks back on the *Arcadia* from these later writers of distinctively Renaissance pastoral works, having seen what their age did to broaden and transform the limited genre of the eclogue of antiquity, it seems likely that a principal reason for the imaginative stimulus they found in the work is the one suggested by the title itself: that Sannazaro was the first Renaissance pastoralist to make his work fundamentally Arcadian. It is this concern with the pastoral setting of the eclogue as a self-sufficient literary subject that J. H. Hanford has pointed to as the seminal new literary idea which marks the vernacular pastorals of the Renaissance, and which led writers in the vernacular to expand their pastoral works beyond the confines of the eclogue form into the forms of the drama and the prose romance.

The creation of the Arcadian mood, of the sense of the enveloping countryside of the eclogues as a reign of "bucolic" peace, has commonly been traced to Virgil in the *Bucolics,* who is credited with giving to the setting of his eclogues idyllic qualities lacking in the country setting of Theocritus's poems, and thus with first making Arcadia a symbolic country of the mind. But if these suggestions are actually in the *Bucolics,* they are certainly not marked and unequivocal; and my own guess is that the real Virgilian source for the Arcadian mood which is one ingredient of this seminal new idea for the vernacular pastoralists of the Renaissance is their own combination of faint suggestions of this kind in the *Bucolics* with Virgil's utopian picture of the Arcadian kingdom of King Evander in Book 8 of the *Aeneid.*

It is a striking fact, at any rate, that, by contrast, Mantuan and other writers of Latin pastorals in Sannazaro's time, like earlier Latin imitators of Virgil, all of whom wrote with their eyes narrowly on their model in the *Bucolics,* show none of the Arcadianism which developed in the vernacular pastorals, and continued to handle the eclogues in what Hanford has called "the Medieval spirit" of their predecessors.[9] Dante's Latin eclogues have in them little, apart from their title, which corresponds to what the word *pastoral* suggests to modern criticism. And in Petrarch's and Boccaccio's Latin imitations of Virgil's *Bucolics,* as well as in most of the later eclogues of Mantuan, it is chiefly the allegorical and didactic elements in Virgil's pastorals which they have responded to, so that they handle the eclogue as a genre for moral teaching, or for political and ecclesiastical satire.

In the *Arcadia,* however, the prose narrative which frames the twelve eclogues is concerned primarily with the Arcadian setting itself and more broadly with the countryside and the various activities of Arcadian life than with the specifically pastoral occupation of tending sheep and goats. The author tells us at length about the landscape; about the country sports and hunting diversions of its people, their religious rites, and folklore and magic charms; and, of course, about their yearning, unfulfilled love affairs. And for most of the first half of the book at least, Sannazaro seems to be presenting his visit to Arcadia almost as an experience in itself, without moralizing this life or assigning to it, in fact, any clearly defined contemporary reference.

But if Sannazaro has turned away from the medieval practice of treating the pastoral life as a fiction to be allegorized for didactic references to contemporary society, he nevertheless, as the book progresses, makes his Arcadia into a symbolic as well as a realistic country. Its symbolic suggestion begins to emerge midway in the *Arcadia* (chap. 7), in an autobiographical passage in which the author introduces himself and explains his role in the book. He has entered Arcadia, we learn, not as a shepherd, but in his own person, as a cultivated young gentleman of Naples made melancholy both by the depressed fortunes of his family under the political vicissitudes of that kingdom and by the sadness of a youthful, unrequited love. In the vain hope of forgetting these sorrows, he has left Naples and journeyed to Arcadia. And he thus retains there his proper name, one honored by his forebears, of "Sannazaro," or it may be, as he prefers to be called, of "Sincero," the name of his poetic persona.[10] Moreover, since the author has visited Arcadia, as he reiterates in his epilogue, "not as a rustic shepherd, but as a most cultivated youth," so journeying there "unknown, and as a pilgrim of love," it is not entirely surprising that this modern cultural sophisticate feels, at times, somewhat alien to the simple, uncultivated life of his Arcadian world.[11]

By this surprising breach of poetic decorum in his nakedly autobiographical intrusion into the narrative, Sannazaro in effect presents himself in the book in precisely the real-life situation of an early Renaissance poet who is imitating the naive poetic techniques of the simple way of life that he has found in the classical pastorals. And when one becomes aware of Sannazaro's bizarre self-consciousness about his role as a literary character in this modern recreation of the ancient pastoral world, and recognizes many of his fellow-poets from Naples, some of whom appear under their actual names and others disguised under shepherd names as they engage in singing their eclogues, it becomes clear that the Arcadia of his book is an only half-realized fictional symbol for the world of Sannazaro's youthful imagination. Preoccupied with love-longing, and with his early dedication to poetry, he has created this Arcadia in his mind, he suggests, under the stimulus of reading the eclogues of antiquity (the only literary source for this country which the book itself acknowledges): it is the mental region in which the related preoccupations of youthful love-dreams and poetic aspirations can find their home, as he abandons his own city-world of Naples and both the political responsibilities of his birth and the strenuous demands of his humanistic education to dwell for a while in this simpler, ancient world and write his vernacular eclogues.

The Arcadia of Sannazaro has not yet been made into what it was to become in the hands of some later Renaissance pastoralists: a picture of the Golden Age, historically actualized in an idealized fiction of the life of ancient Greece. Nor has the pastoral world become what it was to be still later for Milton, in both *Comus* and *Lycidas*: a symbol of the Neoplatonic Life of Contemplation. But Sannazaro has at least launched Arcadia on the long and various new career that it is to have in the modern imagination. Moreover, by making his Arcadia the region for solitude (a situation, incidentally, quite unknown to the shepherds of antiquity) and for wistful and sentimental Petrarchan musing among the consoling presences of rocks, woods, and streams, he has refashioned this setting for Virgil's Eclogues into something neither Roman nor Greek but an expression, instead, of his own romantic temperament and of one characteristic strain in the sensibility of his own nation in the Renaissance.

Hanford suggests one plausible reason that certainly contributed to the Arcadianism by which the vernacular pastoral developed away from the allegorical and didactic qualities of Virgil's Eclogues to a more realistic interest in the mere quality of Arcadian life—the gradual rediscovery in the 1480s to 1490s of the hitherto unknown source for the *Bucolics*: the *Idylls* of Theocritus and the surviving fragments of Bion and Moschus (whose poems were originally thought to be the work of Theocritus himself).[12] Sannazaro was quickly aware of this literary discovery and freely plundered the work of these Sicilian pastoralists in writing both his prose narrative and his verse eclogues. But to his imagination the recovery of Theocritus's work not only made clear the realistic origins of the literary eclogue in the folk songs and folk customs of the Mediterranean islands: it suggested also to his ardent mind some propositions about literary history more momentous in themselves and in their future consequence.

It appears to me that it was Sannazaro—not just single-handedly, I am sure, but certainly more than any other man—who launched us on the belief that there was something like a significant "pastoral tradition" in the genre of the eclogue, in the literature of classical antiquity. And, on the skimpiest of evidence, he created a new and surprisingly generative literary theory out of nothing more than a handful of short poems that represented only a very small part of the large corpus of ancient literature known by his time—two groups of eclogues which, for all practical purposes of literary history, were the work of only two poets of distinguished talent, one Greek, the other Roman, neither of whose eclogues had produced any numerous contemporary imitators in the genre or had established any significant tradition in the later literature of his own nation. And on the basis of nothing more than this handful of ancient eclogues, Sannazaro went on to argue that the form of the eclogue, in its evolution from its folk-beginnings, clearly traceable through the works in this kind by Theocritus, and then through the works culminating in the *Aeneid,* had been one of the really seminal genres to bring about the crowning achievement of the literature of the Augustine age, forming an ancient poetic tradition—extending from Greece to Rome—which should be emulated by any modern writers hopeful of paragoning that literature in the literature of his modern nation.

There is, in fact, no definition of the pastoral as an independent literary genre anywhere in the criticism of ancient times.[13] The concept of the pastoral as a distinctive genre is virtually a creation of the Renaissance. And it was thus that the Renaissance gave a dizzying new spin to the dusty "Wheel of Virgil" of the twelfth-century rhetoricians. The Eclogues were no longer regarded as just the group of poems which formed the initial stage of Virgil's progression through his own literary career: in later eager extensions of Sannazaro's theory, the eclogues came to be regarded as virtually the beginning of a national literature itself.

This belief of Sannazaro's, first asserted in the tenth chapter of the *Arcadia,* seems to have been shared by many, probably most, of the later writers of pastoral works in the Renaissance. But what Sannazaro and his contemporaries had started did not stop there. It took on a vigorous new life in the Romantic Movement, when this handful of ancient eclogues, at this time read in conjunction with their numerous Renaissance progeny, seems to swell until it threatens to engulf all Greek literature except the *Odyssey* and a few myths and romantic tales; so that the world of the classical eclogues seems, to some writers of that time, to have become almost the literary record of the morning world of Greece itself. It was from this modern pastoral tradition that the imagination of Keats created a romanticized picture of ancient Greece that is with us yet: it was a leafy-green Arcadia, peopled by technically ignorant bards who sang superb romantic tales and then died content on pleasant sward, with no other literary company than the shepherds, who everywhere, and spontaneously, sang only of their loves, in full-throated ease.

I would say that this belief in the significance in antiquity of the "classical pastoral tradition" is still far from dead among historians of modern literature. But it is one of the myths of literary history. I think it would have made any Greek or Roman poet simply stare and gasp.

Sannazaro's heady excursus into literary history appears in his tenth chapter. It was thus originally intended as a part of the conclusion of the work, since the first form of the *Arcadia,* preserved in manuscripts, was constructed by Sannazaro on a Virgilian ten-eclogue plan. In this scene a priest leads Sincero to the sacred grove and cave in which shepherds have built their shrine to Pan, the forest-deity of Arcadia. Hanging on a tree by the cave is a

zampogna, or bagpipe, the native peasant instrument which the
Italian poets equated with the seven-reeded shepherd's pipe of
antiquity. It was hung there by Pan, the priest explains, who had
sung to this pipe his unconsummated love for Syrinx, thereby
converting his sighs into sweet harmony. In this passage, expanded
from a few lines in Virgil's Second Eclogue, the myth of Pan and
Syrinx suggests the rise of the most primitive folk-form of pastoral
poetry. This earliest, artless phase of the eclogue, the myth implies,
was the spontaneous and natural creation of shepherds living in
direct contact with the natural world and endowed with the godlike
gift of poetic speech; and the sole subject of these songs which Pan
first created from his syrinx was, just as naturally, frustrated love.

But after Pan's death (and the passing of this primitive stage of
society) the zampogna came to Theocritus. "Thereafter it came, I
know not how, into the hands of a shepherd of Syracuse who,
before any other, had the daring to play it without fear of Pan or of
other God, beside the crystal waves of his native Arethuse." At
Theocritus's death, Sincero learns, he made the shepherd pipe

> his last gift to Mantuan Tityrus: and with failing breath resign-
> ing it to him, he spoke in this fashion: 'You now will be the
> second lord of this; with which at your will you can reconcile
> the quarreling bulls, rendering most grateful harmony to the
> woodland Deities.' Upon which Tityrus, pleased at so great an
> honor, working his pleasure with this same zampogna, first
> taught the woods to echo the name of the beautiful Amaryllis;
> and then thereafter, the burning of rustic Corydon. . . .

And so on, through what looks at first like just a list of the subjects
of Virgil's ten Eclogues. But this list is selected and arranged, so that
we learn first of the more strictly pastoral, bucolic eclogues. And
then, as though Virgil had begun to expand his original endowment
from Theocritus, we learn that he wrote several eclogues which seem
of a different kind (5, 6, and 10, on graver, less specifically pastoral
themes, in a more elevated style): "adding to this the death of
Daphnis, the song of Silenus, the fierce love of Gallus, with other
things which (I believe) the forests yet remember, and will remember
while shepherds exist in the world."

But beyond these poems, still showing traces of their derivation

from folk-tradition and the Theocritean idylls, Virgil was emboldened to write one more eclogue for which the traditional
pastoral pipe could no longer serve him.

> But he by nature having a genius disposed to higher things,
> and not contenting himself with so humble a strain, took in
> exchange that reed that now you see there, larger and newer
> than the others, to be able to sing of greater things, and to
> make the woodlands worthy of the loftiest Roman Consuls.
> Which reed (when having abandoned his goats he set himself
> to instruct the rustic tillers of the soil, perhaps with a hope
> of later singing with more sonorous trumpet the arms of Trojan
> Aeneas) he hung up there, where you now see it, in honor of
> this God who had shown him favor in his singing. After him
> came never a soul to these woods that has been able to play
> it with accomplishment, though many, spurred by ambitious
> daring, have attempted it often times and attempt it still.[14]

To Sannazaro, therefore, the historical tradition of the pastoral
eclogue of antiquity, as that genre had been refined from its
subliterary beginnings by Theocritus and then carried to full literary
elaboration by the greater genius of Virgil, who then passed it on to
modern writers for further development of its potentialities, points
the modern heirs of this legacy to only one exemplary poem—the
proto-epic Fourth Eclogue, in which Virgil had escaped the
confinements of the pastoral conventions and, swelling his eclogue
to a grander style, had first essayed a national theme, in order to
prophesy for his nation the coming renascence of the Golden Age.

Among the humanist poets of Naples, Sannazaro finds, there are
many new shepherd-singers, who are praised later in this tenth
chapter as "the distinguished generation that saw itself plenteously
endowed with so many shepherds of such quality; inasmuch as in
our age it had been granted us to see and hear shepherds singing
among their flocks who after a thousand years would be in demand
in the forest.[15] But none among them is more ready to take up that
larger pipe which Virgil left hanging on Pan's tree than
Sannazaro-Sincero himself. This poetic intention, evidently, is the
reason for his ambiguous attitude toward the pastoral world.
Arcadian life, melancholy songs of love, and the humble style of

vernacular eclogues are allowable to the feverish period of youth. But a young poet nursed in the humanist culture of noble cities visits Arcadia only to learn there that maturity will require of him sterner tasks.

When Sincero, who has been a passive observer in the early chapters, enters the action to reveal his identity and to tell the shepherd Carino the story of his sorrowful love, Carino responds with sympathy. But he then asks Sincero about the rhymes of another kind "that long since I heard you singing in the depth of the night." Though the words have escaped him, the new melody remains in his mind, and in recompense for these poems he gives Sincero an unusual pipe made of elderwood.

> With this I trust that you, if it be not denied you by the fates, in the future will sing in loftier vein the loves of the Fauns and the Nymphs. And even as up to this point you have fruitlessly spent the beginnings of your adolescence among the simple and rustic songs of shepherds, so hereafter you will pass your fortunate young manhood among the sounding trumpets of the most famous poets of your century, not without hope of eternal fame.[16]

Already endowed with the pipe of the *Georgics,* and thereby giving promise of producing in maturity the *Aeneid* of the new Italy, Sincero is prompted to the only eclogue in the book which the author sings in his own person. "When he had said this, he fell silent, and I, sounding my accustomed lyre, began in this fashion." His solo eclogue is a formal love-complaint, written as a sestina, and closely modeled on one of the canzoni of Petrarch.

The lyre is not the shepherds' zampogna; and this word serves notice that Sannazaro's poem will rise above the humble form of the pastoral eclogue and ascend to the higher category of the lyric. But lyres, to which he is now accustomed, are not trumpets, to which he will advance in time; and Sannazaro evidently regards the lyric as a form of middle dignity, somewhat below the heroic poem, but, in its artistic reach, clearly higher than the eclogue. Since the lyre betokens his poetic ascent in the direction of the sounding trumpet, Sannazaro evidently looks on the Tuscan canzone of Petrarch as the modern lyric form that is analogous to the intermediate poetic stage of the *Georgics* in the "Wheel of Virgil" of the medieval critics: it is the genre by which a poet reaches beyond the pastoral toward the epic poem.

Many other effects in the later chapters of the *Arcadia,* particularly in the dark concluding chapters on the national theme of the French conquest of Naples, which Sannazaro added to the revised edition of 1504, show similar indications that one central purpose of his book is to enfranchise the pastoral genre from the low estate to which critics had confined it. The predominant literary suggestions of these later chapters are those of tragedy and sometimes of nationalistic epic. The final eclogues are funeral dirges, the eleventh, the climactic elegy for Massilia, written not in loose, pastoral *versi sdruccioli* but in Dantesque terza rima ("because at the close it behooves me somewhat to rise, abandoning my rude pastoral style"); there is a passage of funeral games, imitated from the *Iliad,* the *Thebaid,* and the *Aeneid;* and the narrative ends with a portentous dream sequence (derived chiefly from Boccaccio and Virgil's Fourth Georgic) in which Sannazaro returns to Naples by a journey under the earth, during which he has revelatory visions of the tragic future of his conquered country—the free city-state of Naples—under the domination of France.

The elegiac "Epilogue: To His Zampogna" resumes earlier laments for the death of the Neopolitan Muses, the ruin of "our Parnassus," and the contemporary extinction of the shepherd songs in the woods. And though it assumes a deprecatory attitude toward these simple eclogues of Sannazaro's green youth, it reasserts in its conclusion what he evidently regards as the central achievement in his modern attempt to carry on the ancient pastoral tradition: he sees himself as the first who has tried to play that new and larger pipe, left hanging by Virgil on Pan's tree, "with accomplishment," and with that daring to which the pastoral genre invites the emergent vernacular literature of a new country and a new, intellectually sophisticated age. Responding to those who have criticized his pastoral work by saying "with precise judgment . . . that in some place you have not well kept the laws of shepherds, and that it is not well for anyone to pass further than befits his station," Sannazaro confesses his guilt. Nevertheless, he tells this book, "for you it can be no small excuse that you have been the first in this age to reawaken the slumbering woods, and to show the shepherds how to sing the songs they have forgotten." Furthermore, he points out—with that engaging, naive candor that justifies his literary name of *"Sincero"*—he could scarcely have been expected to hold himself down to the humble style critics insist upon for pastorals. When he came into Arcadia to sing these songs, he came there, after all, "not as a rustic shepherd but as a most cultured youth. . . . To say nothing of the fact that in other times there have been already shepherds so daring that they have advanced their style even to the ears of Roman consuls; under whose shade you will be able, my zampogna, very well to shelter yourself, and with spirit to advance reasons for your defense."[17]

That Spenser, writing his *Shepheardes Calender* in the early, eclectic phase of the evolution of the English Renaissance vernacular literature, found much to turn to his own use in this seminal pastoral work of the European Renaissance seems certain. The *Arcadia* could not, however, have served in any sense as a model for *Lycidas*. But it is not a model for that poem, in any case, that I am looking for: clearly, there is none. Any ideas about the pastoral genre which the *Arcadia* contributed to the forming of *Lycidas* are, at most, general rather than particular; and the influence may have been indirect, through Sannazaro's limited influence on the pastoral work of Spenser and his stronger influence on that of Tasso, two poets for whom Milton felt a much closer affinity than he could have felt for this pioneering pastoralist of an earlier Renaissance, who had written in a less advanced stage in the development of its techniques for vernacular literature. But it would be surprising if Milton, in the eager exploration of Italian literature he had begun several years before the writing of *Lycidas*, had failed to read, and to be attracted by, this work that had held so admired and influential a place in the literature of the nation toward which he looked, while he laid his plans to journey there, as "the lodging place of *humanitas*, and of all the arts of civilization."[18]

It remains for me to consider one further mutation of the classical eclogue in a much finer work by a much finer poet, Tasso's *Aminta*. The *Aminta* is one of the collateral descendants, in a later generation, of Sannazaro's *Arcadia*, and its influence on the forming of *Lycidas,* as F. T. Prince has shown, is both more direct and more certain.

Milton's early admiration for Tasso was of a kind which he could not have arrived at overnight, but it is not until *Lycidas* that it begins to register as an active influence on his poetry. In the rest of his poetic work, from *Lycidas* on, we can see that Tasso has taken his place beside Spenser—who had himself studied under Tasso for his *Faerie Queene*—as the second of Milton's chief masters among the moderns, in much the same way that, also in *Lycidas,* we can first see Homer emerge from behind Virgil to stand with him as the other of Milton's chief masters among the ancient poets.[19] In the poems of his Italian journey, which came immediately after *Lycidas,* Milton's ardor for "the great Tasso," and for celebrating the "glory of his mighty name" ("*decus nomen . . . ingens*") is written strong in the Latin poems he addressed to Leonora and to Tasso's friend Manso; and I think F. T. Prince is correct in saying that one of the precise literary purposes Milton had in mind as he planned his visit to Italy was to seek out Manso in Rome and Naples "because he wished to find out all he could about Tasso, the only epic poet of modern times of whom he thoroughly approved."[20] These poems express an imaginative identification with Tasso, moreover, which is more than merely literary. It has something of the character of that high Platonic ardency in friendship which first appears in Milton's letters to his Italian friend Charles Diodati during the Horton period, and in the *Epitaphium Damonis*; and it is significant that a principal focus of the strikingly impassioned poem *Mansus* is the fact, stressed in the headnote, that it was to Manso that Tasso had addressed his dialogue "On Friendship."[21] Like his lifelong devotion to Spenser, whom Milton told Dryden he regarded as his father,[22] his feeling of affinity with Tasso was evidently a more complex and personal bond than the purely literary respect and indebtedness that a young English poet, beginning his career in the 1630s, might understandably owe to the greatest Italian poet of the late Renaissance.

My present concern is not with the epic poet of *Gerusalemme Liberata* and the later creation-epic *Le Sette Giornate del Mondo Creato,* but with Tasso the pastoralist, in his verse drama *Aminta.* In

Tasso's work, however, these two aspects do not represent different stages in his career but are concurrent; and the fact that Tasso did not write his one important pastoral work until he was already embarked on a career as a writer of epics accounts in part for the new development in form which the pastoral poem received at his hands. As the precocious son of an accomplished epic poet, Tasso may have concluded that he had no need to serve the traditional probation in eclogues before he qualified for epic poetry; and he began a full-scale epic on classical models at the age of fifteen. Deciding, however, that his wings were not fully fledged for this flight, he laid this enterprise aside and wrote the less ambitious *Rinaldo,* which modern criticism has classified as no epic but a chivalric romance,[23] but which both Sidney, in the *Apology for Poetry,* and Spenser, in his "Letter to Ralegh," regarded as a significant modern example of the genus of the heroic poem. Having completed the *Rinaldo,* and being thus timely-happy and not yet arrived at the age of twenty-three, Tasso returned to the abandoned fragment of his earlier epic and began revising it into the first version of *Gerusalemme Liberata.* He had been at work on it for several years when he interrupted his epic labors, in 1573, to write the *Aminta,* for presentation before the court of Alfonso d'Este at Ferrara, to which he had recently become attached as a court poet.

The Estense court, whose poets had earlier, in the 1460s, established a tradition of neo-Latin pastorals in imitation of Virgil's Eclogues, also had a tradition of elaborate pageants and theatrical entertainments; and it had recently seen the performance of pastoral plays in the vernacular.[24] The first of these, Beccari's five-act verse comedy *Il Sacrificio,* was revived soon after Tasso's work; and taking advantage, it appears, of the duke's absence from Ferrara, which allowed him a temporary respite from work on his epic, Tasso decided to try his hand at a full-scale pastoral drama in verse. One wonders, in fact, whether he might not have reflected that, since a work of this sort seemed the expected thing for a new poet at the court of Ferrara, he might not only pay fuller homage to the ancient poet he most wished to emulate but also perfect some skills that he would need for his epic poem, if he paused, in his brilliant but impetuous career, belatedly to execute his bucolics.

Other Renaissance pastoralists had followed the example of Virgil, not only in his Fourth Eclogue but also at other points in the *Bucolics,* in using their pastorals to air their plans for someday writing an epic poem. Since this convention did not entirely apply to Tasso's literary circumstances when he wrote the *Aminta,* he decided to run a variation on it and to make use of the convention, by an ingenious twist, in order to justify the literary innovations he made in this pastoral work. In view of the fact that his piece was to be performed before the Estense court, whose members were already familiar with his *Rinaldo,* as well as with what he had completed of the *Liberata,* Tasso interpolated in the second scene of *Aminta* a review of his literary career with particular reference to his historically unprecedented situation as a heroic poet suddenly required to turn pastoralist.

In this scene the shepherd Tirsi (Tasso) tells of the effect that had been produced, both on him and on his songs, when he left the simple country life to which he had been born and found himself received as an honored poet in the cultivated world of this ideal court of the Renaissance. His bedazzled eyes saw there for the first time noble men and celestial goddesses, new Linuses and new Orpheuses, and Phoebus and the Muses. And when one seated among those Muses (the poet and philosopher Giovanni Battista Pigna) graciously made him welcome into their company:

> in that instant
> I felt myself made greater than myself,
> Full of new power, full of a new deity,
> And I sang of wars and heroes,
> Scorning the crude pastoral song;
> And though later, at the pleasure of others,
> I made a return to these woods, I still retained
> Some part of that temper: nor indeed
> Does my zampogna sound humbly, as was its wont,
> But in voice more haughty, and more sonorous,
> It rivals the trumpets, it fills all the woods.[25]

It is a pretty difficult thing for a man, Tasso playfully suggests, when he has discovered that he has the talents of an epic poet and is perfecting himself in the arduous skills required for that great genre, suddenly to throttle his talent down to the low, humble tones expected of the simple pipe of pastoral poetry. And if, under constraint and the strong demand of an occasion, his fingers are forced to do it, that very occasion will, after all, find him addressing his pastoral to the same discriminating audience, habituated to the greater Muses, which he had looked to as those who could appreciate the high-classical modern epic that was already taking form in his mind. In these circumstances almost the only thing such a poet can reasonably do, Tasso suggests, is to enlarge both the form and the stylistic reach of the humble genre of the pastoral poem, in order to make it produce some of the poetic effects traditionally reserved for poetry in the major literary forms, and at times even heroic poetry, to which his own career has now been committed.

In the new form he created for the *Aminta,* Tasso follows in the tradition, begun by Sannazaro, of expanding the forms of pastoral writing beyond the confines of the classical eclogue. In its form, in fact, Tasso has cut his poem entirely free from its roots in the verse eclogues of antiquity and has developed it, instead, out of the pastoral drama which, evolving from the short, generally comic dramatic eclogue, had recently appeared as a new form of the mid-century in Italy. His play is actually an amalgamation of a wide range of sources, native Italian as well as classical, and in so far as it derives from the classical verse eclogue, it is more in debt to the Arcadian pastoralism of Theocritus and Moschus than to the graver pastoral work of Virgil.[26] But the Renaissance Italian poets, as we have already seen with Sannazaro, have a well-understood convention of concealing their eclectic hybridizing of Italian with ancient literary forms, by suggesting that the literary models of their modern works are exclusively, or at least primarily, classical. Tasso was enough of a humanist in literary theory to give to the *Aminta* a diffused but recognizable connection with Virgil's Eclogues, to cover his eclecticism by alluding in his prologue to the traditional view that it was through pastorals that a poet took the proper road to the epic, and to give his modern play identifiable suggestions of the classical literary genres. In order to raise the originally low genre of the dramatic eclogue to literary dignity, he devised for the play both a formal design and a style and prosody that would make his pastoral, by a

scheme more artistically integral than the methods Sannazaro had
used for this purpose, reach out to embrace the effects not only
of the lyric but also of tragedy. Though it remained for Guarini,
whose *Pastor Fido* is the direct offspring of *Aminta,* to formulate
the novel critical concept of "tragicomedy," Tasso must have
wished to suggest a tragic, dramatic form of this kind by the
structure of *Aminta,* a drama of five acts in which the act-divisions
are marked by choruses in rhyme, the first two of which are free
adoptions of the verse form of the canzone, a form which Italian
critics had regarded as a modern equivalent to the strophic stanzas
of the choral odes in Greek tragedies.[27]

Though the play manages a happy ending, its pervasive mood is
the melancholy love-longing that had been the dominant character
of the *Arcadia* of Sannazaro. Actually, the aspect of Virgil's
Eclogues which Sannazaro's imagination had centered on in
conceiving his own Arcadia was not Virgil's suggestions in the
Fourth Eclogue for swelling the pastoral to a grander style, though
he had claimed that eclogue as the authority for his innovations in
the form of pastoral literature. What he had responded to most
strongly, among the varied subjects of Virgil's *Bucolics,* was the
generally frustrated loves of Virgil's shepherds, and particularly the
mood of broody sexual yearning in the Second, homosexual
Eclogue, the "Alexis." This mood is also Tasso's preoccupation in
Aminta, and with an imagination bolder than Sannazaro's, and a
more forthright sensuality, he makes his play into one of the most
complete expressions in literature of a youthful sexual daydream.
Virgil's Fourth Eclogue, which had prophesied to Pollio and
Octavius the return of the Golden Age, had undergone some
surprising transmogrifications in after ages, as it foretold the birth
of the Messiah to Emperor Constantine and to Saint Augustine
(not to mention some stranger later bedfellows of theirs); and
once again, in medieval times, as it provided the basis for the
mythical figure of that Virgil who was a great magician. But it
received no stranger transformation than the one Tasso gave it in
the superb first-act chorus of the *Aminta, "O bell'età dell'oro,"* in
which the Golden Age, which Tasso finds embodied in the classical
pastorals, peopled with shepherds who bear classical names,

becomes a longed-for world of complete sexual license, from which all Nature speaks to men its one and only moral law: "If it gives pleasure, it is lawful."

On first reflection, it does not seem that a pastoral on this subject is exactly what one would look to in searching out the literary forebears of *Lycidas*. It is certainly not in the erotic pastorals of the late sixteenth and early seventeenth centuries that Milton found modern examples for his essential conception of what a pastoral poem should be, but rather, as Prince has said, in the high seriousness of the eclogues of Spenser, and, among the Italians, in the graver pastorals, more closely modeled on Virgil, which had been written earlier in the century by Sannazaro and, after him, by Bernadino Rota, who had stiffened the style of Sannazaro's vernacular eclogues by adapting to them the dense diction and the rhetoric and cadences of Virgil. The *Aminta* stands at the breaking point between the neo-Virgilian tradition of these earlier pastorals and the new thing that was made of pastoral poetry by Italian writers at the end of the century, as well as by most of the English poets, after Spenser, who wrote pastoral lyrics in the late Elizabethan and Jacobean periods. After the technical innovations of *Aminta* and *Il Pastor Fido,* as Prince puts it, the Italian pastoral developed away from any dependence on the example of Virgil, "and entered on a new world of its own, preoccupied with the affairs of the Amaryllis and Neaera who are allotted two lines in Milton's poem."[28]

But the mere subject of a poem, or even its morality, can never be the whole story of it to an artist. Moreover, as the opening line of *Lycidas* reminds us, Milton had himself written earlier poems devoted to the myrtles of Venus; and the tone of the lines in which he speaks of his renunciation of Amaryllis and Neaera is, at any rate, rather more regretful than censorious ("Alas, . . . were it not better done . . ."), suggesting that those earlier preoccupations were not wholly gone from his mind when he wrote this poem. They recall to us earlier periods in Milton's youth when he had called Ovid his master among the Latins and (probably a few years afterward) had written love sonnets in Italian, and when, by his own later testimony, his imagination would have responded with-

out any reluctance to the intensely romantic sexuality of the
Aminta.[29]

The poet in him, at any rate, clearly responded to what is Tasso's most original accomplishment in the *Aminta*. This accomplishment resides not in the mere form of the play, since all the
components of that form (the verse patterns, the five-act structure, and even the lyrical choruses between acts) had appeared
in earlier Italian pastoral dramas. It resides, rather, in what
Tasso points to, in the passage I have quoted, as his distinctive
achievement, the rhetorical and metrical virtuosity by which he
makes the Italian language sound, move, and cohere throughout
the play, so that his shepherd's pipe can be made to resonate with
the tones of trumpets and fill all the woods.

The verse form Tasso chose was not in itself a novelty.[30] He
combines unrhymed hendecasyllabic lines, which are the norm for
the dramatic dialogue, with passages of dialogue in heptasyllables,
occasionally with rhyme; and the same mixture predominates in
the choruses, which are more fully but still irregularly rhymed, so
that the lyricism of the choruses seems to flow back into the dialogue and then to arise naturally from it in the choral poems concluding each of the acts.

This mixture of eleven-syllable with seven-syllable lines had
originally been the verse pattern for that noblest form of the
canzone stanza Dante had described as the "tragic" canzone and
which he had regarded as the one Italian stanza form suited to the
"illustrious" style.[31] Tasso's innovation was to conceive the verse
structure of the entire play, and not just of the choruses, in terms
of potential lyrical stanzaic units whose patterns of line length
and flickering rhyme could at any point be shaped into sustained
units of musical phrase. Writing with an ear trained to the formal
patterns of the canzone—a verse form which the cinquecento poets
had liberated from its original requirements of maintaining a fixed
rhyme scheme throughout a complex stanza and then repeating
that metrical pattern in succeeding stanzas—Tasso had a prosodic
mold that inclined him to think in terms of sizable
verse-paragraphs within which he could dispose long rhetorical
periods. But this prosodic mold allowed him to break into those

periods, in a freely improvisatory way, inflecting their movement as he wished by shorter lines that could be made at times to rhyme, so that these musical patterns of sound might also be used to shape the formal movement of his verse. With this fluently lyrical verse instrument, he could write dramatic dialogue that might lift itself at any moment into music for a series of lines long or short, and then lapse back into dialogue. And in his choruses he could deploy his periods into irregularly rhymed stanzaic patterns whose movement could be checked with the shorter lines and then released to flow through the long lines and to form into broader metrical reaches.

F. T. Prince has argued plausibly that in "this liberation of the canzone for dramatic and lyrical verse" in both the passages of semilyrical dialogue and the choruses of the *Aminta,* together with the similar choruses of Guarini's *Il Pastor Fido,* Milton found hints which he turned to use in the irregular verse structures of *Lycidas.* But Prince makes clear that Milton's free use of the verse techniques of the canzone, like Tasso's, builds on the work of a long line of predecessors in Italian poetry. It is in debt to Petrarch, whom Milton acknowledged, together with Dante, as one of his early masters; and it has its origin, ultimately, in Dante's metrical analysis of the canzone in *De Vulgari Eloquentia.*[32] I can only refer my reader to Prince's precise demonstration of the way in which Milton has adapted Dante's metrical principles for this verse form, and Tasso's freer use of the canzone stanza, adding to them a few technical innovations of his own, in order to create the interacting metrical and rhetorical structures of *Lycidas.* The conclusion Prince comes to, from his analysis of this aspect of the formal structure of the poem, is as follows:

> Two technical experiments—the attempt to evolve a poetic diction equivalent to that of Virgil, and the attempt to combine the tradition of the *canzone* with that of the Classical eclogue—marked Italian pastoral verse in the sixteenth century. In England both these experiments bore fruit in *Lycidas.*[33]

To the Italian critics, however, the canzone was more than a complex instrument of verse structure. This Tuscan verse form had behind it a critical as well as a poetic tradition in Italian literature, a critical theory that was more elaborate because this form was of greater interest to the cinquecento critics than the critical theory of the classical eclogue. In this critical tradition the canzone had acquired virtually the character of an independent literary genre, with its own decorums of subject, of structure, and of style. It was of particular interest to humanist critics because they saw in this native poetic form, which had actually been developed independently by northern Italian poets of the thirteenth and fourteenth centuries, an equivalent in their own vernacular literature to what they regarded as one of the major literary kinds of Greek poetry—the genre of the grand lyric.

In writing *Aminta,* Tasso was aware of this critical theory, to which he was later to make contributions of his own, and he exploited it in his prologue to the play. That prologue concludes with two literary propositions announcing, at the start, two technical innovations, both of them violations of the accepted critical decorums for the pastoral, which Tasso has made in building his pastoral work. First, he makes clear that he has decided to break the critics' "Wheel of Virgil" and to reject completely the requirement of a low style for this genre. The prologue is spoken by *Amore* (appropriately, since the device implies Tasso's view of the essential subject for pastorals), who has escaped from Venus and from the tiresome courts and court amours which are Venus's preoccupations. Appearing now in the costume of a shepherd, Love placates the critical rigorists with romantic charm. Here among the shepherds, he explains, he will manifest the miraculous power which is an attribute of his deity: he will "breathe noble sentiments into boorish breasts and sweeten the sound of their speech." Through this miracle all the shepherds are released from having to talk the uncultivated language required by the "decorum of persons" for the genre—and an epic poet is released from having to do anything so artistically uninteresting to him as trying to write constantly in the humble style.

The second technical innovation follows logically from the first and is the conclusion to which the prologue builds. In a reference not only to the device of introducing into a pastoral choruses in the verse form of canzoni, but also, probably, to the pervasive influence

of the canzone stanza on the verse of the dramatic speeches, Tasso
announces that his work will achieve a combination of the low genre
of the eclogue with the noble genre of the lyric. As *Amore* points
out, and as any well-trained critic would recognize, this is a literary
miracle more surprising than any which has hitherto been
accomplished by the supernatural power of Love. But wherever Love
manifests himself, among shepherds no less than among heroes,

> the inequality of my subjects,
> At my pleasure, I equalize. And this really
> Is my crowning glory, and my own great miracle,
> That I can make the rustic *zampogne*
> Equal the most highly skilled lyres [*le più dotte cetre*].

To Tasso, as to Sannazaro, the lyre is the recognized symbol for the
genre of the lyric poem. The lyric is a noble literary form which is
dotto: it requires learning and complex literary skills, and it does not
lower. its flight to the humble style. In Sannazaro's earlier view, as
we have seen, the lyric is a form below the heroic poem, whose
symbol is not the lyre but the trumpet. But both in Tasso's prologue
and in the autobiographical passage in the second scene of act 1, he
seems to regard the lyric as a form appropriate to heroes, the persons
proper to the epic, and capable of tones which can at least rival the
trumpets of epic poetry. And it appears that this is exactly why, at
this stage in his career, he himself wants to employ it, and why, in
order to do so, he is deliberately merging the eclogue into the genre
of its better, the lyric. Such a generic scheme for a pastoral work will
allow him to make full use of his talent for verse that is sensuous and
lyrical, while at the same time permitting him to exercise his skills in
writing the verse of vigor and sonority which he was trying to master
for the epic poem he was working on.

With the conjunction, in the *Aminta,* of the genre of the eclogue
with the genre of the lyric, I come to the final stage of my inquiry
into the literary theory and practice which entered into the shaping
of *Lycidas.* But we might pause, at this point, to consider what this
survey of earlier Renaissance practice in the vernacular pastoral has
demonstrated. In looking at the ideas about both form and style for
this genre which have directed the work of three of Milton's

predecessors—two of them poets whom Milton looked to as masters, and the other an earlier pastoralist who had exercised some influence on the work of both—and by inquiring into just what it was in the Eclogues of Virgil or the Greek pastoralists which they fixed on as a basis for their ideas for writing new works in this genre, we have arrived at a picture of a "pastoral tradition" behind *Lycidas* quite different from the one usually described. This is not surprising. I have been focusing on only one aspect of the evolution of the Renaissance pastoral, on what happened to the literary form and the style of pastoral writing in the vernacular when the imaginations of young poets were seized with an impulse to a higher mood. And the poets with whom I have been dealing have directed me, more-over, to concentrate on only one genetic strain in the broad tradition that derives from Virgil, a strain that has its origin chiefly in Virgil's Fourth Eclogue.

But the critical studies of *Lycidas* which have concentrated instead on Milton's careful observance of the "pastoral conventions," and on the innumerable other echoes of "the classical pastoral tradition" in the text of the poem, have certainly not been mistaken, nor is what they have emphasized any less important to an understanding of the poem. These studies point us to what is simply another, and quite different, genetic component of *Lycidas,* one I have been neglecting, but which is certainly a strong force in the molding of the poem. That other emphasis can direct us now to see things about the artistic choices Milton made in writing his pastoral which resulted in a number of related effects in the poem that combine to form one major component of its structure.

We can see, first, that despite a Renaissance poetic tradition, both Italian and English, which invited a considerable amount of free-wheeling in devising the form for a pastoral poem in the vernacular, Milton, like Spenser, elected the option of making his poem adhere much more closely to the literary form of the verse eclogues of antiquity than many other Renaissance pastoralists had chosen to do. Next, he wished to give his pastoral a further suggestion of its bond with the classical originals by making its style a virtual concentrate of echoes from the specific pastoral conventions, not only of Virgil, but also of Theocritus, and of Bion and

Moschus. (In this respect, as Hanford makes clear in the passage quoted earlier, *Lycidas* adheres more closely to the tradition of the neo-Latin eclogues of the Renaissance than to the new forms of vernacular pastoral literature.)

In addition, Milton has followed the example not of Spenser but perhaps, as Prince suggests, of the Italian pastorals of Bernadino Rota, and certainly the general poetic practice of Tasso and Della Casa, in making the diction of his pastoral dense with echoes of Virgil's language and poetic ornaments—so much so, in fact, that the modern student of English literature who goes from Milton to his first reading of the *Bucolics* sees what look like quotations from *Lycidas* on almost every other page. This heavily classical resonance of the language and style of the poem parallels in suggestion another striking element in the poem which I have discussed earlier—its insistent and repeated reference to the neoclassical critical norms for an eclogue built on classical models, to what is traditional and decorous in this literary kind. All these devices of overt, ostentatious classicizing combine to form one artistic strand that is woven firmly into the texture of *Lycidas* and plays an important part in the growth and movement of the poem and its final artistic effect. Essentially, these repeated suggestions of the "classical pastoral tradition," as Milton keeps alluding to it throughout the poem, serve to articulate, for both Milton and his reader, the aesthetic pressure of that force of "convention" (in the broadest sense of the term) which is one radical component of the life of any work of art.

It will not be a mere pedantic flourish but rather an honest search for an appropriate metaphorical language—a search forced upon me by our modern lack of any generally accepted logical terminology for the most fundamental ingredients in both works of art and our aesthetic responses to them—if I attempt to define the way in which this component of convention operates in *Lycidas* by adapting to my purpose some of the Aristotelian logical terminology the Italian critics themselves sometimes turned to for metaphor when they faced a similar difficulty. In these terms, one might say that the two basic artistic forces that, in their dynamic interplay, generate the artistic structure of the poem function in a way analogous to the operation of the two principles which, in the Aristotelian-Christian cosmology, join forces in the creation of all things in this world. The two principles at work in the process by which all "substances" or self-subsistent things are created are, first, the passive principle of matter and, second, the active, intellectual principle of "form."

In the shaping of *Lycidas* what is conventional in the poem—taken up into the text from earlier eclogues or from the theory of neoclassical critics—functions like the poem's component of matter, its passive principle: it is always there, preexistent but inert, asserting its presence throughout the poem. The new poem can be created only when the active principle of form, first conceived as an idea in the mind of the creator, realizes its potency in act by seeking out the particular matter which it was designed to activate. As it informs this passive, conventional material, the form molds it to coherent shape and at the same time makes out of it an active, substantial thing, existing in itself and performing its vital function in the scheme of things.

The form, however, cannot act alone: unless it infuses the particular passive material which it was created to animate and exerts its molding force upon it, form cannot actualize its own potentiality. But the passive matter also does its own work in the creative process: it exerts a force to pull against the form and to constrain it to its proper mode of action. The dynamic interaction between these two principles is the cause of the distinctive life of every created thing. If the activating form had not been required to pull against the preexistent, passive—or conventional—material out of which things of this specific kind are made, the new thing that had been conceived in the mind of the creator might perhaps have been a new thing, but it could never become what in essence its creator had designed it to be—a new, living exemplar of its species, the pastoral elegy on classical models.

4

The Lyric

In *Lycidas* the new form for the pastoral, the active, intellectual principle which pervades and shapes the whole poem as its informing artistic soul, is the form of the lyric as that genre was conceived by Italian poets and critics of the cinquecento and by Milton himself. The Italians had devised their theory of this genre, one that interested them strongly, by trying to harmonize what they could learn from classical sources about lyric poetry in antiquity with the theory and practice of their Tuscan poets of the trecento in forms of vernacular verse which seemed to them analogous to those ancient poetic forms.

Milton's own concept of the lyric was derived partly from the practice and theory of the Greek and Roman poets, and partly from the Hebrew poetry of the Old Testament, but chiefly from this new critical enterprise by which the sixteenth-century Italians had tried to establish the lyric poem as one of the major, comprehensive poetic kinds. In the theory they devised for it, the lyric was a mode of poetic discourse in which words worked in various kinds of combinations with music in order to produce a special kind of artistic effect. It was this conjunction of music with poetic language which categorized the lyric and gave to verse in this genre an effect different in character from that produced by the other major genres of the epic poem and the dramatic poem, in which language operated in partly different ways (or by different means of "imitation") to produce the effects distinctive to each of those literary kinds.

In the second Book of *The Reason of Church Government,* written in 1642, Milton presents his ideas about the one kind of lyric which strongly appealed to him—the most imposing of its ancient forms. represented by the strophic Pindaric ode and by the more formally

elaborate of the Old Testament poems. It was this form, according
to the Italian critics, one that could be discovered in both the
Greek and Hebrew literatures of antiquity, which found its modern
analogue in the most complex and stately variety of the canzone, a
native poetic form that Guinizelli, Cavalcanti, Dante, and other
Italian poets of the twelfth century had elaborated out of the
simpler *cansos* of the troubadour poets of Provence, and which
had then been brought to finished perfection in the canzoni of
Petrarch.

In Milton's survey of the major literary genres he had under
consideration at this time for the first work of his poetic maturity,
he discusses five literary kinds, with the fullest attention given to
forms of the epic; and he concludes with a discussion of the most
worthy kinds of the lyric poem. The other genres, with their preferred
models, are as follows:

1. the epic poem (following either Aristole's rules or nature):
   a. the diffuse form (*Iliad, Odyssey, Aeneid*, and also, as the
      only modern work mentioned in the whole passage,
      Gerusalemme Liberata)
   b. the brief form (*Job*)
2. the dramatic poem
   a. tragedy (Sophocles, Euripides, *The Apocalypse of St.
      John*)
   b. pastoral drama (*The Song of Solomon*)

In conclusion (3), Milton ponders whether "occasion shall lead to
imitate those magnific odes and hymns wherein Pindarus and
Callimachus are in most things worthy, some others in their frame
judicious, in their matter most and end faulty. But those frequent
songs throughout the Law and Prophets beyond all these, not in
their divine argument alone, but in the very critical art of composition, may be easily made appear over all kinds of lyric poesy to be
incomparable."[1]

This passage shows us several things about Milton's conception
of this highest of the lyric forms. He regards it as a noble genre,
comparable in literary status to the most worthy varieties of the
epic and of the dramatic poem, and requiring sophisticated literary

skills in the true critical art of composition. He thinks of it as a "song," a poem originally conceived to be set to music and actually sung. He regards the Greek odes of Pindar and Callimachus, and the Hebrew poems interspersed through the Pentateuch and the books of the Prophets as examples of essentially the same genre in the poetry of antiquity; but he sees the religious subjects of the Hebrew poems as the "argument" more appropriate to the lyric than the "matter" of the Greek odes. And he thinks the Pindaric odes were written in the "magnific" style. We shall see that these ideas reflect the pattern of thought which is common to most discussions of the high lyric genre by the cinquecento critics, and that the concept of the *magnifico* style derives also from these critics and, in its particular technical details, specifically from the analysis of that style by Tasso.

At this point, as we turn to a survey of Italian critical theories about the lyric, I wish to claim the privileges of an essay, and to allow a few of these critics room enough to speak at some length on their ideas about poetry. Most of their critical writings are very little known to English readers; and to strip them down to a few brief "critical opinions," brusquely excerpted, that would be directly relevant only to my argument about the form of *Lycidas*, would give, inevitably, a suggestion of dogmatic finality in their reasoning on literary matters that would misrepresent their critical thinking and conceal the subtlety, range, and frequent adventurousness of their speculations about literature. And there should be a peripheral value, apart from the immediate application of this criticism to an analysis of *Lycidas*, in taking a little time to investigate the literary ideas of some of the poets and critics with whom Milton associated intellectually while he was making up his mind about what kind of poet he was going to be.

In devising their theory of the lyric, as in their theory of the pastoral, the Italian critics found scant material to build on in classical literary criticism. A number of passages in ancient writers—in Plato, Aristotle, Plutarch, and Boethius—gave them tantalizing information about the strong and psychologically specific ethical "effects" which the different modes of Greek music had produced in their listeners, and which, one might infer, had been produced also by the verses that had been sung in these modes to the accompaniment of the lyre, the flute, and pipes of various kinds. These accounts of classical music had been of fascinating interest to Ficino and other Neoplatonists of his "Academy" in late fifteenth-century Florence; and they continued to engage the imaginations of some humanist literary critics and musicians of the late sixteenth century in Italy, as well as of the humanist group of *Pléiade* poets and musicians who, during the same period, were associated with Baif's Academy in France.[2]

But when Italian critics turned to the literary critics and rhetoricians of antiquity for information about the purely literary characteristics of poems written to be sung to music, and the laws governing the genus and the subspecies of the lyric as a literary genre, there was not much to go on—little more than some unspecific remarks in the *Poetics* and a passage of a few lines in the *Ars Poetica*. Still, that brought both Aristotle and Horace to their aid; and the passages from these two works, together with some brief remarks about dithyrambic poetry in the pseudo-Aristotelian *Problemata,* especially when read in conjunction with the widespread testimony from antiquity about the striking ethical effects of Greek music, were enough to provide the authority they needed for constructing a theory of the lyric as one of the dominant genres of classical poetry. From this theory they could then proceed to demonstrate that the sonnets, ballate, canzoni, and lesser lyric forms which had marked the first flowering of Italian literature in the thirteenth and fourteenth centuries, and which the Italians had in fact derived from the Provençal poets, represented nothing less than the first rebirth in modern times of one of the great poetic genres both of Greece and Rome, and of Jewish antiquity.

We can dispose briefly of the sources in classical criticism for the cinquecento theory of the lyric. In the introductory sections of the *Poetics,* before he proceeded to his analysis of tragedy, Aristotle had included dithyrambic poetry as well as "most music on the flute and lyre" (and, he later adds, "on the syrinx"), along with epic poetry, tragedy, and comedy, in his list of the distinctive forms of imitation in the arts; and in a later section he had pointed out that "tragedy was produced by the authors of the dithyrambs." What is common to all these arts is that they "produce their imitation through rhythm and speech and harmony, either separately or combined." Aristotle then suggests his definition of poetry (which "is up to the present without a name") as "the art which imitates by means of words only," whether in prose or metrical language. And he concludes this preliminary laying down of distinctions as follows:

> There are some arts that employ all the means I have mentioned, namely rhythm, melody, and metrical language, as the poetry of the dithyrambs and of the nomes and tragedy and comedy. These arts differ in that the first two use the three means throughout, the last two use them in various parts. These are the differences of the arts in the means through which they work out their imitation.[3]

These statements are scarcely conclusive for any sharp definition of the lyric genre, but for the later neo-Aristotelian critics who wished to exalt this literary form, the remarks about dithyrambic poetry could, and did, offer suggestive possibilities: that it had been the source from which the great genre of tragedy evolved, and that, because it could employ freely and throughout the devices of rhythm, melody, and metrical language, it was one poetic form which could combine all the means of imitation that were available to practitioners in the separate arts of dance, music, poetry, and drama.

Horace, on the other hand, was more gratifyingly specific from the point of view of the legalistic concerns of Renaissance humanist criticism, though far less suggestive from the point of view of aesthetic philosophy. As he chatted on informally to the Piso family about the poetic art, he delivered himself, by the way, of a few roundly assertive lines, which he did not enlarge upon elsewhere in the *Ars Poetica*, that could easily be read as having the sure ring of dogma and reflecting a definite conception both of the lyric poem as a fixed genre and of its decorums of subject:

> The Muse has assigned to the lyre the work of celebrating gods and heroes, the champion boxer, the victorious steed, and fond desire of lovers, and the cup that banishes care.[4]

It was not, however, until the Italians brought these two separate passages in classical criticism into combination with the critical theory and poetic practice of Dante and Petrarch—and then stirred into them, in a mixture whose proportion varied from one critic to another, some of the half-magical metaphysical ideas about Greek music which derived from the Florentine Neoplatonism of Ficino—that we can see the emergence of the theoretical concept of the lyric genre which engaged the energies of critics in the latter half of the sixteenth century.

In this combination the key work is Dante's *De Vulgari Eloquentia.* This formidably technical treatise "about literary style in the vernacular," which Dante undertook in the first decade of the 1300s and then left half-finished when he became engaged with his *Commedia,* had been lost sight of during the late fourteenth and fifteenth centuries; and it was rediscovered only in the early 1500s by Bembo, whose manuscript copy of it has been preserved, and by Trissino, who published it for the first time in 1529, anonymously, in his own Italian translation. In terms of its effect on Renaissance literary theory and literary history, therefore, *De Vulgari Eloquentia,* like Aristotle's *Poetics,* did not become an operative force until the middle and late sixteenth century. Moreover, when it first appeared, only four years after the publication of Bembo's *Prose della Volgar Lingua,* it seemed to most readers a contemporary document. Dante's ideas in this work looked much like what they had been hearing from other writers of their time: his view that the classical languages and literatures represented the absolute standard for vernacular poetry; his concern to create from the Tuscan dialect a poetic language and a vernacular literature that would conform to the standard of those "regular" languages; and his attempt to categorize the genres of Italian poetry, and to define their decorums of subject, on the basis of the "three styles" of the Greek and Latin rhetoricians. In 1529 these critical purposes seemed so entirely contemporary, in fact, that since Trissino was widely known to be the author of the translation, many believed *De la Volgare Eloquenzia* to be a literary forgery that Trissino had written himself and had fathered on Dante as a way of gaining authority for his own humanist poetic program. [5]

Dante did not know Aristotle's *Poetics*. But he knew the *Ars Poetica:* he refers to it in *De Vulgari Eloquentia* as the "Poetria" of "magister noster Horatius" (2, 3), and he several times quotes passages from it, both in this treatise and in other works. He never saw occasion, however, to quote the lines in which Horace seemed to have legislated on the subjects the Muse had assigned to the lyre; and in his surviving criticism he shows no more concept of the lyric as a poetic genre than he does of the epic or of the theatrical forms of tragedy or comedy, as genres. By the time he wrote the *Commedia,* at least, it would seem reasonable to assume that he must have learned, from Servius's Commentary on Virgil, and, if he knew them, from such other ancient sources as Macrobius's *Saturnalia,* about classical ideas of the epic or heroic poem in the forms written by both Virgil and Homer; but he gives no evidence of any concept of the epic as a form in either his prose works or the *Commedia.* It appears that any clear critical concepts of such generic ideas— perhaps, indeed, of the critical idea of *genre* in its modern sense— belong not to the early 1300s but to later centuries, when critics could read the two Homeric epics, had a much wider, as well as a more accurate, knowledge of the surviving texts of Greek and Roman literature, and, finally, had read Aristotle's *Poetics.*

De Vulgari Eloquentia is of use to our inquiry chiefly because of what Dante says in this work about the relation between poetry and music, and because of its full-scale analysis, which is both theoretical and practical, of the Italian verse form of the canzone. What Dante had to say about these two subjects in his treatise was frequently cited with approval by Italian critics of the late cinquecento; and his analysis of the canzone was discussed, and at times quoted verbatim, more than two hundred years later, by both Minturno and Tasso in their own analyses of the canzone as a poetic form. Furthermore, although sixteenth-century taste, following the lead of Bembo, generally inclined to prefer the canzoni of Petrarch, because of their graceful sensuousness and consistent elegance of style, to the some- times hard-muscled and rugged poems that Dante had written in this form, Petrarch had left no systematic work of literary criticism; so that Dante's treatise remained, for critics of the later century, the most authoritative exposition of the principles, for this verse form and for poetic practice in general, which had been followed by their Tuscan poets of the trecento. It appears to me that it was primarily because of Dante's exaltation of the canzone, on grounds of critical theory, as the grandest of the forms of Italian poetry, together with his minutely detailed practical analysis of its requisite techniques and principles of poetic structure, that the cinquecento critics felt justified in equating the gravest variety of the canzone, as Dante had defined it, with the noblest form of the great lyric genre of antiquity.

Dante's statements in *De Vulgari Eloquentia* about the intimate relation between poetry and music are brief; but they are uncompromisingly definite and are logically fundamental to his entire poetic theory. In the second Book he presents his logically precise definition of poetry as "a rhetorical fiction set to music"; and later (chap. 4) he asserts that "if we take a right view of poetry," it is "nothing else than a metrical composition set to music."[6] He lists the poetic forms of vernacular verse as canzoni, ballate, and sonnets (as well as "other illegitimate and irregular forms"), and he points out that, as the names for these three forms indicate, they are conceived as poems which will require for their performance the assistance, respectively, of singers, of dancers, and of instrumental musicians.

Moreover, though he later qualifies this proposition for the canzone by arguing that the assisting role of the singer and the accompanying music is not of the essence for this noble poetic form as it is for the two lower forms, his analysis of the scheme of logical and metrical structure by which one must "bind up" the separate units of a long canzone stanza is based on the principle that the sequence of the metrical divisions of the stanza is determined by the succession of musical units in the accompanying melody: of the three principles on which "the whole art of the *canzone*" depends, the first is "the division of the musical setting."

In basing his analysis of the poetic art on this fundamental conception of the interaction of words and music in the generation of verse structure and poetic forms, Dante was not, as I have said, guided by any critical concept, ancient or modern, of lyric poetry as a special literary kind, nor was he directed by any Platonic or Neoplatonic ideas about the powerful effects that can result from a conjunction of the sister arts of music and poetry. He was basing his theory simply on the empirical facts of what the new vernacular poetry of Italy had been as it evolved, in the thirteenth century, out of the remarkable school of vernacular verse which had flowered in southern France in the twelfth century. As Dante recognized, both the metrical forms and the literary kinds of Italian vernacular verse were all either imitations of, or further developments from, the verse forms and the genres of Provençal poetry; and originally the poems of the troubadours had been intended not to be read but to be set to music and sung—in the earliest days at least, by the poet himself, to a melody which he himself composed.

Dante's poetic theory, then, was derived from his observation of the historical facts in the evolution of a New Poetry in the vernacular in the two preceding centuries—later in Italy, but before that in the literary form of the Provencal dialect, which he regarded as the "parlar materno" of the various Romance languages and Italian dialects.[7] As he analyzed this kind of verse, and sought for a logical definition of it which would both certify it as authentically "poetry" and justify his argument that it might be made to produce works which could rival those of the classical poets, it appeared to him that the verse in the undisciplined common speech had certain fundamental characteristics that differentiated it from the great Latin poetry he read, and the great Greek poetry he could only read about. Essentially, since it was originally conceived to be sung rather than read, it was verse whose prosodic structure depended not on metrical feet but rather on the harmonic verbal device of rhyme and on stanzaic patterns which had been devised to follow the turns and re-turns of an accompanying melody. Since these basic facts of its verse technique, in his analysis, were what distinguished vernacular poetry from the verse of the "great poets" writing in meter in the classical languages, or "Grammars," who had set the standard of correctness that he wished the New Poetry to emulate, the dependence of the prosody of the new verse on accompanying music must be stressed as fundamental in any practical study of the means by which vernacular poetry might, in its own way, hope to attain to that *eloquentia* which was the hallmark of the poetry of antiquity.

So much for Dante's definition of poetry as "a rhetorical fiction

set to music," which had, I believe, historical grounds that were
largely unrelated to the ideas this phrase suggested to some of the
cinquecento critics who saw in *De Vulgari Eloquentia* an analysis of
the principles of Tuscan lyric poetry. But in actual fact, as contemporary readers of Dante's treatise would have known, the transition
from a view of the new verse as oral poetry composed to be heard as
song, to a view of it as written poetry intended to be read, was
nearly complete by the time Dante's work was written.[8] The poems
of the troubadours had been disseminated throughout Italy in
manuscript collections, and it was in this form, undoubtedly, that
Dante himself had encountered, and carefully analyzed, most of
the Provençal verse that he knew. And though many of the Italian
poems were still being set to music and sung, many of the more
complex ones, including some of Dante's own early poems and
the verse of other poets in his school of the *stilnovisti,* were probably given no musical setting at all, and were conceived as "literary"
works whose intricacies both of philosophic thought and poetic
artifice could be understood only when they were read, and studied,
in manuscript copies.

This was particularly true of the verse form of the canzone, in the
new development which it received in the Italian tradition. At the
earliest appearance of the form in Italy, about 1230, the Italian poets
did not compose the melodies for their canzoni, and by Dante's time
most canzoni were not set to music at all. Nevertheless, as Dante's
analysis of the form makes clear, the canzone was still thought of
by Italian poets as essentially "a song." Although it was a literary
poem, it must be written as a poem which *could* be set to music;
and the structure of the elaborate canzone stanza, as the poet
conceived it, was determined by his sense that, if the poem were set,
musical convention dictated that the stanza be accompanied by two
contrasted melodies, one and sometimes both of which would
normally be repeated within each stanza.[9]

In his attempt to bring vernacular poetry under the critical discipline that had been observed by the "regular poets" of antiquity
(i.e. those whose work had been controlled by the *regulae* of "art"),
Dante first undertakes to categorize its poetic forms according to
a three-stage hierarchy of genres, styles, and subjects evidently

patterned on the "Wheel of Virgil" of the twelfth-century rhetoricians. But his genres of tragedy, comedy, and elegy, with their appropriate illustrious, middle, and low styles, are not—as I have suggested earlier—really genres in the sense in which that term was understood by the critics of the Renaissance; and his descending triad of subjects—Virtue, Love, and Arms—does not actually get fitted to his triad of literary kinds in order to constitute any clear theory of a decorum of subject for each genre. Essentially, his neoclassical generic categories, like those of the "Wheel of Virgil," are based on the rhetoricians' distinctions among the three levels of style; and *tragedy,* as Dante uses the term in *De Vulgari Eloquentia* (and also in the *Commedia*), means simply a poem, like the *Aeneid,* that is written throughout in the high, or "illustrious" style. As Tasso was later to point out in criticizing the "false principles" of Dante's poetics, he did not follow the sound Aristotelian method of basing his literary kinds on decorums of either the matter or the plot (*favola*) but, making an error "common to other writers of that time," defined the poetic genres on grounds of "the verse form and the correspondence of the rhymes."[10]

Tasso here put his finger squarely on what Dante was really doing. Actually, his disposing into generic categories and his marshaling of the right rules of art at the beginning of Book 2 of *De Vulgari Eloquentia* has very little logical relevance to his serious critical purposes in his treatise. These gestures in the direction of the standards by which literati have judged the Latin poets seem preliminary devices of rhetorical persuasion, designed to confer honor on vernacular poetry and gain serious literary attention for it from men of Latin learning. Dante does not actually think of the canzone, the ballata, and the sonnet in any serious sense as forms of the tragic, comic and elegiac genres. He thinks of them as effective new Italian verse forms, with different poetic potentialities. This classification merely enables him to establish the native verse form of the canzone as a poetic form equivalent to the noblest kind of poetry understood by Latin criticism, and therefore entitled to employ the lofty style; and to assign the ballata to the middle style and the sonnet, apparently, to the humble style. And once this honorific undertaking is out of the way, Dante can get down to the practical business he is really interested in: analyzing the prosodic possibilities of the canzone, and showing how, in this verse form, the Italian language can be made to operate in the Grand Style.

From this point on I will focus my discussion on the one variety of canzone which Dante was most eager to exalt: the form he calls the "tragic" canzone, in which the stanza is built on a combination of eleven-syllable and seven-syllable lines, with the hendecasyllabic line asserted at the start and predominating through the stanza. It is this kind of canzone to which Dante gives most of his attention; and this form was the center of attention also of the later analyses of the canzone made by Minturno and Tasso, who found the best Tuscan models for the noblest kind of lyric in the canzoni written in the "tragic" stanza by Dante or by Petrarch. Furthermore, in its later development into the *canzone libera* (as it subsequently came to be called), in which the poem was freed from the requirement of exactly repeating the structure of the first stanza in subsequent stanzas, this metrical variety of the canzone stanza became a mode for free metrical improvisation and formed the prosodic base for Tasso's verse in the *Aminta*. And the same verse form was adapted into English poetry, out of Petrarch's canzoni, by Spenser, who devised an English equivalent for it in a stanza composed of ten-syllable and six-syllable lines, with an added final alexandrine, for his *Prothalamion* and *Epithalamion*. In my opinion, Tasso's *Aminta* and Spenser's two marriage hymns—particularly the *Epithalamion,* which is the most superb prosodic achievement in English poetry before Milton—are the most probable immediate models for the verse structure of *Lycidas*.

Once his preliminary flourishes of tripartite categorizing are out of the way, Dante settles down to demonstrating that the canzone is the most excellent of all poetic forms, nobler than the ballata, and certainly nobler than the sonnet, which, he says, everyone concedes to be inferior to the ballata in nobility of form. Canzoni embrace "the whole of the art of poetic song"; and it is "at once apparent that all that has flowed from the tops of the heads of illustrious poets down to their lips is found in canzoni alone." The highest, or "tragic" style clearly requires the canzone form: "if our subject appears fit to be sung in the tragic style, we must then assume the illustrious vernacular language and consequently we must bind up a canzone," using in the binding the "sticks and ropes" of "pre-eminent words" and "exalted constructions."

To demonstrate the degrees of grammatical and rhetorical exaltation in the construction of sentences, he gives several examples, precisely analyzed. And he is equally precise, and more lavish with examples, in defining the kinds of preeminent words that qualify for the standards of diction of the illustrious vernacular style. Of the three general classes of words—childish, feminine, and manly—only manly words are proper for a canzone; and of the two subclasses of manly words, it should eschew the sylvan and select only the urban. Urban words, however, are of four general kinds, depending on their syllabic structure and their texture of sound; and of these four kinds only two can be called "grand," because the sound of the other two kinds "tends to superfluity."

The poet who wishes to produce from his canzone the most excellent effect, therefore, will reject the inferior classes of "glossy" and "rumpled" urban manly words and will employ only the grand varieties of "shaggy" and of "combed-out" words. These two varieties are, to be sure, different in their sound quality, but this mixture of two contrasting sound textures will be quite desirable in a canzone, and will enable the poet to demonstrate that full range of the art of poetic song which is the prerogative of this all-embracing poetic form. If he learns the methods by which "ornamental" polysyllables that are "shaggy" can "be harmonized in the lines with combed-out words," the mixture in the poem of two sensuously contrasting effects of diction can be made to "produce a fair harmony of structure" in the poem as a whole.

Of the more fundamental principles by which Dante governs the construction of a canzone stanza I will speak in a moment, but his concluding precepts for the use of rhyme in the canzone may be considered here, because they are parallel to his contention that the diction of the poem should combine two contrasting sound effects of roughness and of smoothness. And his *ad libitum* attitude about the rhymes of the poem had consequences for later criticism, because it opened the door for the critical approval of the irregularly rhymed canzone, and for the view, widespread in sixteenth-century criticism, that the big canzone, despite its several requisite laws and decorums, was a freely improvisatory poetic form in which a poet was entitled to many licenses.

Because Dante maintained earlier that the "whole art of the canzone" depends only on the structural divisions of the stanza, and on the prosodic pattern of long and short lines which later stanzas must repeat—although even in these fundamentals he has found so many allowable variations that the reader has been called upon to "admire how much license has been given to those poets who write canzoni, and consider on what account custom has claimed so wide a choice"—he concludes that "rhyme [i.e. a standard rhyme-scheme for all stanzas] does not concern the peculiar art of the canzone." It is "allowable in any stanza to introduce new rhymes and to repeat the same at pleasure." He finds from observation that canzoni are poems in which poets have been particularly prone to exploit the mixed harmonies of different rhyme-sounds: "in this matter almost all writers take the fullest license; and this is what is chiefly relied on for the sweetness of the whole harmony." He concludes that in this matter "every wished-for license should, it seems, be conceded." Roughness of rhymes, however, should generally be avoided, "unless it be mingled with smoothness; for from a mixture of smooth and rough rhymes the tragedy itself gains in brilliancy" (chap. 13).

The opening propositions I have quoted about the obvious nobility of the canzone suggest that Dante regards the preeminence of this verse form, to which he has assigned virtually all the attributes that Renaissance criticism would require of a genre, as a fairly self-evident truism. He nevertheless undertakes, before beginning his analysis, to prove the sovereign nobility of the form by some rather strenuous logical demonstrations. The first of these is the argument that the canzone "produces by itself the effect for which it was made," and thus it "appears nobler than that which requires external assistance." We can observe that ballate, like sonnets, are subservient creatures, since they require the assistance of the performers for whom they are written (dancers or instrumental musicians) to produce their distinctive effects. But the noble canzoni partake of no such menial dependency: "they produce by themselves the whole effect which they ought to produce."

The real significance of this proposition appears later (chap. 8), when Dante attacks the problem of whether, for purposes of exact logical definition, the essence of the canzone inheres in the words themselves or in the music to which it is to be set. His closely reasoned conclusion is that, unlike the less noble poetic forms, the canzone does not make any use of its musical setting for its complete effect: the *Ding an sich* of a canzone is the written words alone, even though they are written for music—because we can observe that those who write the words, when they have set them on paper, and even before these written words have been uttered or set to music, "call their words canzoni." From this empirical evidence, the logically precise definition follows: "a canzone appears to be nothing else but the completed action of one writing words to be set to music."

The real consequence of this scrupulous and sober-faced demonstration, it seems—though Dante does not say so explicitly—is to establish by wholly objective methods of reasoning the conclusion that canzoni alone, among all the forms of vernacular poetry, have full status as self-subsistent works of literature: poems in this form are as fully *poesia,* not just *rime,* and as worthy of being read, studied, and commented upon, as are the works of such regular poets as Horace, Statius, Lucan, Ovid, and Virgil.

But the appropriate musical accompaniment for the poem, as that music was imagined by the poet while he was engaged in the action of writing the words and setting them on paper, was nevertheless an indispensable intellectual component of the act of composing this structure of written words which, when the action was completed, would constitute—in itself, and wholly independent of any musical setting it might later receive—a noble canzone. Dante's minutely detailed practical analysis of the technique of binding up a canzone is based firmly on the first principle that the design of the poem is determined by the "division of the musical setting" into two different melodies, one or both of which would most often be repeated, in succession, through the progress of the stanza. It was this purely hypothetical action, imagined by the poet as he wrote, of setting his verses to the accompaniment of a quite specific binary musical structure—an accompaniment which the completed poem would have no need of, and which, in plain fact, it would probably never receive—that was the determinant of the internal logical and prosodic structure of the canzone and, in fact, of the literary form of the poem as a whole.

This account of the creative process involved in canzone writing, in which the writer devises the form of the poem by listening in his own head to a piece of music that will not appear with the text of the poem when he delivers it to his readers, and which those readers will never know and would not, in any case, need to hear in order for the poem to produce on them the full effect the writer intends it to have, certainly presents some puzzles to our modern critical understanding of the poetic art. But it is a process about which Dante is perfectly clear and unequivocal in this toughly businesslike, almost chillingly pragmatic treatise about how a man must go at the job of writing poems in the spoken language if he wants to guarantee the best results.

I think the answer to the puzzle is suggested at several points in *De Vulgari Eloquentia,* and that it will come to light if we scrutinize what Dante has to say about one of the many technical terms used in his own time, as well as in cinquecento criticism, to denote the basic structural components of the canzone stanza. Of this bristling vocabulary of technical jargon, which was unquestionably not only generally understood but also put to practical use in the writing of canzoni by Italian poets both in Dante's time and in the sixteenth century, I will consider only the term *volta* (= turn). This one term is important to my inquiry primarily because it had consequences for later critical theory, and also, I believe, for *Lycidas.*

The technical terminology for canzone structure was not absolutely fixed, and it not only underwent some changes in later criticism but also could vary a bit in usage from one critic to another. Dante himself prefers not to use the popular term *volta* and wishes to substitute for it the more learned word *diesis;* but in defining the diesis he explains that "this, when speaking to the common people, we call *volta*" (chap. 10). *Volta* is nevertheless the term most commonly used by sixteenth-century critics. The volta, or diesis, in a canzone (to define the term broadly, in a way which will cover both Dante's and later usage) is that section where, after a series of lines fitted to one of the two accompanying melodies, the other melody makes its entrance, so that the prosodic structure of the verse must change accordingly, to accommodate itself to a melody of a different kind.

Dante, who is dealing with the "regular" canzone, in which the structural units occur within the single stanza, whose metrical form is then repeated in subsequent stanzas, designates the separate melodic-prosodic units of the stanza as "odes," and defines the diesis (volta) as that point at which, with a shift to the second melody, the poem makes "a transition from one ode to another." Later poets, however, sometimes applied the word *volta* not just to the transition point at which the stanza made its "turn" to the second melody, but rather to the entire prosodic unit (Dante's "ode") that followed, shaped to the new melody. And if the second melody and its accompanying prosody were then repeated, this section of the stanza was sometimes called the *rivolta* (= re-turn).

But in the more precisely neoclassicizing literary climate of the sixteenth century, Minturno, in his *L'Arte Poetica* (1564), suggested an extension of these Tuscan structural terms that would adapt them to the later, free-style canzone which did not require the repetition of the same verse form in every stanza. While recognizing that critical usage, deriving from Dante's analysis, had hitherto applied the terms *volta* and *rivolta* only to stanzaic subsections of a few lines within a single stanza that followed in sequence and were of the same metrical structure, Minturno proposed extending the reference of these terms to adapt them to entire stanzas of the kind of canzone which changed its metrical pattern from one stanza to another.[11] He suggested that the term *volta* be applied to the whole canzone stanza which used one melody, and if the following stanza made use of the same melody and its cognate metrical pattern, before the poem shifted to a new melody and prosody for the third stanza, that the stanza which duplicated the *volta* be designated as the *rivolta*—a word whose literal meaning, to be sure, was "re-turn," but which might also be thought of as meaning "counter-turn."

I will not, I believe, need to anticipate any further my examination of Minturno's critical theory for my reader to be able to make a shrewd guess at what he is really up to in this reshuffling of some of the traditional terminology for canzone construction. At one point in his dialogue on "melic" (i.e. lyric) poetry, his interlocutor, the poet Bernadino Rota, raises the question of what adjustments can be made to adapt Dante's terminology to the new theory of the canzone as a genre which Minturno has expounded, since Minturno has begun his analysis of the Italian form by saying that he is basing it on the "precepts of Dante in *L'Italiana Eloquenza,* which Dante had used in writing his own compositions." Bernadino notes that, in Dante's analysis of the "regular" canzone, he has described the first part of the stanza, which he called the *fronte,* as constructed, normally, of two or more metrically identical sections, fitted to the first melody and its repeat, and that he had reserved the term *volta* to the latter part of the stanza, in which the poem made the "turn" to shape its prosody to the second melody. Nevertheless, he goes on to suggest, in order to "assimilate" Dante's structural concepts, "as much as we possibly can, to the ancient lyric poets," one might, in defining the structure of the regular canzone, designate the first prosodic subunit of the *fronte* as the *volta,* and its subsequent metrical repeat as the *rivolta.*

In reply, Minturno candidly admits that, in the sense in which these words have been used up to now, they could not properly be so applied. He decides, however, that, "constrained by the lack of appropriate terms," we may "make ourselves content" with this distortion of Dante's usage, because of "the resemblance which we find," in these structural terms of Italian canzone theory, to the terms the ancients had used for the structural divisions of the noblest kind of lyric. It would therefore not be wholly unjustified, Minturno concludes, if we thought of even the earlier Tuscan form of the canzone, whose prosodic pattern was uniform through all stanzas, as a lyric poem built on a three-part scheme for a sequence of whole stanzas in the major Greek lyric. The single canzone stanza, as analyzed by Dante but applying the change in terminology suggested by Bernadino, would then begin with a "turn," followed by a "counterturn," and conclude with a third section in a metrical form different from these two symmetrical units of its opening section.

Minturno is trying to equate the Italian canzone with the Greek poetic form represented by the odes of Pindar and by the most regularly patterned of the choral odes in the Greek tragedies. In his preliminary analysis of this ancient form of the lyric poem, and of its highest examples in Pindar's odes, he has consistently avoided, in fact, the term *ode*, although that word, in its classical literary meaning, had been established in the Italian critical vocabulary of Minturno's time. He has referred to these odes simply as the "canzoni" of Pindar. And in order to demonstrate how the Italian canzone can be "assimilated" to this ancient genre more completely than Dante's analysis or the practice of the earlier Italian poets has yet made clear, Minturno subjects to analysis two canzoni of his own, composed on a sequence of strophic stanzas analogous to that of the Pindaric ode; and he then compares his poems, in their stylistic as well as prosodic principles, to the first of Pindar's Olympian odes.

In these canzoni, Minturno has designated the first two stanzas of the three-stanza structural pattern by the words from Italian canzone terminology which, it so happens, directly translate the Greek terms *strophe* and *antistrophe*: they are the *volta* and the *rivolta*. And he has been able to discover, in the critical terminology of Italian poetry, another native-born term of poetic structure that will serve to designate the third, contrasting stanza in the Pindaric scheme: the Italian word *stanza,* in its original meaning, has, he observes, the sense of a staying, or "standing still." And therefore the third unit in Pindar's "composition in three parts," which classical canzone terminology had designated by the term *epodos,* can find its proper Italian equivalent, ready-to-hand, if it is designated by the Italian critical term *stanza.*[12]

Consequently, by only a moderate regularizing of the Italian poetic practice in the native genre of the irregularly rhymed canzone, and a reapplication of some of the terms which Italians have long used to define its units of structure, this big poem in a series of elaborate, metrically free-swinging stanzas, can easily, if those stanzas are just patterned on a *volta-rivolta-stanza* sequence, be made to manifest fully its inherent equivalence to the great lyric genre, with its *strophe-antistrophe-epode* design, which we see in the Greek canzoni of Pindar. Moreover, in historical perspective, this new development in cinquecento poetry will, if one looks back carefully, prove to be only an outgrowth of a process of literary evolution that had been at least adumbrated, and in part critically

defined, in the trecento, by Dante and by Petrarch, when they first
began to bring the canzone, and all other popular forms of verse in
the Italian vernacular, under the discipline of the rules of art.

It would, however, be unfair to Minturno to suggest that he is
basing this structural analogy between these modern and ancient
genres on a merely fortuitous verbal correspondence between some
Italian and some Greek terms for poetic structure. He is a critic of
wide knowledge in both classical and Italian literature, and also of a
considerable intellectual rigor and honesty in his methods of
argument. Moreover, his criticism, like that of most of the other
major critics of the late cinquecento, has a philosophic base in a
theory of aesthetics and in some conclusions about the processes
that operate in the historical evolution of artistic forms. A brief
glance at his reason for believing that the Italian terms *volta* and
stanza are genuinely analogous to the Greek *strophe* and *epodes,*
because they reflect similar circumstances in the development of
poetry in antiquity and in modern civilization, will serve to direct
me back to Dante for a final look at his poetic theory, and perhaps
for a solution to my puzzlement over how Dante can think of the
canzone as a poem which is conceived essentially as a musical
structure, even though it is intended to be read purely as a literary
structure.

Minturno is persuaded—partly, it seems, on the grounds of what he
knows about the development of vernacular poetry in his own
country—that many of the forms of Greek and Hebrew verse, either
lyric or dramatic, like their analogous forms in Italian poetry, had
their origin in popular rituals and thus were intimately bound up
with folk-song and folk-dance. This assumption is pervasive in the
third dialogue of *L'Arte Poetica* on "melic" (lyric) poetry, the
literary kind whose forms are determined by the conjunction of
words with melody, or "harmony." And it underlies also his dialogue
in the preceding Book on the forms of "scenic" (dramatic) poetry,
because he finds the aesthetic determinant of the dramatic literary
kinds in their historical derivation from the early conjunction of
words with the rhythmic movements of dance, that art which
Aristotle had defined as "imitation by rhythm alone without harmony."

Minturno believes that verse forms like the Greek ode and the Italian canzone, although they later evolved into purely lyric genres, had an analogous origin in communal or ritualistic dance-songs (i.e. the ancient dithyrambs cited in the *Poetics*), and that the coincidence of critical terminology like *volta* and *stanza, strophe* and *epode* in the two literatures points to the operation of the same historical principle in the evolution of poetic forms. The Greek terms for the structure of the ode, he explains, like their Italian counterparts, "conformed largely to the dance," to the turns, counterturns, and stops, "to prolong the song," of the chorus which had originally been used in the performance of the Greek strophic ode.[13] And in his preliminary survey of the historical evolution of lyric forms, which points to the analogies between their first development, in both the Greek and the Hebrew literatures of antiquity and their modern reappearance in the Italian language, Minturno assigns primacy to the popular dance-song in the emergence of the various lyric forms of "our" poetry. He thinks that the new poetry of his own country had its first beginnings in the poets' adaptations of the folk-dance form of the ballata:

> After the ancient lyric poets came ours, who began with writing *ballate*, which, as the word itself signifies, were sung while dancing. Afterward they wrote *sonetti* and *canzoni*, which had their name from the sounding of instruments and the song.[14]

Whether Minturno is correct or not—and I believe he is not—in this assertion about which of the new Provençal verse forms were the first to be attempted by the Italian poets, this statement points us to what must certainly be the meaning of Dante's otherwise rather peculiar observation, in *De Vulgari Eloquentia,* that "when speaking to the common people" about the *diesis* in a canzone, we must call it the 'volta.'" Though at first glance this remark seems to have the bizarre suggestion that the common people might readily participate in, and even have a few ideas of their own about, Dante's high-powered literary analysis of the artifices for constructing the noble canzone, I think it actually refers to the literal meaning of the word *canzone,* and thus to its use as a general term for country folk-songs. Dante must be alluding to a folk-song, of a sort still common among the Mediterranean peoples, which, like the ballata, was sung for group-dancing; and to the fact that in a song of this kind, in which the dance-group made a turn and changed to a different dance step at the point where the singer shifted to a new melody, this point of melodic shift in the song was commonly called the *volta*. If I am right in this interpretation, this incidental remark of Dante's can serve the useful function of dropping us suddenly from the rarified upper atmosphere of his aspiring theory about the austere requirements of this noble poem in the illustrious vernacular, and setting us for a moment on the solid earth which Dante knew was beneath his feet. This casual allusion to the canzoni of the common people directs us to a fact which is suggested at several points in *De Vulgari Eloquentia*—that is, to Dante's recognition that the verse forms of the new vernacular poetry had their origin in popular songs and in folk-songs.

In his exposition of the theory and practice of the canzone, Dante is undertaking to fix as standard the fairly recent literary development by which the Italian poets had elaborated the short stanza forms of most of the Provençal *cansos* into large and metrically complex stanzas, suitable for grave and artistically ambitious poetry: he wishes to demonstrate the high degree of poetic artifice possible in a canzone of this kind, and to specialize the meaning of the traditional, generic name for this poem so as to restrict it to this new verse form alone. However, as he himself points out in *De Vulgari Eloquentia*—and as Minturno repeats, two and a half centuries later, in his own analysis of the form—"though whatever we write in verse is a *canzone,* the *canzoni* alone have acquired this name." He recognizes that, in normal usage, the word *canzone*—which is just the Italian cognate of the northern French *chanson* and the southern French *chanso* or *canso*—means simply "a song." In Dante's time the word would probably denote not an art-song, but rather a popular song based on either plainsong or folk-song melodies, the canzone known to "the common people." And he is fully aware that all the forms of the new art-poetry in the vernacular are still, in the usual, nontechnical sense of the word, essentially canzoni.

This fact, I believe, provides the solution to the problem of how

Dante can think of the great canzone as an entirely literary form made of nothing but written words, but as a poem, nevertheless, whose formal principle derives from the poet's shaping his stanzas to the dictates of two sequential melodies, probably of a standard and popular kind, which he hears in his own head as he writes the words. In his time these popular tunes to which the new vernacular "rhymes" had generally been set must have still been so readily familiar to poets that they were easily imagined by writers as an integral part of the act of composing the verbal music of poems in the spoken language.

Dante was the first modern poet to face up to a technical problem which continued to present a vital and still-open question to the Italian poets and critics of the cinquecento; to the Pléiade poets in France; and in England, not only to their contemporaries among the Elizabethan poets, but also, even in the following century, to John Milton—the problem of discovering the principle of prosodic form that governed the verse lines of the New Poetry in the vernacular languages.

In all the earlier poetry that the Provençal and trecento poets knew, writing a verse line had always been an art of composing it on a certain arrangement of recognizable metrical feet. And the real difficulty in defining the prosody of the New Poetry, as Dante seems to have realized very early, was that the kind of metrical feet which had provided both musical coherence and expressive range in organizing the unrhymed verses of the Latin and Greek poets were no longer being used by the writers of verses in the vernacular. The question for Dante, then, was what was taking their place, especially in poems like canzoni, most of which were no longer actually sung, in order to set lines of vernacular verse apart from prose and give them some of the qualities of "poetry."

The question is not an easy one. And, as far as I know, no writers in Dante's time had yet begun any of those experiments, often of great metrical skill, by which poets tried to adapt quantitative meters directly to modern languages. But the obstacle most of these later writers seem to have come up against is that, for one reason or another, classical metrical feet no longer work in Italian or the other vernaculars. And the question as to what different scheme of foot-

structure forms the natural pattern for the character of the modern
languages is proving elusive. In English, modern poets, reacting
against what Ezra Pound described as the English reader's expecta-
tion of "a hefty swat on alternate syllables," have made us doubt
our earlier belief that the musical nature of the modern English verse
line rested on pseudoclassical metrical feet based on alternate
stresses. Milton, at any rate, as F. T. Prince has demonstrated, held
no such view; and I have yet to identify a single poet of the English
Renaissance who was—or who ever thought he was—writing his
tragedies or narrative poems in a five-stress verse line which might be
called "iambic pentameter."

For Dante, then, the question was what was to be done—or, rather,
what had been done—to give the new vernacular verse lines musical
coherence and flow in the absence of those metrical feet which
formed the basis of all the poetry in which Dante had been formally
educated. He had made his first, tentative attempt to solve this
problem in *La Vita Nuova*. In chapter 25 of that early work, he had
concluded that the determinant of prosodic form in vernacular verse
was the single fact of rhyme; and he had gone on to argue that, since
to organize speech by means of rhyme was rather analogous to
organizing speech, as the classical poets had done, by the metrical
feet which gave structure to their "verses," these "rhymers" in the
common speech might properly be given the name of "vernacular
poets."

But Dante evidently concluded, on further reflection, that the
novel prosodic device of rhyme, though it was so obvious an innovation that it had led to the practice of designating the new poets as
"rhymers," and their poems as "rhymes," was not a sufficiently
comprehensive device for imposing coherence and form on large
verbal structures to provide of itself the real secret to the prosody of
the new verse. It could not, certainly, be the only principle of verse
form which controlled the large canzone stanzas, whose structure
was no longer determined by any fixed scheme of rhymes, but which
nevertheless gave to the ear an effect, quite analogous to that of the
"verses" of the Latin poets, of a sustained musical coherence and
prosodic flow, through a structure of lines long and short, and of
final musical resolution into large, internally shaped verbal units.

In *De Vulgari Eloquentia,* therefore, Dante has discarded his earlier theory that prosodic form in vernacular verse depends solely on its use of the harmonic device of rhyme. He regards rhyme as one of its formal devices but not quite an essential one: the essence of prosodic form in the new verse, and thus of its distinctive poetic genres, inheres in its stanzaic structures, whose patterns, to be sure, are inflected by rhyming words, but whose formal principle is a certain organization of longer and shorter lines, in which the line-length is determined not by metrical feet but by a fixed number of syllables.

But a mere stanzaic pattern of lines having certain syllabic lengths could not, Dante seems to have thought, by itself produce the effects of musical continuity and coherence within the line, of relations and phrasing of that line to other lines in the stanza, or of the other formal patterns of timing, rhythm, and pitch of voice by which the metrical feet of classical prosody had given articulation to the line units and the stanza structures of the Latin poets. To find the source of the prosodic coherencies of this kind in the stanzas of the vernacular poets, he turned to the origin of those vernacular stanza forms, to the poets' initial adaptations, in verses originally written as actual songs, of those popular melodies to the accompaniment of which, in the folk-songs of the people, they had first heard their native language being made to move in the rhythms and harmonies of poetic form.

I can only conclude, from *De Vulgari Eloquentia*, that to Dante and other poets of his time these popular songs were still familiar enough, and the relation of their melodic structures to the stanza forms of vernacular poetry still enough taken for granted, for a purely literary practitioner in these forms to be able to imagine readily the kind of melodies to which the stanzas had been and might well be sung. Thus, even the poet who was writing a grand "tragic" canzone in the illustrious vernacular would still be able to guide his ear, as he disposed his words into the prosodic units of the poem, by the flows and turns of the popular melodies which made up the binary form of those musical canzoni that were being sung, and danced, by the common people, by shepherds and workers in the fields. In Dante's analysis, at any rate, it was certainly those unheard melodies which gave to literary canzoni that sweetness which the reader of the poems would hear in the written words alone.

After this attempt to thrust a depth-probe to the base of Dante's poetic theory, I have still before me an examination of the new theory of the lyric that was evolved by poets and critics in the sixteenth century, and of the additions they made, partly as a consequence of that theory, to Dante's original formulation of the generic principles governing the canzone. For these questions I will first return to Minturno, whose *L'Arte Poetica* offers us a clear, generally conservative presentation of critical doctrines on these subjects fairly widely held in the latter cinquecento, and presents these ideas, moreover, as part of a systematic treatise on poetics. And I will look, finally, at the ideas about the lyric and the canzone found in the critical writings of Tasso. Tasso's criticism is not systematic, nor entirely consistent, despite his efforts to make it so. But it is, like Dante's, abundantly informative about the practical problems of technique as they appear to a poet; and it is sometimes very suggestive about new poetic possibilities, as yet unexplored, that lie in traditional literary forms. It is Tasso's critical ideas, among all the Italian critical theories of his century, that would probably have been of the most compelling interest to the young Milton.

Aristotle's *Poetics* provides the foundation for the system of Minturno's poetics, as one recognizes readily from his disposition of the poetic genres into three broad categories, defined in a terminology, adapted from Greek, which is based on their means of "imitation": "Epic" poetry (i.e. imitating by words alone without the use of harmony or rhythm), "Scenic" poetry, and "Melic" poetry. These categories are basic both to his earlier Latin work, *De Poeta* (1559)—which Sidney plundered freely for *An Apology for Poetry*—and to his later treatise in Italian, *L'Arte Poetica* (1564), in which he deals exclusively with poetry in the vernacular rather than with Italian neo-Latin poetry. To Minturno, in both works, the proper "precepts" for poetry are those observed by the Greek and Roman Muses; and in *L'Arte Poetica* he asserts that he is the first to give full and perfect instruction in poetry, according to these rules, to those who speak only Tuscan and no Latin. In this work his mentors in critical method will be Aristotle and Horace; and he undertakes to demonstrate that their critical principles are those which have been followed by the most admired poets, both among the ancients and among "our" poets, and that these principles have

been exemplified equally by the poems of Homer and Virgil, Dante
and Petrarch.

In his earlier Latin treatise, however, on which he tells us he spent
almost twenty of the best years of his life, there is much of Plato, or
of Neoplatonic ideas, showing alongside Minturno's logically
systematic Aristotelian doctrines about the different kinds of
"imitation," and the categories and decorums of the major poetic
genres. Platonic patterns of thought are most in evidence in the
introductory Book of *De Poeta,* where Minturno is concerned not
with the rules and techniques of poetic forms, but with general
propositions, philosophic and historical, about the metaphysical
character of poetic truth; about the high role of the poet in primitive
civilizations as a teacher of religious truth through his myths, the
"divine" nature of his mind, and the "divino furore" of his poetic
inspiration; and about poetry as essentially godlike creation rather
than imitation. These Platonic doctrines—which it is perfectly
proper, of course, to discuss openly when one is addressing one's
fellow literati, but which should naturally be expressed more
guardedly, and duly labeled as "opinions," when one speaks to the
unlatined laity—are noticeably less prominent in *L'Arte Poetica,*
published only five years later, where Minturno's thinking seems
stiffened by a more thorough-going Aristotelianism.

When he addresses himself, however, to an explanation of the great
genre of the lyric poem, and of the powers of mind that are called
into play when music is blended with poetic language, it is Plato—or
at least a very strong ghost of him—who meets us at the start. In his
answer to Bernadino Rota's opening question about whence melic
poetry had its origin, Minturno speaks round and clear:

> From Heaven, and from the gods. Seeing that God the creator of
> the heaven and of the earth, both of things visible and of those
> that are not seen, had created the gods and humans, and had
> adorned them with wondrous gifts, it was only reasonable that
> both the one and the other generation should make declaration
> of such degree of the beneficences from him received as they
> were possessed of.

And accordingly the spheres, finding voice through the gods (i.e.
their watchful and perceptive celestial intelligences), forthwith made

harmony; and men, as soon as they are born, remembering their other life in heaven (as was the opinion of Plato), have wished to imitate "the practice of those who inhabit the heavens."[15]

These, then, are the generations—begotten upon mankind by the moving heavens and their angelic inhabitants, through those divinely bestowed powers which link men's minds to the gods'—of that sphere-born, neo-Aristotelian, thoroughly classical and equally Italian, literary genre of the lyric poem.

The opinion of Plato's that Minturno cites here was actually Plato's. And his crossing of Plato's creation myth with phrases from the Nicene Creed might seem to reflect no more unorthodox a Christianizing of Plato than would derive from the parts of Plato's thought in the *Timaeus* which earlier centuries had built into scholastic theology. But the amalgam of Platonic and Christian ideas in the passage as a whole, especially its allusion to man's prenatal existence in one of the spheres, sets up resonances that reach well beyond what had long been found acceptable, at least as public doctrine, to the church which numbered Minturno among her bishops—and which, moreover, in the year before *L'Arte Poetica* was published, had just concluded, with Minturno in attendance as one of the Italian delegates, the final decisive sitting of her Council of Trent.[16]   The Platonized Christianity of this passage has High Renaissance overtones which suggest neither church Christianity nor the historical Plato. It looks much more like that "ultimate Plato" (to lift a phrase from Wallace Stevens) whom Marsilio Ficino, Pico della Mirandola, and their Florentine associates thought they had discovered by reading the Platonic Dialogues in the light from Plotinus and other ancient Neoplatonists, and by interpreting them against the background of what they regarded as the original source for the religious ideas common to Plato and the Jewish Scriptures— the magical treatises of the Hermetic Books.

The suspicion that Minturno's view of the thought of Plato—whose Dialogues, in fact, he knows at first hand and can read in the Greek texts—has been tinctured by the richly iridescent lights from Ficino's Latin translations and commentaries is confirmed when one notes, at the beginning of the dedicatory epistle to *L'Arte Poetica,* some propositions about the primal poet-theologians that could have no

other source than this new, Christianized brand of aesthetic
Neoplatonism which had been the invention of Ficino and his
Florentine Academy. In that dedication, echoing ideas he had
expressed more fully in *De Poeta,* Minturno asserts that poetry is
actually divine, the very art of God; that the poet, like God, is a
creator; and that the historically original theologians have been
poets:

> To this fact the writings of the primal theologians,[17] as much
> among the Hebrews as among the other nations, give testimony,
> to all those who read the books of Moses, and of the Prophets;
> and of Orpheus, as of Linus; and of Mercury [= Hermes Tris-
> megistus, or Mercurius Termaximus], of Homer, and of the
> Pythagoreans.

Nevertheless, although he begins his dialogue on melic poetry with
these heady propositions about the supernatural origin of man's
natal impulse to blend poetic speech with music and, through this
conjunction, to apprehend once more his recollected life in the
celestial spheres, by renewing the kinship of his mind to the minds
of the angels who contemplate the Divine Ideas, Minturno does not,
in *L'Arte Poetica,* allot much space to exploring these metaphysical
auras which surround the lyric genre. These ultimately Platonic
doctrines are fundamental to his philosophic concept of this poetic
form; but once he has propounded them firmly, he sets them aside,
in a manner quite usual for a learned cleric in a Catholic culture, as
though these metaphysical speculations belonged properly to some
less public part of his mind, and he had not really undertaken to
expatiate upon them in this logical, orderly, pragmatic treatise
addressed to the part of the laity that has read no Latin.

Minturno proceeds briskly to his Aristotelian business of defining the essentials of the melic genre: specifying its decorums
of subjects and of persons; distinguishing its various subspecies
in the poetic forms of Italian literature (fourteen of them, no
less, in a hierarchy graded from the canzone, down through the joke,
and on to the epigram); and establishing the rules and techniques for
each, on the grounds of examples and quoted passages that illustrate
the practice of both the Italian and the Greek and Roman poets in

analogous lyric forms. And in his final Book he goes on to give a good deal of detailed practical instruction, based on analyses of passages from poems ancient and modern, in the technical components of the graded levels of each of the "three conventional styles"—constructions, rhetorical devices, diction, and the ingredients of prosody in the various stanza forms, meters, and kinds of rhyme.

The whole—even though we are looking at only one dialogue from Minturno's complete whole—adds up to quite a performance, a sustained and coherent piece of systematic critical thinking of a sort that has no parallel at all in English literary history. But it is a fairly representative Italianate critical treatise of its century, a good deal less adventurous in its theory and less subtly imaginative in its literary responses than some others, but cumulatively impressive in its lucidity, its logical order and consistency, and its mastery of anc ancient and modern literary texts (and sometimes also of textual scholarship) both in general and in close detail.

We can pass over Minturno's specificities about poetic technique and his treatment of lyric kinds other than the canzone. And I have already touched on one important part of his theory of this chiefest of the lyric forms. For our purposes we need give attention only to some of his propositions about the decorums general to the lyric kinds, and therefore to the canzone, and to a few enlargements he makes on Dante's specifications for that poetic form.

It is Horace's lines in the *Ars Poetica* that serve Minturno for his view of the decorum of persons in the lyric poem. In his preliminary discussion, in Book 1, of the persons who are properly to be imitated in each of the three major genres, he decides that the melic poem deals "with those who are worthy of praise." And later, in his third Book, when distinguishing the species of the lyric poem from other forms of the melic genres, he explains that "the ancient poets sang to the lyre the praise of gods and heroes," and that, although melic poetry included such other species as the dithyrambic poem in praise of Bacchus, sung to the sound of pipes, and the nomic poem, sung to the cithara, it was only the form sung to the lyre that was called "lyric." But his general definitions of the subject of melic poetry have a way of gravitating only to that first in Horace's list of the subjects which the Muse has assigned specifically to the lyre, "the praise of gods and heroes." When Bernadino Rota inquires what the faculty of the melic poet consists in, Minturno's answer is, "Properly, in speaking praise and in praying."[18]

When he comes, however, to defining the general "matter" of melic poetry in his third Book, he has a well-formulated definition, of an Aristotelian-cum-Horatian kind, which establishes for the lyric a certain dignity and scope of subject; a range of tone that embraces two kinds of actions and their related moods; and a principle that the poet's mode of discourse in this genre can vary by mixing narrative with passages of dramatic speech. The poem in this kind is

> an imitation of actions which are sometimes grave and honored, sometimes pleasurable and cheerful, comprised within an entire and completed subject of a certain magnitude; the which is made delightful with verses that are not, certainly, simple and bare, but clothed and adorned by harmony, which readily, and by their nature, are accompanied by music and by dance: sometimes simply narrating, sometimes introducing others to speak, sometimes following both the one and the other mode; to the end that it produces equally delight and profit.[19]

In the list of the "essential parts" of a lyric poem that follows this definition, the part which Minturno puts foremost—as Aristotle had done in his analysis of tragedy—is the "favola," the plot or "action." To the question as to whether lyric poems can properly be said to be based on an "action," Minturno replies that, like every true genre of poetry, they must be, and that, as with the other genres, the action must be "perfect and one." For the lyric poet, the favola is "the matter which he undertakes to describe," and it is "clearly apparent" that this subject "cannot be long." As examples of the kinds of favola proper to the lyric, Minturno runs through a considerable list, which includes speaking praise or blame, accusing or defending, in praise of either gods or men; telling of divine things or human; commending the honest or reprehending the ugly; praying; and dealing with true or grave things. He winds up the list by pointedly inquiring whether it could be said that a man who has done any of these things is someone who has performed "no action."[20]

Nevertheless, despite this broad spread of the kinds of "matter" appropriate to the many kinds of lyric, Minturno concludes that the truest provenance of the genre is religious. He inclines to genetic assumptions in his definition of literary forms; and he therefore feels that these forms manifest their most natural, and consequently most essential, basis in human character when we examine them, in the freshness of their prime, as they first appeared in early civilizations. In his summary definition of "Materia Lyrica," he begins with a survey of the uses to which the lyric had originally been put in both classical and Hebrew literature, and he concludes:

> From this it can clearly be seen that the matter of this kind of poetry was from the first fixed entirely in things divine, and that, descending afterward to human actions, it lapsed into the bosom of amorous prattle, and of the vanities of this word, as one can see in the songs of Anacreon, and in not a few of those of Horace. However, to the extent that it may sing of chaste love, and properly address itself to the praise of beauty, Petrarch, head and source of amorous poetry in his rimes, will be the master to us.[21]

In order to establish the preeminence of the grand canzone, however, it is not to the canzoni of Petrarch, but rather to Dante's theory and practice in this form that Minturno looks for his proof that this is the noblest of the Italian lyric genres, and for his precepts about its decorums of subject and of style. In fact, he shows a little reluctance at admitting Petrarch into consideration at all, since Petrarch's propensities as to subject matter, despite the fact that his amorousness had always been brought to heel by Virtue, have led, Minturno feels, to a certain slackening of the sinews. In his view, though with due honor to Petrarch, the tendency was ill-advised. For when one recognizes the essential equivalence between this form and the Pindaric ode, it is evident that the canzone must be braced for sterner stuff; and Minturno intends for it a more arduous literary future than even Dante had envisaged.

Minturno was not the first critic to find a correspondence between the noble canzone, in what Dante had called the "tragic" stanza, and the form of the Greek strophic ode, although he may have been the first to suggest that the Italian verse form might imitate exactly the

stanzaic pattern of its ancient prototype. This analogy, and also the
similar analogy—though this parallel is of lesser interest to Minturno
and to most other critics—between the canzone is simpler stanzas
and the "monostrophic" Latin ode of Horace, are widely current
propositions in late cinquecento criticism. We have already seen how
Tasso, in the *Aminta,* could exploit these doctrines as though they
were critical commonplaces, in order to validate the innovations that
he made in the verse form and style of his pastoral play. And the
same analogy was argued, in later decades of the century, both by
critics who acknowledged their debt to Minturno and by others who
seem to have arrived at the conclusion independently, or from other
sources.[22] In fact, if one is reading through Italian critical treatises
of the period to discover what they have to say about the canzone as
a lyric genre, one of the handiest ways to find out what one is
looking for is to keep an eye out for the phrase "Pindaro, principe di
Lyrici."

It is on the basis of the verdict of antiquity that Pindar was the
foremost of the lyric poets, combined with Dante's demonstration in
De Vulgari Eloquentia that the canzone is the noblest of the Italian
lyric forms, that Minturno maps the program by which this genre, in
future, can achieve what he regards as its manifest destiny. Although
he recognizes that Pindar's strophic verse form had also been used
for the choruses in some of the tragedies of antiquity, and although
he follows many of Dante's precepts for the construction of canzoni
and is interested almost exclusively in the stanza form which Dante
had described as the "tragic" canzone, Minturno does not use either
that label or Dante's argument that the canzone is the Italian verse
form proper for the tragic genre. It is not toward tragedy that
Minturno thinks the canzone should aspire. In his analysis, its
destiny, once it is disciplined by rules that will manifest fully its
generic equivalence to the Pindaric ode, is to become a genre for
heroic poetry.

When Bernadino Rota raises the question of just how, since the
word *canzone* is applied to all poetic compositions which are sung,
one can specifically define that form which "because of its
excellence is called the *canzone* [= grand song]," Minturno replies,
"because it should be a composition magnificent and splendid, and
divided into parts concerned with a single sentiment. Such are the

canzoni of the ancient lyric poets, especially of Pindar, and of ours,
particularly of Dante and of Petrarch." And to the question of why
this one form "holds the first place" in Italian poetry, Minturno
answers, "Because for dealing with things grand and heroic no other
lyric composition is so worthy as this one." He then reviews Dante's
triad of subjects, Arms, Love, and Virtue; and though he concedes
that all three of these matters are dealt with in canzoni of different
styles, he concludes that it is best for the form to be specialized
to the one subject which most befits it,

> since it seems it is especially adapted for writing about that
> which appertains to virtue. And it was this, certainly, that Dante
> both adhered to in the precepts which he gave us in *L'Italiana
> Eloquenza,* and put into practice in writing his own
> compositions. And even though Petrarch spent the greater part
> of his *Canzoniere* in speaking of the delights of love, none the
> less, in the whole course of his writings he never descended to
> the vile pleasures of the base rabble.[23]

To summarize the logic of Minturno's theory: the canzone, in the
stateliest of its forms, as Dante's theory and practice have
demonstrated, is already seen to be preeminent among the Italian
forms of the lyric genre. Horace had said that the Muse assigned to
the lyre "the praise of gods and heroes"; and this principle, if it is
harmonized with Aristotelian precepts for the decorums of persons
in the various genres, leads to the general proposition that lyric
poems should imitate "those who are worthy of praise." The
practice of antiquity gives historical confirmation to these precepts,
since in both Greek and Hebrew literature, the primal lyric forms
had been wholly devoted to things divine, from which they later
descended to treat the actions of men.

Dante, in his analysis merely of the Italian genre, had recognized
that, in its variety of styles and verse forms, it might deal with the
full range of human concerns; but he had preferred to exalt only the
"noble canzone," in the most stately of its stanzaic variants,
composed exclusively in the illustrious vernacular, which celebrated
man's aspirations to Virtue. And the stanzaic structure of this
grandest of Italian songs, as Dante had analyzed it, and even some of
the technical terms in current use for its prosodic units show
significant correspondences with the stanzas and the structural

terminology used in antiquity for the canzoni of Pindar. Pindar had been recognized by the ancients as the foremost practitioner of the lyric genre, and his canzoni in praise of gods and heroes were poems essentially heroic in both matter and style, which blended verses that were grand and splendid with the music of the lyre.

For the future, then, the clear pattern of literary history, which seems to operate rather like Natural Law, dictates the course the canzone should pursue. It should part company with the soft Lydian airs of Petrarch, which have only weakened its noble frame, return to the more austere prototype of Dante's poems, and by emulating fully the *strophe-antistrophe-epode* pattern of Pindar's canzoni, strike an ancient lyre to heroic strains in order to shape the illustrious vernacular to the new genre of the "Pindaric canzone."

This new genre, like any authentic one, will have its inherent rules to discipline it to that decorum which is the grand masterpiece to observe. But its acceptance of the Pindaric verse form, which it has already approximated, will entail only a slight restriction on that quality of free-ranging "license" which, as Dante had shown, was a distinctive trait of the Tuscan canzone, one that had been "conceded" to the form by common consent because such freedom was a direct manifestation of its noble character. And in Minturno's view, if the genre rises to heroic stature by taking unto itself the full rights of the Pindaric ode, it will find open to it new freedoms for expansiveness and improvisation, freedoms that would be wholly proper, because these further licenses were decorums antiquity had conceded to the Pindaric lyric genre.

The example of Pindar, in fact, will specifically invite the vernacular canzone to poetic licenses as yet unattempted in Italian rhymes. And in the clear enthusiasm Minturno shows for Pindar's innovating licentiousness, for his disregard of literary precedent in the lyric kind, and even his ignoring the essential Aristotelian principle of restricting the "matter" of a poem to a single action, as he allows his energies to range at loose rein over wide poetic spaces, one can see the basically legalistic and prescriptive character of Minturno's critical theory suddenly begin to buckle and bend as it responds to the pull of that aesthetic ideal of "Variety" which forms one of the two intellectual poles of Italian critical theory in the sixteenth century.

Even in the work of the critics like Minturno, who are strongly drawn to the opposite, neoclassical pole of "Art"—the laws, rules, decorums, and genres established by the poets and critics of Greece and Rome—one can usually see points at which variety, whether explicitly acknowledged or not, manifests its attractive power. Variety is the way of "Nature," in contrast to "Art," and on their critical theory it can exert its force, often unexpectedly, to make the classical hard lines of their neatly ruled critical structures soften and bulge into something like the curves and swells of Baroque.

It is exactly this effect, in Pindar's odes, of poetic energies ranging free at the extreme limits of a controlling form that Minturno finds invigorating and would like the Italian canzone, by a close imitation of Pindar's poetic form, to achieve for itself. From his survey of the historical evolution of lyric verse in antiquity at the start of his dialogue on melic poetry, he finds it clear that Pindar's distinctive achievement had been to enlarge the lyric poem beyond its original, simple form, to stanzas made of "a great variety of verses." But Pindar's enfranchisement of the genre had not been merely one of prosody: in both the "matter" and the structure of the form his work provides the example for a ranging expansiveness and an almost unpredictable variety. To turn from the example of the poems of Horace, or of the Greek lyric poets Alcaeus, Stesichorus, Simonides, and Anacreon, to the odes of Pindar, Minturno finds, will provide a salutary warning against overhasty dogmatism about the matters that can be comprehended by this genre: "anyone who will look well at the works of Pindar will not confine within short and narrow bounds the matter of the melic poet." And he goes on to drive home the warning with a rather whirling list of the variety of subjects Pindar's canzoni managed to bring within the bounds of the lyric.[24] Further, as his later analysis of the sonnet demonstrates, it is precisely by this attribute of an improvisatory ease and discursiveness, in subject, style, and structure, that the canzone manifests its difference from the more limited and rigid sonnet form and acquires the richness and amplitude which appertain to heroic poetry. Unlike the sonnet, the grand song is a form in which one "dilates" and "adorns" the poem by "bringing in other things from outside," and clothes the entire varied structure with a "richness of vesture."[25]

If the Italian canzone is to become truly Pindaric, this distinctive principle of bringing in things from outside should lead it, Minturno believes, to follow Pindar's example by introducing, as a generic component of its structure, the specific discursive device of formal "digressions." And if the genre is constructed on the fundamental principle of shaping the poem to an "action," which is "perfect and one," those points at which the poet suddenly breaks free and departs from "the matter which he has undertaken" will be clearly apparent. These digressions are particularly to be desired because they can give to the canzone one of the effects distinctive to heroic poetry: that characteristic trait of the long epic poem Milton alludes to, in *The Reason of Church Government*, in designating this genre as "diffuse"—a confident ease and amplitude of mind on the part of the epic poet which inclines him to depart at will from the sequential narration of his argument, and to give variety to his poem by digressing into episodes which are byways to the course of his central plot.

In Minturno's view, that "mode of discourse which is called digression well becomes all the epodic *canzoni*" (i.e. those in which a contrasting epode stanza follows after the identical *strophe-antistrophe*, or *volta-rivolta* stanzas); but for the specifically "Pindaric" variety of the epodic canzone, the digression, being of the essence, "is, in these poems, strictly required. This will be found true by anyone who reads the canzoni of Pindar, and the Odes of Anacreon or of Horace which might be set in comparison with them." He prefers, however, to set the lesser odes aside, and to direct his attention solely to the one poem he has introduced, at the start of his analysis of the canzone form, as the classical archetype for the genre—the ode in which Pindar celebrated the first victory of the horse of King Hiero of Syracuse in the chariot race at Olympia. This ode will adequately exemplify the general requirement for the "matter" of the genre of the "Pindaric canzone," for which "no other matter, certainly, is so well becoming as the grave and illustrious, which is called heroic." But it is exemplary chiefly because it provides a striking illustration of that other device by which the "Pindaric canzone" produces its heroic effect—the epic digression.[26]

While Minturno, in analyzing the classical prototypes for the Italian form, has begun by placing emphasis on the effects of compression and brevity characteristic of the Hymns of Orpheus and of Homer, which deal with the praise of gods, he finds this Olympian canzone of Pindar's an even more admirable model for what the Italian canzone should become; and it is this model that he has tried to emulate in the two canzoni of his own, one on the death of the Marchese of Pescara, and the other on the victory of Emperor Charles V at Tunis, which he offers as exhibits. Pindar's canzone not only has observed the necessary compression and brevity in dealing with a single, complete action, one which, like the *favole* necessary to all the lyric kinds, "cannot be long." In its splendid digression, his canzone has also gone beyond celebrating the deeds of heroes in the victory of the king's horse in the Olympian *palio,* and has ranged up to the gods, with heroic discursiveness, as Pindar "departs from the matter which he has undertaken, but with a digression which is suitable to it," in order to expatiate upon the festival at Olympia and to narrate at length the myth of Pelops and Tantalus.

In the same manner, Minturno points out, he has allowed his own canzone of lament for the Marchese of Pescara to digress from its proper "matter," and to introduce the chorus of the Muses, in order amply to narrate and praise the Marchese's glorious deeds. As he completes this analysis, Bernadino Rota, duly persuaded, draws the conclusion as to what structural device it is, in canzoni of the specifically "Pindaric" form, that enables them to produce their distinctive effects as a genre of heroic poetry: "These digressions, therefore, in the canzoni of the lyric poets, like the episodes in the heroic poem, and in the tragedy and the comedy, make the work more magnificent and more rich." [27]

There is, finally, one question about Minturno's theory of the new Pindaric form of the canzone which I cannot answer with certainty, and that is whether he has in mind any definite musical accompaniment for poems in this kind, and particularly, whether he conceives of a musical setting that will attempt to imitate the Greek musical forms to which Pindar's odes had originally been sung. He is not specific on this point in *L'Arte Poetica,* beyond his covering proposition that the aesthetic determinant for all lyric poems resides in their "blending" of the voice, in poetic modes of speech, with musical "harmony," or with "melody." *Harmony* is the term

Aristotle had used in the *Poetics* to define the nature of music, and his term reflects the Greek view that expressive form in music derived from the pattern of harmonic interrelationships between the note-intervals which distinguished the different musical modes.

But Minturno also uses the term *melody,* which reflects a modern concept of expressive form in music; and it is evidently this concept to which his own musical thinking inclines, as one sees from his adaptation of the Greek word *melos* (song) to provide the generic name for the lyric poem. For the most part, he seems to shuffle the terms *melody* and *harmony* casually together, as though the two musical concepts are, if not exactly equivalent, at least interrelated components of musical form as he conceives it. I see no evidence that he has yet come upon any of the ideas about ancient Greek music which Italian theorists were beginning to explore in the late sixteenth century, suggesting that the musical "harmony" Greek writers spoke of was not at all the same thing as the chordal harmony characteristic of modern polyphonic or harmonic musical forms. Moreover, once Minturno gets beyond his general propositions, applicable to all subspecies of the lyric, about the effects resulting from the blending of poetry with music, he seems to have little concern for the specific kinds of music to accompany poems in the different lyric forms.

Minturno has also dropped from both his general theory of the lyric genre and his specific theory of the canzone Dante's basic principle that the intended musical accompaniment for the canzone is the determining factor, for the poet, in shaping the literary form of his poem. (He struggles with Dante's explicit statement on this point, which evidently makes no sense to him, and decides to read it metaphorically rather than literally.) When he defines the specifically "lyric" quality of verse technique in these poetic forms, he locates the source in the words alone. In the general definition of the class of the melic poem I have quoted, he specifies that the verses must be so "clothed and adorned by harmony" that they will, "readily, and by their nature," be "accompanied by music and by dance." And in his formal definition of the canzone, he states, as the final requirement, that the verses of the poem must be so made that they are "apt for singing."[28]

Minturno obviously thinks of the "Pindaric canzone," on grounds of these general requirements for all melic poems, as a singable grand song, which may, and on theoretical grounds ideally should, be set to music and sung. But if he has in mind any particular kind of setting for these poems, I would guess that the music he is thinking of, in the early 1560s, would have been polyphonic. And that guess finds support in Minturno's tendency to think of music as a combination of the expressive devices of both melody and harmonic effects. But if he has entertained the possibility that these canzoni might go the whole way in their assimilation to the Pindaric ode, and be sung by a single voice to a lyre, in music which attempted to reproduce the effects of some of the Greek modes, he gives no evidence of it in *L'Arte Poetica*.

Minturno has responded strongly, in his philosophic definition of the lyric genre, to the ideas of Plato, or of Ficino's Plato, about the virtually supernatural mental powers that can be brought into play when musical "harmony" is conjoined with poetic speech. But he shows no particular interest in those other passages in Plato's Dialogues, which had been of great interest to Ficino, that recorded the remarkable and specific ethical "effects" which had been produced by the several modes of ancient Greek music. If these passages in Plato, or in other ancient writers, had engaged Minturno's imagination, he would certainly, in that careful reading of the odes of Pindar which he more than once recommends to his reader, have paid more attention than he does to one striking fact about both the *Pythian* and the *Olympian Odes*—that Pindar frequently prescribes in the text of an ode that the poem be given one or the other of two kinds of musical setting: some are to be sung to the flute, in the Lydian mode, and others to the lyre, in the Dorian mode.

If it had entered Minturno's head that Italian poems in his new genre of the "Pindaric canzone" might be set to a kind of music which, by imitating the Greek musical settings of Pindar, could powerfully join with the poetic effects of the verse to reinforce the ethical effects of these poems in praise of Virtue, he would scarcely have missed, as he does, the hint for such a musico-poetic effect which lay right before his eyes in Pindar's first "Olympian Ode." In this ode, the one Minturno selects as the shining example of the

specifically heroic quality of the Pindaric canzone, the first antistrophe specifies that the Muse must take from its resting place a
lyre strung to the Dorian mode. And in antiquity it had been the
Dorian mode which had possessed the almost magical power of
infusing in its listeners the specific mood of heroic valor—as ancient
testimony reported, and John Milton was later to explain (in describing the army of Satan as it prepared for battle):

> Anon they move
> In perfect *Phalanx* to the *Dorian* mood
> Of Flutes and soft Recorders; such as rais'd
> To highth of noblest temper Hero's old
> Arming to Battel, and in stead of rage
> Deliberate valour breath'd, firm and unmov'd
> With dread of death to flight or foul retreat,
> Nor wanting power to mitigate and swage
> With solemn touches, troubl'd thoughts, and chase
> Anguish and doubt and fear and sorrow and pain
> From mortal or immortal minds.[29]

I conclude that Minturno, in 1564, either had not encountered any
of the new theories about Greek music which engaged the attention
of some groups of humanists in both Italy and France in the last
three decades of the century, or, more probably, is a critic who
simply does not have any very strong, or precise, interest in the
musical art. For this reason, although he would like to see the Italian
canzone become as fully Pindaric as possible, he is content to detail
only the literary techniques required for the evolution of the genre,
and leave the competent musicians the task of giving these poems
the kind of musically appropriate setting normally given such poems
in his time. But I have raised the question about his theory of the
canzone because other Italian critics, both at the time Minturno
wrote his two treatises and in the following decades, were beginning
to be interested, as they explored the analogy between this Italian
form and the Greek lyric ode, in assimilating not only the poetic
structure but also the musical accompaniment for canzoni more
closely to what they conceived to be the practice of antiquity; in
specifying, as a characteristic of the genre, the instruments to which

the poem should be sung; and even in experimenting with having these poems actually sung solo to the sound of the lyre.[30] As we shall see in the criticism of Tasso, some of these musical theories of the late cinquecento eventually exerted their influence on the purely literary theory of the Italian canzone as a lyric genre.

Our inquiry comes to conclusion—appropriately, since we are here dealing with criticism that we know Milton read seriously—with the critical ideas of Tasso: about the lyric, the range and characteristics of the styles fitted to this genre, and finally about the canzone as a poetic form. Tasso's views on the first of these subjects, except for some ideas scattered in shorter critical pieces, are expressed chiefly in his two sets of *Discorsi*. The first of these, the *Discorsi dell'Arte Poetica, ed in particolare sopra il Poema Eroico,* an ardent work composed in his early twenties while he was at work on *Gerusalemme Liberata,* was originally a set of three lectures Tasso delivered to the Academy at Ferrara in the late 1560s, but not published until some years later, in 1587. Near the end of his career he rewrote these early discourses into a more comprehensive and solidly reasoned six-book work, which he published in 1594, the year before his death, under the title *Discorsi del Poema Eroico.* Finally, for his full-scale discussion of the form of the canzone, we shall look to Tasso's Platonic dialogue of the 1580s, *La Cavaletta.*

Plato, or his Christianized Florentine reincarnation, is the most fundamental source for Tasso's philosophic thinking and also, as one sees at a number of points in his criticism, for many of his philosophic concepts about the nature of poetry: he is "the divine Plato," "the father and (if it be permissible to speak so) the god of philosophers."[31] But on such practical critical questions as the nature of the genres and the techniques appropriate to the different literary kinds, Tasso, like almost every Italian critic of his age, felt the invigorating force of the new principles for literary analysis which had recently come to light in the *Poetics.* Writing to Orazio Ariosto, he gave this summary estimate of Aristotle's treatise:

> We do not have, in any work which has been written in any of the three finest languages, any greater light on the art of poetry than in this one. We must not take poetic teachings more will-

ingly from any other, nor allow ourselves to be deceived by
false persuasions and by apparent reasons; for every little error
that is committed in the principles as we go beyond, becomes
very great toward the end. Thus Aristotle's principles remain
sound and not thrown to the ground.[32]

Consequently, in the *Discorsi,* in which he is occupied primarily
with the practical problems of form and technique in literary
composition, it is Aristotle—together, of course, with Horace, and
with the full array of Greek and Latin rhetoricians whom Milton lists
in the passage from *Of Education*—who is Tasso's most common
preceptor. But if the *Poetics* was a shining light for analysis of the
heroic poem and its cognate form, the tragedy, the genres that were
Tasso's real concerns in the *Discorsi,* it did not, as we have seen, cast
more than stray, flickering beams on the genre of the lyric poem.
For the analysis of this poetic form Tasso's chief guides were his
own strong talent in works of this kind and the Italian poetic
tradition which derived from his acknowledged master, Petrarch.

The introductory sections of the *Poetics* serve Tasso briefly for
his preliminary demarcation of the lyric genre in the opening book
of the *Discorsi del Poema Eroico,* where he paraphrases Aristotle
but expands on his text to include specifically, within this category,
the various forms of pastoral poetry:

> Poetry has many species: and one is the epic; the others, the
> tragedy, the comedy, and those poems which are sung to the
> lyre, or to pipes, or zampogne and other pastoral instruments;
> all the which appertain to imitation.[33]

But when he comes to deal more particularly with the subjects and
style fitted to the lyric genre, it is Horace and the rhetoricians who
provide at least his point of departure. In the following passage,
which I will cite first in its revised form in the *Discorsi del Poema
Eroico*, he investigates the question of whether the lyric may sometimes treat the same matters as the heroic poem, and whether, if it
does, its traits of style should be the same.[34] For his answer, Tasso
starts with the *Ars Poetica* and a glancing allusion to Pindar, dips
into the practice of the orators, cites Cicero's *De Oratore*, and then,
as he faces up fully to the question, concludes by depositing us
squarely in Petrarch's bosom:

I answer that the lyric and the epic poet may chance at times to treat of the same things, that is, of gods, and of heroes, and of victories, but they do not always use the same conceits [*concetti*]; wherefore from the variety of the conceits, rather than from that of the things treated, arises the difference in style between them. Although Horace in the *Poetica* assigned certain subjects to the lyric poet, he nevertheless ranges freely, as does the orator, through all the things and all the matters proposed. And although he may sometimes show a fear of singing of great things, as Horace has shown, his proper subjects, nevertheless, are the praises of gods and heroes, and of Bacchus in particular: though dithyrambic poetry, which is called melic by Marcus Tullius, divides from poetry of this kind. Be that as it may, he makes use of some conceits of his own which are not suitable for the tragic or the epic poet. I would not say, therefore, that lyric poetry derives its form from the sweetness of the numbers, or from the exquisiteness of the words, or from the pictorial vividness of the imagery, or from the other colors and other lights of the diction, as some have adjudged; but rather from the pleasantness, from the grace, and from the beauty of its conceits, from which the diction is suffused at times with an indefinable something [*un non so chè*] [35] of wantonness [*lascivo*] and of smiling.

After this conclusion, for which Horace's *Ars Poetica* can scarcely be held accountable, it is no surprise to turn the page and learn that "just as Virgil excelled all the ancient heroic poets in gravity, so has Petrarch excelled all the ancient lyric poets in charm [*vaghezza*]."

A passage like this serves warning that we cannot expect from Tasso the kind of precise, logically coherent answers about the determinants of the lyric genre that we get from a critic like Minturno. He is not, to be sure, writing a systematic poetics, like Minturno's two treatises: his two sets of *Discorsi* are primarily expositions of his own theory and practice in epic-tragic poetry, and they deal with other genres only by the way, in terms of their relation to, or their distinction from, the heroic poem. What this passage clearly suggests, however, is that Tasso simply does not have any firm, systematized conception of the lyric as a distinct genre. He can talk as though he does: he can seem to accept the conventional demarcations between the lyric, and the epic and tragic poems; he will speak in terms of the usual neo-Aristotelian generic concepts of the matters, persons, style, verse form, and even, at times, the kinds of action, or plot, which befit the lyric poem; and he will cite, with some approval, the passages of presumed authority on these questions in the *Poetics* and the *Ars Poetica*. But if we follow at any length the workings of his mind when he is speaking of "la poesia lirica," it is soon evident that the term *lirico* denotes for him some quality in poetic expression that the generic categories of Renaissance neoclassical criticism, however well they serve him for his analysis of the epic and the tragedy, cannot adequately define.

The principles of cinquecento Aristotelianism fail him most clearly when he attempts to classify the lyric by one of the propositions most fundamental to that literary theory: the distinction between poetic forms on grounds of the objective "matters" which each undertakes to "imitate." It is on the decorum of subjects for the lyric that Tasso seems least willing to commit himself. This kind of poem should, no doubt, have as its proper subject the praise of gods and heroes, as Horace has said, and perhaps especially of Bacchus. But its essence, to his mind, seems to inhere less in the particular "things treated" by the poet than in a certain attitude of mind toward his poetic subject—a rather dégagé attitude, in fact, about the matter of his poem, which disposes the lyric poet to an easy discursiveness that sets his imagination ranging at large "through all the things and all the matters proposed." And in one passage in the earlier *Discorsi* Tasso comes close to saying outright that the "matter" of the lyric simply doesn't matter; that its distinctive character inheres rather in its style, which must be "fiorito" and "ornato." Such flowery ornateness is necessary because in this genre "the poet appears most often in his own person," and since the matters he chooses to treat "are, for the most part, low and abject [*vile e abietto*]," they would remain so if they were "not adorned by flowers and by caprices of wit."

A few pages later (in the original version of the passage I have cited from the later *Discorsi*) he states firmly that "the matter of the lyric is not fixed," and that this form is characterized by the improvisa-

tory discursiveness by which the poet, like the orator, "treats every
matter which occurs to him." But he is even more explicit than in
the revised passage in asserting that the determinant of the lyric
poem resides in certain *concetti* (conceits) of a kind not common to
tragedy and the epic. And he is insistent that, if these *concetti* are
not to be confused with the actual subjects of the poem, the
"things" that it treats, neither are they to be identified with its traits
of style:

> Nor is it true that that which constitutes the poetry is the
> sweetness of the numbers, the exquisiteness of the words, the
> charm and the splendor of the diction, or the pictorial quality of
> the imagery and of the other figures. It is rather the tenderness,
> the graceful beauty, and, so to speak, the amenity of the con-
> ceits; and it is upon these qualities that all those other things are
> then dependent. And one sees in these poems *un non so chè* of
> smiling, of floweriness, and of wantonness, which is unsuitable
> in the heroic poem, and in the lyric is natural.

What the lyric poem really treats of, it seems—its distinctive poetic
"matter"—is not any of those objective "things" in which neo-Aristotelian criticism sought the determinant subject matters of the
various literary genres: it is rather certain kinds of "concetti" in the
poet's own mind. The word *concetto* is a key term in Tasso's criticism, one he uses in a sense partly his own. It almost never seems to
have the sense of "concepts," or "themes," or "subjects," meanings
the word often has in other criticism of his time. It finds its exact
English equivalent in the contemporary Elizabethan usage of "conceits" in the plural sense (derived from the use of "conceit" in the
singular to mean "imagination")—as in the following lines of Marlowe's *Tamburlaine:*

> And every warrior that is rapt with love,
> Of fame, of valor, and of victory,
> Must needs have beauty beat on his conceits.

The "concetti," then, which Tasso regards as the determinant that
"constitutes the species of lyric poetry" are the elements in a certain
emotional state and imaginative cast of mind on the part of the poet,
the entire way in which his mind "conceives," and imaginatively
transforms, whatever subjects he has taken in hand for poetic treat-

ment. The elusive essence "lirico," which Tasso seems clearly to recognize but cannot precisely express in critical terminology—what this kind of poem really "imitates," we could say, if we are willing to stretch the Aristotelian term to a meaning that Tasso himself would not have given it—is a particular poetic mood: a purely subjective state of relaxed, cheerful emotional harmony, grounded in a benign sensuality that disposes the mind to gaiety and to graceful imaginative play, a mood which is recognizable to the poet himself as a distinct, coherent psychological entity.

With this creative mood beating on his conceits, the poet will normally, but not inevitably, be inclined to deal with a certain range of subjects, and these conceits will incline him, almost inevitably, to treat "every matter which occurs to him" with those flowery and ornate qualities of style that are usually regarded as characteristic of lyric poetry. But the poetic subjects chosen are merely, we might say, "objective correlatives" for the smiling and wanton mood which is the poem's true subject, and the stylistic qualities merely its outward and visible symbols—things contingent and consequent upon the "concetti" that constitute the creative mood itself.

With this view of what constitutes the essence of lyric poetry, it is not surprising that Tasso could not make much headway when he tried to define the form in terms of the analytical concepts of cinquecento criticism; that, when he tried to pin it down with a string of emotive adjectives, it seemed still to slip through his fingers as "un non so chè"; and that he makes the clearest sense about it in his criticism when he uses the term *lirico,* as he often does, to denote a certain poetic style, as though it were only through the interacting artistic effects of words built into poetic structures that language could adequately express something so complex and intangible as the lyric state of mind. The concept of lyric poetry which Tasso's criticism seems struggling to express had to wait for its full critical formulation until a later age, the age of Romanticism—that period which, throughout Europe, looked to Tasso as one of its cultural heroes. The theory took shape slowly through the nineteenth century, in the poetry and poetic theories of the French Symbolists, until it achieved full critical definition, at the end of the century, in the late work of Stéphane Mallarmé, and in England, somewhat earlier, in the criticism of Walter Pater.

It was Pater, in his widely influential *The Renaissance: Studies in Art and Poetry,* who made the classic critical formulation, for modern English literature, of the concept of lyric poetry which I think Tasso had apprehended only poetically. In Pater's analysis, poetry, although it "works with words addressed in the first instance to the mere intelligence, and deals, most often, with a definite subject," is always, like the other arts, "striving to get rid of its responsibilities to its subject or materials," in order that "the mere matter of a poem . . . should be nothing without the form, the spirit, of the handling: that this form, this mode of handling, should become an end in itself, should penetrate every part of the matter." On these grounds Pater regarded lyric poetry as "at least artistically, the highest and most complete form of poetry," because in this literary kind "the matter, the subject, the element which is addressed to the mere intelligence, has been penetrated by the informing, artistic spirit" so completely that it is scarcely possible for the mind to distinguish between the poem's subject and its expressive artistic form. For this reason, he concluded, the lyric poem is the ideal poetic genre: it is the one form most nearly achieving that enterprise which Pater saw as the common effort of all the literary forms—and, in fact, of all the arts—to "aspire to the condition of music."[36]

But neither Tasso nor Milton had their schooling in literary theory under Pater and the French Symbolists. The literary theorists whom Tasso had read, and whose doctrines he makes most direct use of in specifying the traits of verse in the lyric kind, are the ancient rhetoricians who had categorized the grades of literary style. It is on their formulations of the middle, or *mediocre*, style, much more than on the generic concepts of contemporary neo-Aristotelian criticism, that Tasso based his clearest and most precise descriptions of the nature of lyric poetry.

Milton's direct indebtedness to Tasso's technical analysis of the different kinds of style, in *Paradise Lost* and in his mature poetry in general, has now been demonstrated conclusively by other critics, most notably F. T. Prince and John Steadman;[37] and it remains for me to summarize only those of Tasso's stylistic theories and prescriptions which have direct relevance to what Milton is doing in *Lycidas.* Tasso's stylistic principles have their origin in the ancient critical doctrine of what Minturno had referred to as "the three conventional styles"; but at times in the early *Discorsi dell'Arte Poetica,*

and more fully in the *Discorsi del Poema Eroico,* Tasso inclines to
the classifications he found in the treatise *On Style* attributed to
Demetrius Phalareus (the "Phalareus" of the passage in Milton's
Of Education), which had distinguished the types of style into four,
rather than three: the "plain," the "graceful," and (in Demetrius's
subdivision of the third category of the "lofty" style) the "forceful," and the "magnificent."[38]

Tasso did not, of course, decide on his four-part gradation without
consulting all the ancient authorities, both Greek and Roman, on the
disputed rhetorical questions of the number and nature of the styles;
their classes and subspecies; the distinguishing *virtù* and the corresponding vices of each; the proper terms by which they should be de-
nominated; and, in fact, the logically proper terminology for the
concept of "style" itself. In an entertaining passage in the revised
Discorsi, he surveys the extraordinary throwing about of brains on
these problems—a contention in which the Greek and Roman
theorists have lately been joined by such quarrelsome contemporaries
as Julius Caesar Scaliger—by those who, following on the fundamental work of Aristotle in the *Rhetoric,* have undertaken the categorical
enterprise of setting up precise divisions among "the forms of
speaking." He easily discards Hermogenes' classification into seven
forms as self-contradictory and unwieldy; looks with some approval
on Cicero's classification, in *De Oratore,* into the three "genera" of
high, middle, and humble, because it is "briefer and more expedi-
tious;" and then goes on to summarize Demetrius's arguments for his
four-part division, and his principles about which of these styles
may, or may not, be mixed with the others.

But even after Demetrius had arrived at this sensible formulation,
it seems, he had been forced to contend with opponents who wished
to subsume his four kinds of style into only two general forms of
speech, which were then divided into two paired subclasses, the two
halves of which might be mixed with one another, within the pair,
but not with either of the subclasses of the other pair. Demetrius,
Tasso says, thought this scheme "worthy of a smile," because he saw
that not only these two pairs but all the other kinds of style had, in
plain literary fact, been effectively mixed together; and "he recognized that in the verses of Homer and in the prose works of Plato
and Xenophon and of many others, there is much magnificence

mixed with much gravity and much beauty. Such and so great is the difference between the felicity of composition and the subtlety of disputation."

No more have the authorities been able to agree even on the term which should be used to denote those qualities in speech that assume these gradations. Are we to describe them, with Demetrius, as the different "characters" of speech; or with Cicero as the "genera"; or as the "species," or "forms"; or, following Hermogenes and Plutarch before him, as the "ideas"? "But these," Tasso concludes, "are quarrels about names; and if only we understand, and are understood, it matters little whatever they may be called." If, to be sure, the forms of style are truly species, then "it is proper that they be subject to genera; and if that is true, the sublime and the lofty genera will have, as their species, the grand, the beautiful, the splendid; and the grave form, which is full of dignity, will have . . ."—and so on. Finally, after running through some more of this, Tasso sums up: "I say that the forms are mixed together in such a way that it is a hard thing to find them ever separated, except for those which are opposite to one another. So that we may compare speech to a piece of wax, which takes divers signs and divers figures."[39]

Tasso's most usual terminology for the four grades of style, and the genres to which he thinks them fitted, are: the *magnifico,* proper to the epic; the *grave* (a term he prefers to Demetrius's "forceful"), which is appropriate for the dramatic speeches of tragedy; the *mediocre,* which befits the lyric in the demanding verse forms of the canzone and the sonnet; and the *umile,* about which he has little to say but which he seems to think suitable for lesser verse forms like the ballata and the madrigal. Though he inclines to the term "middle" (*mediocre*) for the style typical of the lyric, he often denotes this style by such other terms, taken from Demetrius, Quintilian, or Cicero, as the "graceful," "beautiful," "flowery," "moderate," or "temperate"; and frequently just by the term "lyric." He regards each of these styles as fitted to a certain genre, however, only in the sense that this style is the dominant one in works of that kind, establishing the overall tonal effects proper to that literary form. Tasso follows Demetrius in maintaining that all of these styles may be—and, in fact, usually should be—mixed together in a single work, with the exception of the magnificent and the humble styles, which, being opposites, would, if they were brought into combination, confound one another.

We need to be concerned only with Tasso's specifications for the middle and the magnificent styles: these two styles, he maintains, are properly to be mixed, in both the lyric and the heroic poems, by the introduction of passages or episodes in which the poet departs from the predominant style appropriate to the poem, in order to write, for a while, in a style either higher or lower than the one generic to this poetic kind. This mixture of styles within a genre is particularly to be desired because it produces in the work the artistic effect of "variety," an effect which Tasso, like many cinquecento critics, esteems, because it is by variety that art is bent to follow the way of nature. Nature is operative at such moments, because a natural discursiveness of mind can lead a poet to touch on some subjects which, by the strict rules of art, are not in the class of "things" truly proper to the genre of his poem; and such subjects will necessitate a change from the poem's generic style.[40]

One of Demetrius's doctrines which Tasso adopted, particularly evident in his definitions of the middle or lyric style, is the proposition that subject matter, the "things" the poem deals with, is actually one of the components of style. For the middle style and the lyric genre, these things are not, properly speaking, the "matter" of the poem in the strict, Aristotelian sense of that term: rather, they are components of those imaginative "conceits" which, to Tasso, determine the lyric genre, and are thus elements of the poetic style itself. In Demetrius's analysis of the graceful style, and of the devices which produced its characteristic effect of charm [cháris], he had explained that "the grace [chárites] may reside in the subject matter, if it is the gardens of the Nymphs, hymeneals, love-stories, or the poetry of Sappho generally." Subject matter of this kind, he maintains, "even in the mouth of Hipponax" will have "a gaiety of its own."[41]

Tasso adapts this passage directly in the early *Discorsi*, merely substituting Petrarch for Sappho, for his description of the stylistic qualities of lyric verse: "The graces which particularly suit lyric poetry, and which have been virtually loaned from it to heroic poetry, are the hymeneals, the loves, the glad forest groves, and the gardens and other things of the like with which the poetry of

Petrarch is filled." In the revised *Discorsi*, rewriting Demetrius more freely, he explains that the "ideas" of speech are many; but when the heroic poet looks away from those effects of magnificence or of tragic gravity which are his principal concern, and directs his eyes to that beauty which is the effect of the lyric "idea" of speech, he will seek "the beautiful, and charming, and graceful words which are most appropriate to this form; and from which Petrarch, and Tasso [his father, Bernardo Tasso] , and the others composed their compositions, interweaving the loves, and the nightingales, and lilies and privets and roses, in the marvelous texture of the Tuscan rhymes."

The middle style is distinguishable, then, primarily by certain subjects which fill the poet's conceits—subjects inherently suggestive of amorousness, elate sensuousness, and the fresh springtime joys of the fertile earth; and it is these subjects, when they are combined with smooth-flowing numbers and with an analogously connotative diction, selected for an effect of discriminating elegance, and then are elaborately interwoven by a freely discursive imagination into a final harmonious richness of texture, which give release to the otherwise indefinable mood of smiling and wantonness that is the hallmark of lyric poetry.

In the final Book of the revised *Discorsi,* Tasso goes on to specify such technicalities as the kind of rhymes, sentence structures, and even consonant sounds that are most apt for the lyric style. For rhymes, one should incline to words full of those vowels which are sweetest in sound, a technique he illustrates with a passage of verse concluding with the rhyme words *sedea, gloria,* and *nembo.* He points out, however, that in these lines the final rhyme, which is untypical, being full of consonants, "is here added for tempering; since the beautiful form [i.e. style] should be at the same time the temperate, and that form shuns the checks in speech that are produced by a conjunction of the hardest letters," as in those words in which many *s*-sounds can be heard. Tasso agrees with Demetrius, moreover, in feeling particularly friendly to the use of liquid consonants in the beautiful style, "because the greatest grace and beauty are still wont to arise from those letters which are called liquids, and from the *l* more than from the others; still more, when many words begin with that letter, there is produced from this a most sweet composite, which by the Greeks was called *melisma*."

In sum, the technical effects more suited to this style than to any others are "the sweetness and smoothness of the rhymes, and the tender, soft, and delicate composing of the words and of the verses. Wherefore the verses are the more commended when they are interrupted and perturbed as little as possible in the sentence structure and the word order; so that they are truly elegant and sonorous, and painted, both with metaphors and other figures, almost, as it were, like gems intextured in a work of gold and silk of divers colors."

But if the middle style had been virtually given on loan from the lyric to the heroic poem, the epic might cover that loan by allowing verse in the lyric forms of the canzone and sonnet to make use, at times, of the lofty, or magnificent, or heroic style which was its own property. We cannot, therefore, conclude our survey of Tasso's analysis of the formal structure of lyric poetry without a brief look at his specifications for "lo stilo magnifico."

Tasso's own exposition of the technical tricks of the magnificent style is anything but brief. Although the lyric style was certainly his birthright as a poet, it was the magnificent style that he was most eager to acquire mastery of, and to expound critically, for the furthering, and also the critical defense, of his work as an epic poet. Both in the *Discorsi* and in shorter critical pieces he is tireless at the task of dissecting the techniques of magnificence in verse; of defending and acknowledging his own debt to the stylistic innovations by which Giovanni della Casa had either adopted or invented Italian poetic equivalents for the technical ingredients of Virgil's epic style; and of advancing della Casa's achievements by further technical innovations of his own, derived from close analysis of the verse of Virgil, the Homeric epics, and Dante, and from some of the techniques for oratory, which he sought most often in the *Rhetoric* of Aristotle and the treatise of Demetrius.

In Tasso's analysis, the identifying mark of the magnificent style was the effect he called *asprezza*—roughness, harshness, or arduousness. It was this quality, central to heroic poetry and its attendant poetic artifices. that most clearly set the *magnifico* style apart from the somewhat analogous grave style, which employed many of the same devices, best suited to tragedy. The grave style was comparable to the magnificent in its sustained dignity; and it was certainly, in the term Demetrius had applied to it, "forceful." But its dignity was less sublime and its mode of speech simpler and purer than that of the magnificent style. While in an epic poem the poet "speaks more loftily in his own person and discourses as though with another tongue, like one who feigns to be rapt out of himself by divine inspiration," in a tragedy the poet speaks only through dramatic characters who are moved by strong emotion. He will thus need the simpler and more forthright manner of the grave style, since persons under the stress of the passions tend to speak directly, without those intricacies and artifices of speech which make the truly heroic style such rugged going for poet or speaker, hearer or reader.

"Rugged going," in fact, brings us close to the center of the range of meaning in Tasso's special term *asprezza*. In the metaphor which he uses to define its operative force—and which he took from Demetrius, who had applied it to the prose of Tacitus—its effect is "like one who stumbles while walking through rough paths; but this roughness smacks of *un non so chè* of magnificence and greatness."[42] The rather odd phrasing of this final clause, paralleled in some other passages in which Tasso tries to explain the exact feel of poetic asprezza, tempts me, in fact, to the speculation that, since Tasso's responses to poetic effects of rhythm and sound were intensely physical, he may actually have thought of this asprezza in verse as a poetic effect by which the reader could be made to sense kinesthetically, literally in his muscles, something of that invigorated arduousness of the body which attended the labors of epic heroes.

The components that produce this effect in the heroic style, in brief summary, are, first (on the stylistic principles of Demetrius), certain subject matters: "the magnificence lies in the things, when one treats and describes some great and illustrious battle, terrestrial or naval, and when one discourses of heaven and of earth." The conceits, which give to such subjects their proper poetic transformation, must be "high and illustrious, carefully sought out, elaborated, and almost, as it were, violent." Only by such bold and challenging conceits can this style attain its proper end of arousing in the mind astonished admiration and marvel. Since the verse movement must be roughly energetic, the easy, fluid sentence structures and normal word order which give the middle style its naturalness and lucidity cannot here be the rule. In fact, effects of initial difficulties in meaning, and at times deliberate obscurity, are proper to the

magnificent style. Such difficultness, since it betokens avoidance of
the merely facile, will have the effect of suggesting the poet's intense
seriousness. But these obscurities in the style will also function as
ingredients in its pervasive quality of roughness, since hardships of
this kind impose intellectual checks on the too easy reader, make
him stumble, and thus, as it were, rouse him to more arduous enterprises of the mind.

The most essential devices of *asprezza* in the *magnifico* style, however, are a certain collocation of technical tricks in verbal sound, in
the composing of words within a line, and in the prosody of the
verses, which will work together to produce a verse movement and
texture that is harsh and rugged, broken, by a variety of checking
and braking effects, into unpredictable stops and sudden starts. The
following passage from the *Discorsi dell'Arte Poetica* comprises virtually Tasso's full bag of tricks for creating the distinctive auditory
and metrical dynamism of the heroic style:

> Magnificence is increased by *asprezza,* which is born of the con-
> course of vowels, of the breaking of the verses: of an abundance
> of consonants in the rhymes; of the accentuation of the rhythm
> at the end of the verse, either with words striking for vigor of
> accent, or by abundance of consonants. There is an increase,
> likewise, in the frequency of the copulas, which strengthen the
> speech like sinews. To transport the words some times, though
> but seldom, to a sense contrary to their common usage may
> impart nobility to the speech.

Of these devices, the concourse, or collision, of vowels, which had
been much discussed by the classical rhetoricians, comprises two
different effects of prosodic jolt, effects quite common both in
Italian and in the inflected classical languages. It includes, first, the
conjunction of open vowels at the end of a word and the beginning
of the following word, forcing the reader to make an elision in order
to preserve the rhythm of the verse line; and, second, a conjunction,
between successive words, of two vowels which are not to be elided,
requiring a pause, virtually a caesura, in the reading of the line, in
order to give the proper value to each. Of the other devices listed
here which are not self-explanatory, the "breaking of the verses"
(*rompimento dei versi*) is one to which Tasso assigns special impor-

tance. It is the metrical trick of a bold enjambment, continued
through a succession of lines, in which verse after verse is broken
over its line-end, and (in Gerard Manley Hopkins's striking phrase)
"rove over" into the verse following, so that it breaks that verse as
well with a full medial stop. Tasso's feeling for this prosodic effect
is quite as vivid as that of Hopkins: he sometimes describes such
lines, by a similarly dynamic metaphor, as "versi spezzati [shattered,
fragmented], which enter, the one into the other." And he shows a
similarly acute physical response to the magnificently heroic verse-
racket that can be produced, in the Tuscan dialect, by the doubling
of consonant sounds in the significant penultimate syllable of the
rhyme words: "beyond all the other things, however, which produce
grandeur and magnificence in the Tuscan rhymes, is the sound, or
the clamor, so to speak, of the double consonants, which in the end
of the verse, strike upon the ears."

   This virtual hyperaesthesia to the effects of sound in language
leads Tasso, in the closing book of the late *Discorsi,* to round off his
analysis of the magnificent and grave styles by specifying for them,
as he had for the middle style, the particular consonant sounds
which are most fitting to each, and especially those most productive
of the heroic *asprezza.* The *magnifico* style should, of course, eschew
the *l* so natural to the middle style, since the effect of beauty inherent in its liquidity would be alien to this style's phonological
essence. But the magnificent style, and possibly the grave, may,
Tasso seems to be saying, participate with the lyric style in one
consonantal effect, "which perhaps befits that form"—the "use of
many words which, having the *m* as their initial letter, are appropriate to mourning." The distinctive consonantal prerogatives of the
magnificent style, however, are the letter *s,* which, as we have seen,
the lyric style must shun, and the letter *r.* These two consonants
may also be employed by the grave style; but since "*s* and *r* are most
harsh beyond all the other letters, they will nevertheless take their
place most handily" in *lo stilo magnifico.*

   There is, finally, one proposition of Tasso's about the middle style,
and the particular effect produced when it is used in combination
with the magnificent style, which I think would have been especially
interesting to Milton—the peculiar aptitude of that style for expressing the mental state of temperance. As we have already seen, in an

incidental remark about the effect of a mixture of rhyme-sounds in lyric verse ("the beautiful style should be at the same time the temperate [*temperato*] "), Tasso uses the words *temperato* and *temperamento* in their most common Renaissance sense, to denote a mixing of diverse elements in such a way that extremes are moderated and diversities brought into harmony. It is only rarely, to my notice, that he uses these words with any suggestion of the further, precisely musical connotation ("tuning," or "harmonizing") which they frequently have in the early work of Milton. But in the passage I have cited the *temperato* effect which he sees as characteristic of the middle style is to Tasso an expression not of a fixed mental state but of a mental process in action—as in his example of verse lines in which a single consonantal rhyme word is introduced in order to temper, or moderate, the excessive sweetness of a series of vocalic rhymes.

In the following passage from the early *Discorsi* he defines the temperate—or, more properly, the tempering—effect of the middle style in much the same way. His initial proposition is that since "lo stilo mediocre" is placed midway between the magnificent and the humble styles, it is thus the mean (the literal meaning of his term *mediocre*) in which the extremes of the two styles can be moderated. But as he continues it is clear that he is really thinking of the effects produced when these styles are mixed together in a single work and when, after a passage in one of the other styles, the middle style enters to assert its generic mood. Since Tasso, as a poet, had little or no interest in the humble style, and since his own practice, in both his lyric and epic poems, was to combine the lyric and heroic styles, he gives most of his attention to the effect produced when the middle style appears in juxtaposition to the magnificent. The passage may serve as a summarizing conclusion to our survey of Tasso's critical ideas about lyric poetry:

The middle style is placed between the magnificent and the humble, and partakes of the one and of the other. This does not arise from the mixing of the magnificent and the humble, which together confound one another; but it arises either when the sublime remits itself, or the humble exalts itself. The conceits and the diction of this form are those which exceed the common

usage of everyone, but they still do not carry so much of force
and of sinew as is requisite in the magnificent. And that in which
it particularly exceeds the ordinary mode of speaking is the
charm in the exact and florid ornaments of the conceits and the
diction, and in the sweetness and tenderness of the composition.
And all those figures of an accurate and industrious diligence,
which the humble speaker does not dare to employ, nor the
magnificent deign to, are by the middle speaker put to use. . . .
The middle style does not have such force for stirring the mind
as has the magnificent, nor does it persuade of that which it
narrates with such vividness, but it more greatly delights with a
gentle tempering [*un soave temperamento*].[43]

Our final stop on the journey back to *Lycidas* is Tasso's one full
exposition of the theory and practice of the Italian canzone in his
Platonic dialogue, *La Cavaletta, o vero de la Poesia Toscana.* The
Dialoghi, although they are works on which Tasso expended much
effort, do not, in my view, nor in that of most modern critics,
represent Tasso at his best. Many of them, like the one before us,
were written either during or just after the period of his psychotic
seizures and his confinements in Santa Anna; they show neither the
vividness nor the clarity of his prose writing in the two sets of
Discorsi. The intellectual evasiveness and inconclusiveness of statement which pervade many of them, and show at times in *La Cavaletta,* often seem less the calculated literary effect of Tasso's pose of
Socratic irony than a direct reflection of the fuzziness and uncer-
tainty of his own mind. We know, however, that Milton read the
Dialogues: the *Mansus* headnote records his enthusiasm for the dialogue "On Friendship," and it is hardly likely that he would have
failed to read also, in the same volume, a dialogue subtitled "On
Tuscan Poetry." There is, furthermore, no reason to assume that
Milton's estimate of them was the same as my own. Tasso himself
valued them highly as works of art; and they are, at the least, docu-
ments of considerable biographical interest to anyone who feels, as
Milton clearly did, a strong interest in Tasso personally, both his
temperament and the workings of his mind.

As a coherent work, at any rate, *La Cavaletta* will receive poor
justice at my hands. I will ignore the whole first half of the dialogue—a detailed analysis of the sonnet and of other smaller verse

forms—as irrelevant to my purposes, and will discuss only the latter half, which deals with the canzone. In that section, my interest will be chiefly in Tasso's evaluation, at the start of the discussion, of Dante's classic analysis of the canzone, and in his concluding suggestions for writing a canzone on a new model. Much of the rest of the dialogue seems to me quite undistinguished, and though I will occasionally allow my reader the fun of watching Tasso maunder on without being exactly clear about what he is trying to say, most of what I pass over will be simply filler or, at best, humanist commonplaces about the value of poetry.

In *La Cavaletta* the speakers are Orsina Cavaletta, a gentlewoman of Ferrara who was a close friend of Tasso's and a poet; Ercole Cavaletto, her husband and a man of letters; and Tasso himself, who appears under the pseudonym, used in several of the dialogues, of "Il Forestiere Napoletano"—"the Stranger from Naples"—a title Tasso evidently derived from "the Athenian Stranger" who is the speaker in Plato's *Laws*. In the latter part of the dialogue, when Orsina, feeling herself fully instructed in the art of the sonnet and the ballata, asks Tasso to instruct her, now, in the art of the canzone, he at first declines: having found himself carried away beyond his intent by the early course of the discussion, and feeling a bit weary, he asks Ercole Cavaletto, who has mostly remained silent, to assume the burden. He has been silent, Ercole explains, only because the discussion up to now has been a little beyond him. This new artifice of the sonnet which Tasso has expounded, and particularly the ideal of a sonnet written in the loftiest style, in the manner of Giovanni della Casa, was not taught by Dante, nor has it been the normal practice of Petrarch and later poets. He wonders whether there can properly be an "art" for a practice so irregular. Since the books of Dante's *De Vulgari Eloquentia* that discussed the sonnet have been lost, the art for a sonnet of this kind, if it actually does exist, would have to be sought elsewhere. For the "art of the canzone," however, Ercole feels on much surer gound. In this part of the discussion, therefore, he tells Tasso, "do not expect to hear from me anything that is new, nor, perhaps, from Orsina, who, although she has diligently studied Petrarch, and the other more recent poets, does not disdain the precepts of old." Orsina agrees, but she says that, much as she values these teachings, she doesn't really understand them very well.

Encole undertakes her enlightenment. Repeating the critical com-
monplace that it was Dante who first brought this noblest of poetic
skills under the discipline of "rules," thereby making the writing of
canzoni truly an "art," he launches upon a lengthy summary, in
close verbal paraphrase, of Dante's exposition in *De Vulgari Eloquentia,* beginning with Dante's definition of poetry as "a rhetorical
fiction set to music," and continuing through a detailed explanation
of his prosodic analysis of the structural subunits of the canzone
stanza, the technical terms for each, and the rules to be followed in
binding up these metrical units into a noble canzone. Ercole pauses,
at times, to apologize for both the length and the fullness in detail of
his exposition of these precepts of old, but both Tasso and Orsina
assure him that they are hanging on his every word, and they com-
pliment him for the brevity, comprehensiveness, and clarity with
which he has explained all of Dante's rules for this poetic form. As
Ercole concludes, Tasso expresses satisfaction, on behalf of both
himself and Orsina, at being now adequately informed in the art of
the canzone.

He then begins to needle Ercole, raising questions with light irony
about certain things which "you have said, or rather Dante, with
whose words you have virtually spoken, displaying so marvelous a
memory." His own memory, he says, has been failing him since his
recent long infirmity, but because Ercole has "these precious riches"
fully at his command, he would like to profit by further instruction
on some questions which these doctrines of Dante have suggested to
his own mind. Among other things, he questions Dante's proposition
that the rhymes do not belong to the proper art of the canzone,
because this precept does not seem fully consistent with the precise
instructions for rhyme patterns in this poetic form that Dante gives
in a later part of his treatise.

But Ercole stands firm on the legalistic position that those rules
which Dante has explicitly stated as precepts are the true precepts
for the art of the canzone, "because art is of things certain, and such
are those things in Dante's mastery in which he has instructed us."
As for these other considerations about the rhymes—or rather, obser-
vations, which are perhaps just Tasso's personal opinions—they are
not "art." Incidental techniques of this kind are not matters about
which one can present arguments of certainty; and such "uncertain

and inconstant things, which at some times are brought together under rules and at others are not, are not admissible to excellent mastery or good artifice."

Tasso is not persuaded. Though his memory for Dante's prose writing is weak, he finds that he is able to remember Dante's poems quite well, and offering for exhibit the canzone Dante had presented as the model for the "tragic canzone," he proposes to inquire whether this certainty which Ercole has admired in Dante's critical precepts is also to be found in Dante's own verses. Confronted with this poem which is then analyzed by Orsina, and prodded by Tasso's questions, Ercole is brought to concede that not everything in Dante's poem can be squared with Dante's precepts for the art of the canzone. But art, Tasso suggests to him, deals only with things certain, and thus with universals, those things of which one can have certain knowledge. The poet must use not only art but also judgment, which deals not with universals but with particulars that are subject to sense and are infinite in number.

Ercole, admitting this distinction between the different provinces of art and judgment in the making of a poem, accepts the point: "it cannot be denied that the poet is in some things *artificioso,* and in others *giudicioso.*" Tasso agrees: "for me it suffices that the poem neither can nor should be, either always or in all things, artificial"; and he asks, therefore, whether "the room which is taken from art should not be conceded to judgment?" "To inertia, rather," is Ercole's reply. Tasso yields the point: although Dante, in *De Vulgari Eloquentia,* had distinguished the great, or Regular, poets from those who write their compositions by chance and not by art, even these classical poets who composed mainly by art and judgment must have owed a part of their poems, although they had the skill to conceal the fact, to chance or fortune, which rules in things unstable and uncertain. Orsina gracefully rounds off this passage of the discussion by suggesting that such a proposition would seem appropriate to the poetry of Dante above all others, since it was he who had maintained, in the *Inferno,* that Fortune was that angelic Intelligence set in governance over the human sphere.

Tasso then returns to his demonstration that in writing his poems Dante often violated his own dogmatic critical rules for the art of the canzone, offering others of Dante's canzoni in evidence and

analyzing them against his precepts for combining the structural
units of the canzone stanza. Orsina and Ercole join, with apparent
enthusiasm and startling competence, in this closely technical enterprise: and for some time the air is filled with Dante's critical
nomenclature for the different prosodic sections of the canzone
stanza, with argument about the *fronte,* the *versi,* the *volta,* the feet,
the key, and the *sirima* or *coda.*

Orsina then touches on Dante's rule that the arrangements of these
stanzaic units should accord with the divisions in the musical setting
of the poem, and on this matter Tasso raises some questions. He has
listened to the musical settings of some of Dante's canzoni that have
been made, after the poetic fact, by contemporary composers; and
he is not sure they have always followed Dante's prescription that
the change in the musical setting should coincide with the *volta,* or
the metrical division of the stanza. He would like, he says, to ask
some excellent musicians about this.

"Perhaps," says Ercole, "you are going to be like Socrates, who
learned music in his old age."

"I wish that in that I could be like him," Tasso replies, "or in the
virtue of his soul."

After some more discussion of the relation of the musical setting
to the poetic form, Tasso excuses himself from further exploration
of this problem, "because of the slight knowledge that I have of
music."

The dialogue now takes a new tack, as Tasso begins to examine
Dante's definition of poetry as "a rhetorical fiction set to music."
Since he concludes, from the wording of this definition, that Dante
did not consider the musical setting to be of the essence of a poem,
he ignores this clause and argues that the true artifice of poetry is
"the artifice of a fiction." In this respect the poet is like the orator,
who deliberates on things that are uncertain. Art, Tasso suggests,
may therefore be analogized to form in the philosophic sense of the
term, "and the things with which art is concerned, are rather like
matter; and even though matter is uncertain, this does not diminish
the certainty of form." But form must sometimes be bent to the
recalcitrance of its matter, as it is by the judgment of the artificer.
Thus, Tasso concludes, "I will quite readily concede to Alighieri that
the grave poets are the regular ones, if only you will concede to me

that the rules are not of such rigidity or toughness that they cannot be twisted, in one way or another, so as to be a bit supple and flexible."

Orsina concedes readily, the more so since she hopes that Tasso may sometime be pleased to commit to writing his own artifice, directed to the taste of those now living. But Tasso declines; he is not one to prescribe rules, except, perhaps, to himself. It is just that, considering the rules given us by others, he very much doubts whether it is expedient to adhere to them completely.

Tasso then reverts to Dante's definition of poetry as a rhetorical fiction. A fiction is a deception; the truest poetry is the most feigning; and so on, at considerable length. After listening to quite a bit of this, Orsina pointedly remarks that, although the reasons he has adduced for these propositions are sufficiently new, the ideas he is advancing "nevertheless conform to the opinion of many."

Undeterred, it appears, by this accurate observation, Tasso discourses on. But at last he talks his way back to Dante—to the poet's need to subject his essential artifice of creating fictions to the discipline of some rules; to the fact that poets, nevertheless, frequently pay little attention to their own stated critical principles; and finally, to his summary estimate of Dante's rules for the art of the canzone in *De Vulgari Eloquentia*. Dante, we are told, "observed very little any of those rules which he himself had given." And neither, coming after him, did Petrarch, in his vernacular canzoni. No more have they been observed by more recent writers in this form: not by Bembo, nor by Bernardo Tasso, nor by Giovanni della Casa.

The mention of della Casa, who has sought more than anyone else to achieve grandeur in the canzone, leads Tasso into a prolonged analysis of one of his canzoni in the grand style, at the end of which, in a conclusion bolstered, it seems, by the approximate applicability of Dante's precepts to della Casa's poem, Tasso arrives, rather surprisingly, at this final judgment of Dante's precepts for the canzone: "Therefore the art given to us by Alighieri is true the greater part of the time: none the less, it has some exceptions, by which it seems to me that one may enlarge the rule, and accept the qualification of still more unequal verses." He adds, however, that this opinion of his is not so firm that he does not at times shift to the opposite position, which can likewise be defended.

The dialogue does not conclude, however, with this imperfectly Socratic resolution of the questions raised by Ercole's dogmatically literal précis of *De Vulgari Eloquentia*. Tasso moves immediately to open new questions, as yet unthought of, about arts other than poetry which enter into poetic creations, and finally (in Milton's words, in *Of Education)* about "what religious, what glorious, and magnificent use might be made of poetry, both in divine and human things." The passage introducing this new course of the discussion is suddenly pregnant with hints of arcane mysteries, of profundities about poetic creation which are deeper far than the mere rules for the "art" of poetry, and of secrets which perhaps it is not lawful to reveal—hints, it must be said, that the succeeding passage of the dialogue does little to justify, or even to make clear. Inconclusive and ineffectively managed as it is, this momentary rumble of hermeticism about the poetic art has a recognizable source in Ficino's Neoplatonic doctrines of the holy mystery of poetic inspiration and poetic creation, whose secrets are known only to the poet initiate and are never fully revealed in his public statements to the vulgar: ideas we have seen already in the criticism of Minturno, which Tasso also presents in some passages of his *Discorsi.*

After his equivocal endorsement of *De Vulgari Eloquentia*, Tasso continues:

> *T:*   But these are not my sole doubts [about Dante's rule for the canzone]; I have still others that are greater, which I fear to make known.
>
> *Ors:*   In our company anything can be said quite safely, because all will remain just as hidden as you shall think fit.
>
> *T:*   I will say, therefore, reassured by your good faith, that the art of rhyming taught us by the poet was that which he wished to teach publicly; and that there are other arts more secret, which for the most part were not known, for the most part not revealed to the vulgar. [44]

After this premonitory rustle of dark and distant wings, the glimpse Tasso permits us behind the Veil of the Temple comes as something of an anticlimax:

> *Ors:*   And what are these, by the life of the Prince?

T: I will not say what they are, but what I believe they are.
These, in my opinion, are Rhetoric and Dialectic.

The faked melodrama of this brief passage dissipates quickly, however, as Tasso digresses to demonstrate the faults, in comparison
with the methods of Aristotle's *Rhetoric,* of the system for handling
logical topics, or "common places," put forth by Giulio Camillo,
who had been "the first, after Dante, who made bold to show forth"
these hitherto secret arts; and for some time the discussion seems to
wander inconclusively and, finally, to be running down into some
standard humanistic critical doctrines about the obligation of the
poet "to persuade princes to unity and peace, and the public good,
and the war against the infidels."

Tasso concludes by drawing the conventional distinction between
the canzone, in which "one spreads," and the sonnet, in which one
"compacts," with the one analogous to the Greek or Latin ode and
the other to the epigram. But to consider that question more particularly, he feels, would be, at this point, too much of an undertaking. Orsina agrees: she could not think of imposing such a burden
on one who has sustained the greater part of a discussion which, at
the start, she had thought to direct herself. Courtesies and gratitudes
are exchanged. All have profited, Tasso concludes; and if what he
has said has proved not unpleasing to them, he himself will be
pleased to have raised doubts on certain matters and, on others,
to have confirmed his own opinion by their judgment. The dialogue
appears to have reached its end.

Then, as an afterthought, Orsina ponders a further question about
the canzone. As as he rises to this question, one he had earlier cast
aside as both inessential and beyond his competence, Tasso unexpectedly takes the stage to propound, in conclusion, his own revision
of Dante's antiquated, though admittedly classic, analysis of the
canzone.

"If my opinion is worth anything," Orsina tentatively suggests,
"we should not neglect, as you earlier indicated you wished to do,
the music, which is the sweetness and almost, as it were, the soul of
poetry."

"But did we not accept," Tasso replies, "that definition of Dante's
which conceded its place to the music? . . . Therefore the genus of

poetry, and, as it were, the matter, will be the fiction; and its form
will be rhetorical and musical." And as Orsina nods her agreement,
he continues with what seems, at first, a mere exposition of a passage in *De Vulgari Eloquentia.*

> But if I am not deceived, the latter of these forms was added by
> him as not essential but accidental to poetry, in which there are
> some modes of speaking bare and without sauce [*condimento*],
> so that they customarily are gladly listened to or read for them-
> selves; and there are others which have need of this sauce: a
> difference which Dante himself showed that he recognized when
> he said that the canzoni accomplished by themselves everything
> which they should accomplish, which the ballate do not do,
> because they have need of musicians: whence it followed that
> the canzoni should be esteemed the more noble.

On reflection, however, Tasso finds that this opinion of Dante's
"gives occasion for new doubts" about the certainty of his precepts
in *De Vulgari Eloquentia:* first, because this proposition by which
Dante demonstrated the sovereign nobility of the canzone is not
actually true; and, second, because he can think of another sovereign
literary form, one historically unknown to Dante, to which Dante's
precept that the canzone fulfills its end through its words alone
seems more accurately to apply. The form of the ballata, to fulfill its
end, has need of dancers as well as musicians; and the sonnet needs
accompanying musicians; but canzoni, although they need neither of
these forms of assistance, do certainly need singers. We may rectify
this inaccuracy in Dante's argument, then, if we say that the mode
of the canzoni "seems to be most noble, beyond all the others of
this species and of this genus, because they have need solely of
someone who sings them; but the sonnet, in addition to song, requires instrumental music." Nor do the canzoni themselves reject
instrumental music, since Aristotle, in the *Problemata,* says that
"they are heard more agreeably to the sound of the lyre."

With this lead-in from Dante's precepts of old, the dialogue proceeds to its conclusion, which I quote in full:

> *T:*   But over and above the canzoni there is another poem, of
>   another genus, which has no need of being sung. And per-

chance this mode was known by Dante, in the way in which one has foresight of future things, when he said that up to his own time no one had sung of arms, those things of which one is wont to sing and write in epic poems, in such wise that the song in no way detracts from the value of the things written, but conjoins with it rather. Nevertheless, they are sufficient in themselves, for which reason not just songs but books may be required for them. In such poems the *ottava rima* is customarily used, as that which, being more uniform, admits less variation in the musical settings.

Ors: I once heard the verses of Virgil sung in this way to the lyre.

T: And it [the *ottava rima*] can do without the singing better than any of the aforementioned compositions can, for which reason it is much more suitable for narration. For the same reason that the irregular, as Aristotle says, is accommodated to the grandeur of sorrow and of suffering, that, on the other hand, which is regular, as are verses entirely hendecasyllabic, is less suited to lamentation. This mode, therefore, it seems to me, should be deemed the most noble. And what do you say to this?

Ors: I am easily persuaded. And that other [the canzone] which he called the most noble was perhaps so called because of some similarity between that mode and the heroic, which by him is called tragic . . . [citing the lines in the *Inferno* in which Virgil refers to the *Aeneid* as *"l'alta mia tragedia"*].

T: And in that he followed the judgment of Plato, who before him called Homer a tragic poet.

Ors: In the following so great an author one cannot err.

T: Let us, therefore, if it does not seem unacceptable to Signor Ercole, say that tragedy may be a subordinate genus of that which is properly the tragedy; and of the epic; and of these small compositions which partake of the tragic passions, and of tragedy's nobility.

Ors: Everything which Signor Ercole does not deny we will take as granted.

T: The canzoni, however, have need of music, as it were, for a sauce. But what shall we seek for to be this sauce? that which pleasures lascivious youth in the round of feasts and the dances of acrobats? or that indeed which usually befits men of gravity and ladies?

Ors: This, rather.

T: Therefore, let us put by all that music which, degenerating, has become soft and effeminate, and we will ask of Striggio, and Iacches, and Lucciasco, and some other excellent masters of excellent music that they seek to recall it to that gravity from which, going astray, it has often overflowed into quarters of which it is more meet to be silent than to speak. And this grave mode will be like to that which Aristotle calls *doristi*, which is magnificent, inflexible, and grave, and accommodated more than all the others to the lyre.

Ors: This doesn't displease me; but really nothing can be delectable when it is uncompanioned by sweetness.

T: I blame not sweetness and gentleness, but there needs must be tempering; for I hold that music is like one of those other arts truly noble, each one of which is dogged by a parasite similar to it in appearance but in its working very dissimilar: and just as the art of cookery fawns on medicine; the slanderer, on the orator; the sophist, on the philosopher; so does wanton music on the temperate.

Ors: Among so many parasites not only men but the arts themselves are in much danger, and the one and the other in great part corrupted.

T: Therefore our poet will be on his guard lest, on the one hand, he fall into the subtleties of the sophists, which have stuffed many compositions that are pleasing to the world; on the other, that the sauce of the music be neither distempered nor overpowering. But as Tyrtaeus was among the Spartans, so must he be among the Italians, or rather, among the Christians, in the present wars between them and the Turks, and the Moors, and the others who have lost the light of the true faith; and singing now about the left, now about the right, he should so propose, for example, as the motion of the first heaven, which is moved from the east to the west, or indeed, from the right to the left, and as those of the others as well, which are moved in divers ways; to the which two motions our soul corresponds, in the will and the appetite.

The hand at work, however shakily, in this lush peroration is unmistakably the fine Italian hand of Torquato Tasso. But the voice is the voice of Plato. If the echoes of *The Republic* sound clear to an amateur of Plato like myself, they would not have been missed by the young English poet of Tasso's era who had become, during his years of study just before and after his residence at Horton, Plato's enraptured disciple. We may conclude, therefore, with some words of Socrates' which Tasso has drawn on for his Renaissance remaking of Dante's original analysis of the canzone. In the third Book of the *Republic,* after deciding which kinds of poetry must be banished from his state, Socrates turns to consider the different kinds of melody and song, and the modes that accompany and enforce the effects of the poets' words. He will have no need, he tells Glaucon, of the harmonies expressive of sorrow, of the mixed or tenor Lydian and the full-toned or bass Lydian modes.

In the next place, drunkenness and softness and indolence are utterly unbecoming the character of our guardians. . . .

And which are the soft and drinking harmonies?

The Ionian, he replied, and the Lydian; they are termed the "relaxed."

Well, and are these of any military use?

Quite the reverse, he replied; and if so the Dorian and the Phrygian are the only ones which you have left.

I answered: Of the harmonies I know nothing, but I want to have one warlike, to sound the note or accent which a brave man utters in the hour of danger and stern resolve, or when his cause is failing, and he is going to wounds or death or is overtaken by some other evil, and at every such crisis meets the blows of fortune with firm step and a determination to endure; and another to be used by him in times of peace and freedom of action, when there is no pressure of necessity, and he is seeking to persuade God by prayer, or man by instruction and admonition, or on the other hand, when he is expressing his willingness to yield to persuasion or entreaty or admonition, and which represents him when by prudent conduct he has attained his end, not carried away by his success but acting moderately and wisely under the circumstances, and acquiescing in the event. These two harmonies I ask you to leave, the strain of necessity and the strain of freedom, the strain of the unfortunate and the strain of the fortunate, the strain of courage and the strain of temperance; these, I say, leave.[45]

With Tasso's modernization of Dante's precepts for the canzone we come full circle from Dante's original critical definition of it as a poem he conceived as "tragic" only in the rhetoricians' sense of being written in the lofty style, which had outgrown its initial dependence on accompanying music so as to stand on the written words alone but in which the poet who composed the words still shaped the stanza by imagining its traditional musical setting to two contrasted melodies. In Tasso's future program for the form, newly modeled out of *De Vulgari Eloquentia* by the humanist criticism of the cinquecento, the canzone, considered first as the written words alone, would be tragic in a sense more accurately classical than Dante's, exploiting the improvisatory freedom of its irregular verse form to express the fluctuating modulations of grief, and thus the nature of the tragic passions and their nobility as Aristotle had conceived them. But the poem, Tasso argues (and here his theory accords with Minturno's, and with the conventional analogy between the canzone and the Pindaric ode), would also be in some sense heroic, since tragedy is properly a poetic genus subordinate to the literary form of the epic poem, as it is to the tragic dramatic poem and to the lyric poetic forms. The canzone's noblest destiny, he suggests, will be to give voice to the historical imperatives of Christian warfare. But, in Tasso's view, this poetic form is expressively incomplete if it remains merely the words written to be read: it must recover, as an artistic element integral to the poet's conception of his poem, its original component of song.

For the song appropriate to a heroic-tragic canzone, however, one will need a new music, as yet unwritten. This musical setting will emulate the ancient Dorian mode, the mode of courage and stern necessity, although its austerity should be mixed with the sweetness of another mode for an effect of temperance. And thus the ethical power of the music, sung in a mode accommodated to the lyre and, it may be, actually accompanied by that instrument, will reproduce the ethical "effects" of these modes in antiquity, bringing in harmony the divergent motions of man's will and his appetite so that their joined forces can combine with the persuasive powers of the poem's fiction, and of its rhetoric and its logical argument, to move the hearer of the canzone to heroic action. By this conjunction of two arts, the poem will recreate that synesthetic blending of poetry with an ethically compelling music which Italian critics of the sixteenth century regarded as the distinctive artistic accomplishment of the noblest form of the great lyric genre in both the Greek and the Hebrew literatures of antiquity.

Having completed this critical full circle, we may return to Milton, and to his poem. In surveying the ideas about the lyric poem and the canzone in the criticism of the Italians, I have given these men room to speak for themselves and to reason in their individual ways, so as to show the far-from-legalistic ways their minds worked when they confronted literary questions, and thus to demonstrate my initial proposition that Italian criticism of the cinquecento presents us with a method of critical reasoning and critical debate, not with a body of critical doctrine or a set of poetic dogmas.

Read against this background of the actual thinking of some of the Italian critics—those "commentators" on Aristotle and Horace whom Milton recommends to his prospective students—the passage in *Of Education* with which we began our inquiry appears in a new light. Seen by itself, or read only against our knowledge of literary criticism in England, Milton's brief, bald statement of the fundamentals of poetic knowledge—of the controlling demands of a decorum grounded squarely on the "laws" of the three "true" literary genres, taught to us by the sure authority of Aristotle and Horace and their Italian commentators—suggests a critical position that seems much closer to the neoclassic dogmatism of Thomas Rymer and some other English critics of the Restoration or early eighteenth century than it does to what we actually find in the Italian critics whom Milton has recommended as the literary guides we should follow. In English literature, however, the actual Italian critical writings of the sixteenth century did not, as Milton implies in this passage, exert any wide or significant influence on writers during the period of the Renaissance.

The Aristotelian analytical method and the prescriptive conclusions of Italian criticism (rather than the critical works themselves) reached England in force only in the late years of Milton's career, after the Restoration. But at that time the critical ideas of another country and an earlier age came to England largely by way of seventeenth-century France, where the neo-Aristotelianism of cinquecento literary theory and method had suffered constriction and rigorist codification from the new enterprise of French culture in mid-century: the remarkable endeavor, directed by Cardinal Mazarin, to reorder the entire mentality of the French nation, and even the language spoken by its people, by grounding all French thinking on the restrictive concept of Law. Thus transformed, the ideas of the Renaissance Italian commentators on Aristotle and Horace finally registered on English criticism in the form of a new, bright, and cocky neoclassicism alien to the critical temper of its origins: as a movement of legalistic retrenchment and reform in literary expression that was in conscious reaction against the very spirit of the Renaissance.

To an English reader, then, the blunt positiveness of Milton's pronouncement on poetic decorum most readily suggests the formalist critical rigors of this later age which, in fact, was seeking to turn its back on the England of the Renaissance. But Milton's tract *Of Education,* as its preface makes clear, was not intended as a full-scale treatise on that great theme of Renaissance humanist speculation. Conceived originally as only a brief pamphlet designed for publication, along with other pamphlets, as a part of Samuel Hartlib's projects for educational reform, this work of Milton's, including his much-quoted statement on poetic fundamentals, is little more than a schematic outline for an educational program, virtually a syllabus *raisonné.* And in that syllabus he prescribed actual reading of the cinquecento Italian critics in order to learn from them what decorum is, in the fluid and creatively open way in which they conceived it; and to learn also of the chief literary genres, and of what laws truly applied to each, from critics who conceived these laws less as binding codes than as guides that would enable a writer to have an initial scheme for the poem he planned as a coherent literary structure, and to recognize what had been or might prove to be the potential range of expressive possibilities in each literary form.

To read these writers, moreover, is to be instructed not merely in what these genres had been in the past. Defining the genre in antiquity and seeing what it had once been capable of is just the way they get their feet on the ground. What all of them are really interested in—even as conservative and rather academic a critic as Minturno—is the new things these genres might come to be in the literature of a new nation and a new age.

I hope I have been able to suggest a little of the intensity and fervor with which these critics go at the business of writing criticism; because in their quite different voices they all write as though they are caught up in an urgent, passionately exciting enterprise, and as though literature, with all its ancient forms, is marching with them into the dawn. The world is all before them.

5

Lycidas

Lycidas lies neglected, and I have contracted for a new analysis of
the poem. As a point of departure, I will consider the analysis of the
form of the poem which has been widely accepted by Milton
scholars, the one by Arthur Barker.[1] In Barker's analysis *Lycidas* is
built within a frame structure of an opening and a close, which deal
with Milton's act of writing the poem; and within this frame, it is
constructed as a series of three "movements," each beginning with
an invocation, or reinvocation, of the classical pastoral Muse, and
each building in a continuous crescendo to its conclusion. These
three movements form a logical progression. The first (ll. 15–84) deals
with Lycidas as poet-shepherd; the second (ll. 84–131), with Lycidas
as priest-shepherd of the church; and the third and final movement,
which begins at line 132, deals with the apotheosis of Lycidas as he
is received into heaven.

This analysis has much to recommend it. It describes a development in subject which certainly occurs as the poem proceeds
and is accomplished by Milton's molding and shaping of his central
symbol of the shepherd's life. At the start of the poem the symbol
of the *pastor* has its traditional, Virgilian suggestion of a young,
apprentice poet, and thus can embrace the early educational careers
of both Edward King and John Milton; and in the latter part of the
poem, as Milton himself recedes and the focus narrows onto King,
the symbol of the shepherd modulates to the later meaning which it
often had for the Renaissance pastoralists and picks up its
specifically Christian reference in order to define King's calling as
a *pastor* of the church. Barker's analysis also distinguishes three
sections in the poem that begin at what are clearly structural breaks
in the text, the three points where Milton invokes the Muse. And his
analogy to a series of musical crescendoes is promising because it

126

corresponds to the fact that each of these sections begins with an effect of subdued emotion and builds to greater intensity.

But Barker's theory breaks down on several counts. First, it offers no explanation for Milton's explicit indications that the poem is written in at least two different styles, that of the "higher mood" and that of the oaten pipe of the pastoral. The build to greater intensity within the first two sections is not a crescendo within a single unit of musical structure but rather a progression in which the poem modulates from one style to another, so that at the end of each of these sections it has to be forcibly returned to the pastoral tonality with which the section had begun. Second, this analysis does not account for Milton's plain indications in the text that he has built two digressions into the structure of the poem. And the theory breaks down most surely in trying to make the whole passage from line 132 to the end a continuous unit, the final "movement" of the poem. This analysis cannot explain two facts about the third movement: first, that Milton specifically defines the opening lines of this section (ll. 132–53), not as the beginning of new poetic material, but rather as a relaxed interlude between two peaks of intensity. These lines are written, he tells us, for the purpose of "interposing a little ease." Further, the view that everything from line 132 to the end forms a continuous artistic unit leaves out of account the fact that line 165, after the initial invocation which begins the dirge, represents the sharpest structural break in the poem. With the words "Weep no more, woeful shepherds, weep no more," Milton clearly boxes up all the rest of the poem, sets it behind him, and turns away from the subject of grief for Lycidas' death to the formal conclusion that will change the tone of the poem to final serenity.

But the analogy to musical structure is promising.[2] I suspect that the fallacy behind Barker's theory is his assumption that sections which are conceived as units of a musical structure must be conceived also as units of a logical structure, and that the supposed three movements must therefore represent a progression in their subject or their content of idea. We might, however, try taking Barker's metaphoric analogy to music more literally, and entertain the possibility that Milton is constructing the poem as a piece of music whose sections progress according to a musical rather than a logical plan. There is indeed some presumptive evidence that he may be; his imaginative fixation on music is pervasive, from the Nativity Ode on, in his earlier poems. He wrote *Lycidas* while he was living at Horton with his father, who, as "Ad Patrem" reminds us, was a musician and had been a composer. And Milton has told us that during this period he interrupted his studies in the Greek and Latin classics only when he went to London to buy books, or "to be acquainted with some new discovery in mathematics or in music, in which I then took the keenest pleasure."[3] Moreover, he had made integral use of Henry Lawes's accompanying music in evolving the poetic structure of *Comus,* written only three years before. If Milton conceived *Lycidas* as essentially a musical structure, it is possible that he has arranged the different sections of the poem with a concern more for their effects of tone than for their logical content.

There is one passage in the text which makes clear that this is exactly what he is doing, and that he is quite willing, even, to ignore the fact that what the passage actually says is factually irrelevant to the circumstances of King's death, so long as the lines serve the purpose of setting the particular tonality that he wants at this point in the poem. This passage is the one that begins at line 132 ("Return, Alpheus, the dread voice is past") and extends through line 153 ("Let our frail thoughts dally with false surmise"), a passage in which, exploiting one of the conventional devices of the pastoral elegy, he invokes the wooded valleys to bring the most beautiful of their wildflowers to "strew the laureate hearse where Lycid lies." But actually, as line 153 points out, this is a foolish thing to speak about under the circumstances: there is no laureate hearse, and no body; and no funeral ceremony is taking place. As the following lines make clear, the body has not been recovered and is still being "washed far away" by the "shores and sounding seas." Therefore, it is a rather pointless "false surmise" to speculate for twenty lines at this point on what flowers should now be laid on the bier. However, no matter. Milton tells us why he put the passage in: he did it to "interpose a little ease" between the two passages which give climactic expression to the grief for Lycidas's death. The purpose of the passage, then, is altogether tonal, and these lines serve no function whatsoever in either the narrative or the logical structure of the poem.

Let us take a different tack, then, following this lead, and see whether we can analyze the structure of *Lycidas* in terms of a musical pattern; and then, if this works, inquire further whether there is any correspondence between this musical structure and any recognized literary genre. In taking this approach to the poem we are, after all, doing only what Milton himself suggests to us, because in the concluding lines he tells us pretty clearly the principle on which the poem has been constructed:

> Thus sang the uncouth swain to th' oaks and rills, . . .
> He touched the tender stops of various quills.

"Various" here has its Renaissance meaning of "different," or "varying." This song has been made, in other words, by the method of playing on different pipes of the shepherd's syrinx, by using different poetic effects which correspond to different musical keys, or to different tone-colors in registration. And I have already pointed to other indications in the text that the poem is written in two styles, which, like different musical tonalities, would define different states of feeling: lines 87–88 for example:

> That strain I heard was of a higher mood.
> But now my oat proceeds. . . .

The word *mood*, in seventeenth-century English, still retained the pronunciation of its Anglo-Saxon original, *mod,* and was thus interchangeable with the musical term *mode*; and a reading of this word in its musical sense is enforced by the musical suggestion of "that strain I heard."[4] Moreover, as we know from Milton's other words, both early and late, he was fascinated by what he had read in Plato and the Florentine Neoplatonists about the way in which the different modes of Greek music could be used to induce different emotional states in the hearer. Let us, therefore, try to analyze the poem as a structure of different modes, or musical keys,[5] one modulating to the other as Milton plays on the different pipes of his musical instrument.

The first section of the poem proper, the dirge for Lycidas, begins at line 15 with the invocation to the classical Muses to "begin," an invocation which draws an explicit musical analogy to an opening chord struck on the strings of the lyre: "Begin, and somewhat loudly sweep the string."

"Somewhat loudly" echoes at the start of the poem the phrase "paola maiora canamus" in Virgil's invocation for his Fourth

Eclogue, and thus accepts the option, authorized by Virgil, of pitching this poem in a stylistic strain higher than the low style normal to eclogues. But Milton's invocation is not addressed, as Barker has described it, to "the classical pastoral Muse," to those "Musae Sicilidae" whom Virgil had invoked in his own eclogue. The pastoral Muse is Pan, whose streams of inspiration are the Sicilian "Alpheus" and the "fountain Arethuse," together with the Italian "Smooth-sliding Mincius," whom Milton calls to his aid when the "Sicilian Muse" is invoked at later points in the poem; and Pan's instrument is not the lyre but the seven-reeded syrinx, that instrument on which the "uncouth swain" is seen to be playing in the closing lines. Nevertheless, although much of the rest of the poem suggests, as a controlling metaphor for the work, the analogy to a shepherd's song sung to the syrinx, or to the analogous oaten pipe of native English shepherds, Milton's initial invocation is made not to Pan but rather to the high Muses of Parnassus, those sisters whose streams of inspiration flow from "the sacred well" of Helicon, "that from beneath the seat of Jove doth spring," and who sing to the lyre of Apollo.

The distinction between these two orders of Muses was, as we have seen, part of the traditional poetic vocabulary of Renaissance pastoralists. This distinction is pervasive in *The Shepheardes Calender*, and was stated in the passage cited from the "June" eclogue, where, for most of the work, Spenser confesses himself unfit for the skills bestowed by the Muses of Parnassus,

> For they bene daughters of the hyghest Jove,
> And holden scorne of homely shepheards quill;

and where, being mindful of the "danger" which Pan incurred when he "with Phoebus strove," he contents himself with "pyping lowe" in the simpler arts bestowed by Pan alone. But when Spenser rises to the high style in the eclogues for "April" and "November," it is the Parnassian Muses he calls to his aid, and the sacred well of Helicon.

Milton's opening invocation to the "Sisters of the sacred well" thus asserts that *Lycidas* will renounce the low style of rustics and aspire—even higher, it may be, than the *paola maiora* song addressed to Virgil's Sicilian Muses—to the lofty style, and to the learned literary skills which only these Muses confer. And the word *sacred*, together with the following line, in which Milton compares the spring of Helicon to the River of Life in *Revelation* proceeding from beneath the throne of God, implies that the source for the powers which inspire poetry of this kind is literally divine.

Moreover, to the Italian poets, as we have seen from Sannazaro and Tasso, the lyre is the established poetic symbol for the genre of the lyric poem, a genre requiring the high literary skills which, in *Aminta,* can make the rustic zampogna of a shepherd sound forth like "the most learned lyres," and even, at times, "emulate the trumpets" of the epic poem. The phrase "somewhat loudly sweep the string," then, suggests at the start that the controlling poetic form for *Lycidas* may be the genre of the high lyric. And the distinguishing trait of the lyric, to the cinquecento critics, is that it is a poem in which words are shaped, in some artistically integral way, by the sister-art of music.

"Somewhat loudly," however, looks rather peculiar as a description of a purely literary effect; and it is also an oddly gauche translation of the meaning of *paola maiora canamus* in the context of Virgil's lines. If, however, we translate that phrase back into Italian (which is, I believe, its origin in Milton's mind) we come up with a musical term that makes complete sense in Milton's passage. The song is to begin with the Muses sounding the lyre *mezzoforte*, "somewhat loudly."

After this initial suggestion of the genre of the poem, and of the level of style to which it will aspire, the dirge begins with the stylistic effects traditional to the pastoral elegy, making use of its machinery of idyllic nature description and the mythological decoration of nymphs, fauns, and satyrs, and working for a tonal effect of pathos by playing these suggestions of the sensuous and imaginative delights of this easy Arcadian world against the sad fact of death. This tonality, played *mezzoforte,* continues down to line 37, where there is a clear change to *forte*. In fact, Milton puts it in almost those words:

> But O the heavy change, now thou art gone,
> Now thou art gone, and never must return!
> Thee, Shepherd, thee the woods and the desert caves,
> With wild thyme and the gadding vine o'ergrown,

> And all their echoes mourn,
> The willows and the hazel copses green
> Shall now no more be seen
> Fanning their joyous leaves to thy soft lays.

The change in these lines is a change in dynamics only and not in
style. The style of pastoral continues on through this passage,
characterized by the sensuousness of the nature description, and by
two other traits distinctive of this style, which Milton suggests by
analogizing pastoral verse to the flow of "smooth-sliding Mincius,
crowned with vocal reeds." It is marked, that is, by the prosodic
effects of even, fluid verse movement, and by the crowning verbal
sonorities of echoing vowels and consonants which are implied, with
a connotative suggestion of organ harmonies, in the phrase "vocal
reeds." And this pastoral style, with its tonal effect of gentle pathos,
continues on through the lines that follow, with their mythological
ornament of nymphs and the "wizard stream" of Deva.

The stylistic components of this first musical style in the poem are
pretty much those which Tasso, and Tasso's chief sources in
Demetrius and Aristotle's *Rhetoric,* had specified for the "middle,"
"graceful," or "lyric" style. We see here many of the required subject matters for the imaginative "conceits" of "lo stilo mediocre":
the nymphs, the dawn and springtime sensuous delights of a fertile
nature, and "the glad forest groves" ("fanning their joyous leaves").
Generally normal word-order and predominately coordinate sentence structure support the unperturbed prosodic flow of the
verses, which are, as Tasso specified, "tender, soft, and delicate."
And this uncomplicated syntax permits full play to the "sweet"
sound effect of the long, open vowels, to the predominantly vocalic
rhymes, and to the use of nasal and liquid consonants, especially
l-sounds, which predominate in a few lines, producing, in Tasso's
phrase, "a most sweet composite."[6] In emotional temper, the
imaginative world of this opening section, upon which, in the *forte*
passage, grief makes only its first, brief intrusion, has that relaxed,
"smiling" quality which Tasso regarded as the essence of the lyric
state of mind.

The lyric mood of *Lycidas* lacks, to be sure (in the sexual
connotation of this ambiguous word) Tasso's other ingredient of
"wantonness" (*lascivo*) and also "the loves" which are a significant

item in Tasso's list of subjects for the lyric conceits. Such loves would be factually inappropriate to the subject of Milton's opening section, the early lives of Edward King and of Milton in his youthful association with him, as the poem itself makes clear when it briefly introduces the loves, in the persons of Amaryllis and Neaera, as the youthful preoccupations of "others," but not of Milton or his friend. The "hymeneals," however, which Demetrius and Tasso had specified as a related subject-component of the middle style, do make their appearance later in *Lycidas;* but for the same reason they find their place only in the concluding section, where they are transformed into the suprasensual "unexpressive nuptial song" which King will hear at last in his heavenly apotheosis.

The section of *Lycidas* in this opening key comes to a musical cadence with the rhetorical close of line 49: "Such, *Lycidas,* thy loss to Shepherd's ear." The following section begins in the same key, in the conventionally pastoral questioning of the guardian sea-nymphs. The same traditionally pastoral machinery, and the "mean" or "lyric" style, seem, at first, to be continuing also into lines 58–63, as Milton goes on to describe the death of Orpheus. But in the middle of this passage there is a change of key. Actually it is a modulation to a new tonality—the new "strain" we hear, which is "of a higher mood" and guides the poem away from its opening key of pastoral lament. In Milton's usage the word *high* frequently carries the double meaning the word *alto* has in Italian (and also in its Latin root, *altus*). It means both "lofty" (often with the further sense of a raised voice speaking loudly and with intensity), and also "deep," or profound.[7] Musically, then, the "higher mood" is one more stylistically elevated, more vocally intense, and more philosophically serious.

This new key is first heard in the last three lines of the passage on Orpheus:

> What could the Muse herself that Orpheus bore,
> The Muse herself, for her enchanting son
> Whom universal nature did lament,
> When by the rout that made the hideous roar
> His gory visage down the stream was sent,
> Down the swift Hebrus to the Lesbian shore?

This new style, introduced by back-vowels, gutturals, and harsh

consonants, by intensive diction with suggestions of ugliness and
violence, and by sudden heavy rhythmic stresses, is carried on into
the broken rhythms, the strong stresses, and the intensive language
of the succeeding lines.

In this section the new strain of music sounds with moderate
intensity in the opening:

> Alas! What boots it with uncessant care
> To tend the homely slighted shepherd's trade,
> And strictly meditate the thankless Muse?

After the aside on Amaryllis and Neaera, however—lines which, in
the manner of a musical modulation, conclude the transition to the
new key with a backward echo of the "loves" that belong to the
sportive conceits of the earlier, pastoral tonality—the new strain
rises, *crescendo*, to the harsh climax of lines 75–76.

The dominant tone of this new style is one of bitterness and anger.
And its literary materials, in this section, are drawn from the lofty
genres of epic and of tragedy. We see, first, the conventional theme
of Homeric epic poetry or, more specifically, of the *Iliad*: the moral
imperative to the clear spirit of man, when roused by the spur of
Fame, to live an arduous life, a life which would reach its hoped
fulfillment when the hero, at that dramatic moment known to
Homeric critics as his *"aristeia,"* "burst[s] out into sudden blaze"
and wins the "fair guerdon" of earthly glory. And the tragic death
which, in the *Iliad,* so often cuts short these heroic aspirations, is
here treated with other literary echoes, which frame the epic
suggestions of this first digression with suggestions of the Senecan
tragedy of the Renaissance: the "gory visage" of Orpheus, torn by
"the rout that made the hideous roar," at the start of the passage,
and the intensive diction and stock Senecan machinery in the later
climactic lines:

> Comes the blind Fury with th' abhorrèd shears,
> And slits the thin-spun life.

After this *fortissimo,* or at least double *forte,* in the second key,
however—in fact, by a sharp break in the middle of the last
line—Milton begins a modulation to the smoother verse movement
and the calmer tonality of the opening; and this transition back
toward the lyrical style concludes the first section of the poem:

"But not the praise,"
Phoebus replied, and touched my trembling ears:
"Fame is no plant that grows on mortal soil,
Nor in the glistering foil
Set off to th' world, nor in broad rumor lies,
But lives and spreads aloft by those pure eyes
And perfect witness of all-judging Jove;
As he pronounces lastly on each deed,
Of so much fame in heav'n expect thy meed."

This, then, is the musical pattern of the first section: a beginning *mezzoforte* in the pastoral style (middle, and "lyric") working to a *forte;* then a change of key and a double *forte* in the second style (lofty, and heroic-tragic); and a concluding modulation back toward the lower dynamics and more lyrical movement of the verse in the opening key.

The chief model for the new style of this first digression is certainly Tasso's prescription for the *magnifico* style, that style he thought proper to the epic poem, of which tragedy was a subordinate component. The passage, in its echo of the *Iliad* and its subsequent reference to God's judgment and heavenly reward, shows, first, the subject matters which Tasso, following Demetrius, regarded as components of the conceits of the lofty style: "magnificence lies in things, when one treats and describes some great and illustrious battle, . . . or when one discourses of heaven and of earth." It also has the suggestion of violence in these conceits; and, in its opening and its climactic lines (64–65, 70–73, and 75–76), the dramatic "breaking of verses" which contributed to the characteristic roughness of the magnificent style. Further, in many of the lines Milton seems to be making concentrated use of those harsh consonants, *r* and *s* which Tasso regarded as significant devices for producing the poetic *asprezza*.[8] The lines also show, at some points, Milton's deliberate use of some of those compressions and obscurities in expression (absent entirely from the normal word-order and easy lucidity of the lyric style) which create difficulties for the reader and produce that rough-going which, to Tasso, was one index of the rapt intensity of the higher mood:

Fame is the spur that the clear spirit doth raise

     (That last infirmity of noble mind)
     To scorn delights, and live laborious days....

The second section of the dirge, which extends through the speech of St. Peter, follows a musical pattern similar to that of the first section; and it is organized by this tonal design, rather than, as Barker has argued, by a logical shift to the subject of Edward King as churchman, a subject which does not enter the poem, actually, until the latter part of this passage. The artistic pattern of the opening, as Milton's "oat proceeds" once more, is set by the return to the literary conventions of the pastoral, and to the mean style—first, in the passage in which the nature deities are queried about their responsibility for the tragedy, lines that are relaxed and pleasant, developing particularly the "smiling" quality which Tasso prescribed for the lyric style and giving Milton a chance for fanciful imaginative play ("wanton," in the other sense of the term) with mythology and for agreeable sensuous description of calm airs and sleek Nereids playing on level seas. The passage is, in fact, quite similar in tone—or, as Tasso would say, in its "conceits"—to the earlier description of driving "afield, under the opening eyelids of the morn" and "battening our flocks with the fresh dews of night." But, just as in that first section, we come on a sudden *forte* at the mention of the death, and a reintroduction of some of the prosodic vehemence and harshness of sound (again, with the use of *s*'s and *r*'s) that belong to the *asprezza* of the lofty epic-tragic style.

     It was that fatal and perfidious bark,
     Built in th' eclipse, and rigged with curses dark,
     That sunk so low that sacred head of thine.

The following, more lyrical lines return, however, to the middle style in the passage describing the entrance of the river Cam, "the reverend sire," who comes "footing slow." These lines begin Milton's development of another convention of the pastoral elegy, the procession of allegorical figures of mourners at the bier. But here, just as in the first section, while we seem to be operating securely within stylistic conventions of the pastoral, the poem swings out on the second of its digressions. As it does, its style modulates again, beginning with the hint of the new tonality in the words "stern bespake," and shifts to the second key. For the following twenty lines of St. Peter's speech we hear only the harsh tone of the "dread voice" which shrinks the easy flow of pastoral poetry.

In its specific echoes of literary genres other than the pastoral, St. Peter's speech precisely parallels the literary suggestions of the earlier passage in the "higher mood." The first passage carried suggestions of classical epic and classical tragedy, of the *Iliad* and the tragedy of Seneca. St. Peter's speech has similar suggestions of Christian epic and Christian tragedy. It echoes, first, *La Divina Commedia*, the startlingly theatrical scene in Canto 27 of the *Paradiso* in which, amid the serene sensuousness of the circling harmonies of Paradise, St. Peter suddenly flushes red in the face and explodes in a fit of temper over what men on earth are doing to *his* church ("il loco mio, il loco mio"). And the conclusion of his speech, that much-debated crux of the poem in which St. Peter threatens the impending divine vengeance of "that two-handed engine at the door," seems to me almost certainly conceived as a deliberately apocalyptic passage, one which, like the apocalyptic imitations in final cantos of the *Purgatorio* that Milton is here echoing, is intended to be partly clear and partly obscure, in the manner of biblical writing in the apocalyptic genre, but to refer unmistakably, nevertheless, to the impending stroke of the two-handed sword of St. Michael, the Avenging Angel. To Milton, therefore, these lines would carry suggestions of St. Michael's central role in the battle in *The Apocalypse of St. John*; and *The Apocalypse* was a work he regarded as "the majestic image of a high and stately tragedy," analogous in its literary form to the tragedies of Greek literature.[9] From the point of view of structure, then, the two digressions in the "higher mood" are symmetrical in their suggestion of the major literary forms of epic and tragedy, and in the "magnificent" effect of subject-conceits too weighty for the norm of pastoral poetry.[10]

But my primary concern is with the tonal effect of the "dread voice" of St. Peter. I have commented earlier on the stylistic qualities of this digression, on its frequent ugliness in verbal sound, its brokenness of verse movement and violence in rhythmic stress —which give it the quality of dramatic speech rather than pastoral song—and its climactic prophecy of the awesome spectacle of God's

avenging wrath. Actually, however, these "dread" effects do not
emerge in the poem until the latter part of the speech. As the phrase
"stern bespake" suggests, Milton probably thought of the beginning
of the speech as written in the "grave" style, which Tasso regarded
as similar to the magnificent but simpler and more lucid, and therefore more proper to the dramatic speeches of tragedy. As St. Peter's
anger mounts, however, the lines show the breaking of verses, the
harshness of sounds, the conceits of violence and of awe, and certainly the deliberate obscurities, which mark the magnificent style of
heroic poetry. Although this digression is similar in its stylistic
effects to the earlier digression on Fame and sudden death, and
similar also in its tone of bitter anger, it is far more intense emotion-
ally. As Milton reasserts this second key for the last time in the
poem, he seems to be working for the effect of a final triple *forte* in
this tonality.

After the *fortissimo,* the section breaks off sharp in this key and
does not end with any modulation back to the key of the pastoral.
Instead, Milton writes the interlude we have already looked at; and
his statement that he has done this "to interpose a little ease" indicates why he felt the passage was needed at just this point in the
poem. He intends, when he subsequently returns to the pastoral
style for the conclusion of the dirge, to build to another triple *forte*
in the characteristic tonality of this other style, and therefore he
decides on an interlude of relaxation, *piano* or at most *mezzoforte,*
interposed after the climax in the second of the two contrasting keys
on which the dirge has been played, before he starts his final crescendo in the opening key.

For an analysis of the technique of this flower interlude, Milton's
copy of *Lycidas* in the Trinity Manuscript is helpful, because the
revisions he made in these lines show the artistic principles he
was following. His original version of the passage did not include
lines 142–50 (from "Bring the rathe primrose that forsaken dies"
through "And daffodillies fill their cups with tears"). As he first
wrote the passage, the flower interlude, "Call the vales," was precisely an interlude. After this moment of "ease," and without any
transition, he came on again full force in the tragic lamentation of

> Ay me! whilst thee the shores and sounding seas
> Wash far away . . . .

But he evidently decided that the sharp break from the complete cheerfulness and ease of the flower passage to that dramatic outburst of grief was too violent a wrench, and he therefore added the nine lines beginning at line 142. These lines, the manuscript indicates, were revised twice and seem to have given Milton more trouble in the writing than any other passage in the poem. But it is clear what he is doing in them: he is writing a musical modulation, a bridge-passage which changes key from the effect of sensuous delight in the flower description of the preceding lines to the effect of sorrow in the following lines, by introducing the latter effect, first, as an undertone. His method is to describe flowers that all have connotations of sadness:

> Bring the rathe primrose that forsaken dies . . .
> And every flower that sad embroidery wears.

In describing the technique of these lines as that of a musical modulation, however, I am not using the term merely as a critic's metaphor, one that attempts to suggest a literary effect by analogizing it to the effect of a similar device in the techniques of a different art. I am implying, rather, that in writing these lines Milton actually had this musical device in mind and was consciously devising an equivalent for it in poetic technique. His use of the phrase "Return . . . , return . . ." at the start of the passage, together with his use of the word *interpose,* in the phrase defining its intended effect, provide parallel indications that the initiating conception for the flower interlude in *Lycidas* was musical rather than literary. On one level of suggestion, the word *return* echoes a technical term for a device of poetic structure—the word *rivolta* (= re-turn) which, as we have seen, was the term used by Italian critics to define one of the structural units in the canzone.

In the *rivolta* of a canzone, the stanza, in response to a change in the accompanying music, shifted its metrical form, and moved into a new prosodic unit that represented some kind of repetition, or return, to the prosodic pattern and the accompanying melody of earlier lines. But this "return" of the pastoral style from the beginning of the dirge has a further, and more precise, parallel to the musical concept of the *ritornel* (or *ritornello*) in early seventeenth-century music. As used by Italian composers, *ritornel* was the term for an instrumental section of a solo song in which the accompanying instruments played alone, either for an interlude after the voice had temporarily stopped, or for an instrumental conclusion after the singer had finished ("Return Alpheus, the dread voice is past . . ."). It was known as a *ritornel* because, as in the *rivolta* of the canzone, this instrumental interlude, or conclusion, made a *da capo* return to the musical material with which the composition had begun.[11]

But the term *ritornel* was also applied in the early seventeenth century to the musical form of the *intermedio* (or *intermezzo*) as it was used by the early composers of the new form of the *dramma per musica.* And in this musical meaning the phrase "Return . . . , return . . ." at the start of Milton's flower interlude is exactly parallel to the suggestions of his phrase "interpose a little ease." I think that behind the word *interpose,* as Milton uses it here, lies the Italian musical term *intermedio,* in its literal meaning of something placed in the middle, between two other things. The new musical form of the *dramma per musica* was conceived by the Italian composers of the early seventeenth century as a modern musical recreation of the true form of the stage tragedies of ancient Greece. In these works the *intermedii* were instrumental interludes, of a musical character different from that of the music which accompanied the solo voices of the tragic actors, inserted between the acts of the drama; and they were intended to have the function, for the audience, of affording a brief moment of pleasant and desirable emotional relaxation ("a little ease") from the intensities of the tragic action.[12] In some of the earliest of these prototypes of the *opera seria,* Peri's *Euridice* and Monteverdi's *Orfeo,* the *intermedii* were designated in the published scores as "Ritornel."[13]

I think, therefore, that Milton conceived the flower interlude both as a *rivolta* passage in a grand canzone—that passage by which, according to Dante's analysis, the writer changed the prosodic pattern of the poem in response to a division he was hearing in the imagined musical setting of the song—and also as a poetic adaptation of an *intermedio,* or *ritornel,* in the new Italian music drama. And I believe that the change of poetic tonality at the end of this interlude, in the passage about sad flowers which he added in his final revision of the insert, was thought of by Milton as a literary adapta-

tion of the musical technique of a tonal modulation by which his
intermedio would provide a bridge-passage to the forceful reassertion
of the key of tragic lamentation in the succeeding lines.

After this transition the final outburst of grief still comes with
dramatic suddenness, opening with the plangent cry "Ay me!" the
immemorial tragic formula for a cry of woe, derived directly from
the Italian *oimè* (*ahimè*), and ultimately from the Greek *ómoi*. In
this final triple *forte* in the lyric style, Milton makes smooth-sliding
Mincius roll like the sea and cuts in every one of the "vocal reeds" in
the organ:

> Ay me! whilst thee the shores and sounding seas
> Wash far away, where'er thy bones are hurled,
> Whether beyond the stormy Hebrides,
> Where thou perhaps under the whelming tide
> Visit'st the bottom of the monstrous world;
> Or whether thou, to our moist vows denied,
> Sleep'st by the fable of Bellerus old,
> Where the great Vision of the guarded mount
> Looks toward Namancos and Bayona's hold:
> Look homeward, Angel, now, and melt with ruth;
> And, O ye dolphins, waft the hapless youth.

These lines are remarkable for their sustained prosodic coherence
and impulsion, which drive the verse, check it, build tension
by rhetorical suspensions, and finally release the accumulated
force of the verse-paragraph in the two concluding lines, letting it fall, at last, to the firm but lilting cadence of the closing
line. The lines are striking also for their steady, even flow, achieved
by the use of long vowels, which give the verse a movement and
metric more quantitative than accentual, and for their resonant
verbal sonorities. Verse music of this kind had scarcely been heard in
English before Milton—only, I think, at a few moments in the blank
verse of Marlowe's tragedies—and to my ear it suggests less the
prosodic patterns of English decasyllabic verse than the power,
weight, and sonority of the hexameters not just of Virgil but more
particularly of Homer. I will venture the speculation, in fact, that
what Milton was hearing as he shaped these lines was the roll and
sonorousness of the hexameters of the *Odyssey* (that poem preemi-

nently about the sea), rather than the tauter, more sharply inflected verse movement of the *Iliad*.

The verbal sonorities in these lines, furthermore, seem to show some such conscious choice of particular sounds for particular effects of mood as we have seen in earlier passages in the poem; and they appear to have been arranged, also, according to a pattern of tonal progression within the passage. In the first five lines, where the diction suggests both forceful, violent action (as Lycidas's bones are "hurled" far away by "stormy" seas) and a shudder at the horror of this death ("the bottom of the monstrous world"), we notice Milton using the same sound devices of back vowels and *s*'s and guttural *r*'s he had used earlier in the lines on the "gory" death of Orpheus, and on the sinking of the "perfidious bark" (ll. 61–63, 100–02), in order to create a tonal effect of harshness and energy. But in the following, calmer lines ("Or whether thou . . ."), where the effect is less of tragic violence and horror than of pathos ("ruth"), as the body "sleeps" and is "wafted" by dolphins, Milton changes his tone colors by shifting to predominantly front vowels and making a conspicuous use of the consonant *m,* that consonant which Tasso had regarded as particularly efficacious for effects of plaintiveness in lamentation.

In its structural effect, the end of this passage ties back in idea to the speech of St. Peter by means of the massive implications which Milton compresses into the three lines describing the vision of St. Michael, the Warrior Angel, standing in eternal watch over Land's End in Cornwall. Cornwall was in ancient times the land of King Arthur, the Christian warrior-king who had first driven out the Saxons and unified the English nation. As Milton's master, Spenser, and other Elizabethan writers had maintained, the myth that Arthur was not dead and would return from Avalon when he was again needed to lead his people had become a reality under the Tudor monarchs of the Renaissance, who publicly claimed descent from Arthur. It had found its full actualization in the figure of Queen Elizabeth, under whose reign Protestant England, as God's Chosen People, had once again donned the whole armor of God and led the Church Militant to heroic victory in the defeat of the Spanish Armada.

Milton's vision of St. Michael, the traditional symbol of the Church Militant, as the guardian angel of the English nation, on vigilant watch over Cornwall to protect England against Catholic Spain, the arch-enemy not yet finally vanquished (as he "looks toward Namancos and Bayona's hold"), thus echoes Spenser's epic theme in the first Book of his *Faerie Queene*—the heroic, historical role to which the English nation had been called as God's chosen leader in the Holy War of the Reformation. And Milton's bold imaginative stroke in admonishing the Warrior Angel to "look homeward," and "melt with ruth" at the death of Edward King, joins the two peaks of the poem by tying the climax of the pastoral lament to St. Peter's invective against the corruption of the English church, and to his prophecy that God will not long leave these abuses unpunished. Traditionally, St. Michael is also the Avenging Angel, and it is his sword which is the "two-handed engine" that will smite down England's corrupt pastors. Milton thus raises his earlier satiric attack on ecclesiastical abuses to epic dignity as an aspect of the heroic subject of the manifest destiny of the English nation.

Although these lines make no specific allusion to Arthur, they would almost certainly carry at least this general historical suggestion, one that preceding generations had widely popularized, to Milton's English contemporaries. And I venture the further speculation that, in his own mind, Milton intended this reference to his nation's elected historical destiny, a reference pregnant with suggestiveness but still partly veiled, to serve also as a darkly apocalyptic hint of the central theme of his projected epic poem, that major work which, as the Latin poems of his Italian journey suggest, he expected to present as his next English poem after *Lycidas*.[14] As we can see both from Virgil's Fourth Eclogue and from Spenser's protoepic pastoral "October," it was traditional for the young shepherd-poet, when he aspired to his higher-style pastoral, to make in such an eclogue his first disclosures—sometimes rather veiled, and designed to be fully revealed only in his subsequent work—of the "argument" for the future epic work then beginning to take form in his mind. And the only likely guess we can make about the theme of Milton's unwritten epic on Arthur or some other ancient British hero (the epic subject foremost in his mind in the Latin poems subsequent to *Lycidas*) is that the poem would have treated this historical fable so as to give it symbolic reference, in the manner of Spenser's Arthurian epic, to the historical imperatives of the final, and victorious, phase of England's contemporary Holy War. This was exactly what Tasso had done in his *Gerusalemme Liberata* with the historical narrative of the First Crusade, and it is significant that in the passage on Milton's poetic plans in *The Reason of Church Government,* the only modern exemplar for a "diffuse epic" which he is contemplating as a model for his own work is Tasso's epic poem.

The concluding section of *Lycidas,* which follows the dramatic climax of this triple forte in the lyric-pastoral key, presents none of these pregnant obscurities of meaning or complexities of rhetoric and verse texture. With "Weep no more, woeful shepherds, weep no more," the poem returns to that normality in word order, free flow, and clear openness of statement which to Tasso and to most of the ancient rhetoricians were distinguishing marks of the middle style. In shifting from the subject of grief for Lycidas's death to the new subject of his heavenly apotheosis, as a Neoplatonic guardian deity or *daimon* for the locality where he had died, Milton's conclusion to the lament follows a structural design which had had its original beginning in Virgil's Fifth Eclogue, and which had formed the pattern also for the eleventh eclogue of Sannazaro's *Arcadia,* for Marot's elegy on Louise of Savoy, and for Spenser's "November" dirge in *The Shepheardes Calender.* This final section of *Lycidas* is written throughout in a single style; and from its beginning, in the sure, sweeping movement of the opening line, which tunes out both the horror and the pathos of the climactic lines of the dirge with "Weep no more," the section develops, now, a single, unified tonal effect from the pastoral key (and from Milton's own Christian and Neoplatonic transformation of those "hymeneals" which Tasso and Demetrius regarded as one of the subject-conceits of the lyric style). By the device of dropping the undertones of pathos in the contemplation of death which had earlier been the minor tone in the passages written in this key, and developing only the dominant character of cheerful, calm lyricism, Milton now exploits this style to produce tonal effects of satisfaction and quiet hope, and of a serene and finally triumphant joy.

The poem concludes with the *congedo,* or the *commiato* (the leave-taking), which is the normal ending for the form of the Italian canzone. This epilogue, which the Italian poets had developed from the concluding *tornadas* Provençal poets had originally addressed to the jongleurs who would set the music to their lyrics and sing them, was conventionally a short address to the reader, which often commented on the completed canzone and on the author's stylistic methods and personal motives in writing it. In *Lycidas* Milton uses his *commiato* to complete the purging of grief which the final section of the poem has undertaken ("Now Lycidas, the shepherds weep no more") by the dramatic effect of suddenly removing his personal voice from the poem. At this point a new speaker takes over, someone not involved with Milton's personal feelings about King's death, who looks on the scene from outside. As he coolly describes Milton in the act of spending an entire day, from morning to evening, writing the poem, he detaches us from all the personal feelings the poem has expressed, and sets them off, finally, in a frame of calm objectivity. The effect of serenity and final cadence with which the poem ends derives not only from the characteristically Virgilian effect, repeatedly used in the concluding lines of the *Bucolics*, of the picture of a quiet sunset and the hope of happier things on the morrow, but also from what seems a clear adaptation of the musical device of a *rallentando*. This device checks the strong impulsion of the swelling verse movement in the lines about Lycidas's heavenly apotheosis through a paced, final cadence that moves the poem to its conclusion *adagio molto* and in quiet:

> And now the sun had stretched out all the hills,
> And now was dropped into the western bay;
> At last he rose, and twitched his mantle blue:
> To-morrow to fresh woods, and pastures new.

I think, then, that this pattern of musical structure is the fundamental formal principle which controls the artistic design of *Lycidas,* and that the structural pattern of the poem derives from the unifying symbol which is finally made explicit in the concluding lines, that of a solo song, sung to the accompaniment of the varying pipes of the shepherd's syrinx. This symbol, however, had been suggested by Milton at the start, in the name he gave to *Lycidas* and in the note he added to his manuscript and included for its later publication in his 1645 volume of *Poems* in his headnote to the poem: he defined *Lycidas* as "a Monody," that is, in the musical sense of the term, a song written for a solo voice.

This conclusion, however, does not finally answer the question I set myself at the start of this study—the problem of the literary form of the poem as Milton conceived it. Musical form, however analogous some of its structural devices may be to those used in poetry, is still not literary form. A modern poet—Stéphane Mallarmé, or Ezra Pound, or T.S. Eliot—might well say, "So what?" and leave the matter there. In fact, it has been one of the continuing enterprises of modern literature for the past century to invent new literary forms by building them on principles derived from music. But I doubt that such a proceeding would have seemed satisfying to Milton, or to any other humanist poet of the Renaissance. And though he has modeled his poem overtly on the established genre of the elegiac eclogue of antiquity, he has so manhandled this form that he has ended up making the poem do things which, as he himself tells us, are not suitable for a pastoral elegy at all. Clearly, then, the answer I arrived at earlier—that Milton intended *Lycidas* to be a new exemplar of "the pastoral elegy on classical models"—is not fully satisfactory, and it cannot be our final answer to the question of the literary form of the poem.

But once we try regarding *Lycidas* as a transmutation of the eclogue into the generically related form of the grand lyric, all of paradoxical elements in the poem fall neatly into place. As his poetic schema for the poem Milton has chosen the most dignified form of the lyric as that form was defined by the Italian critics—the form of the free-style canzone stanza, composed of hendecasyllabic lines with a mixture of heptasyllables, which was regarded as the modern analogue to the strophic choral odes of Pindar and the Greek tragedians, and to the Hebrew hymns in the Old Testament. With such an archetype (as adapted to English prosody by Spenser, in his marriage hymns), Milton would have had before him an established and fairly well-defined literary form, whose rules and decorums (and licenses), as defined by the cinquecento critics, would authorize practically all of the structural and stylistic effects which this analysis of *Lycidas* has shown to be actually present in the poem.

The stylistic norm of *Lycidas* is the mean, or middle style which most Italian critics regarded as proper to a lyric. This style had been described, in fact, as the *lirico* style by Tasso, whose technically precise specifications for that style and its underlying "conceits," or poetic mood, Milton is clearly employing in writing the specifically pastoral sections of the poem. But Milton avails himself of the privilege of introducing into the poem two digressions of the sort which the example of Pindar's odes had led critics to regard as a proper structural component—in fact, in Minturno's view, a component that was "strictly required"—for this highest form of the lyric poem. In the writing of these digressions Milton has taken advantage, furthermore, of the fact that Italian critics had maintained that this sort of lyric could at times rise to the effects of heroic poetry. (In Minturno's view, in fact, it was specifically by its digressions that the "Pindaric *canzone*" attained its distinctive heroic character.) Accordingly, Milton has written his digressions from the pastoral norm in the lofty style, and has used, as the subject of these episodes, literary materials which have suggestions not only of epic poetry but also of the tragic poetry that was held to be an essential ingredient of any serious heroic poem. (In fact, this specific verse form for the lyric poem had been known to Italian critics, from its initial definition by Dante, as the "tragic canzone.")

Although Tasso had regarded the middle or *lirico* style as the norm for the lyric genre, he had suggested—and demonstrated in his own poetry—that the canzone stanza used in the grander species of lyric might at times sound forth the trumpets of the *magnifico* style of epic. And the style of Milton's digressions shows many of the devices of roughness and vigor which Tasso had recommended as means for producing the effect of *asprezza* that he thought essential to the epic style. Finally, in choosing literary models for his passages in the heroic style—a style which appears for the first time in *Lycidas* as an entirely new effect in Milton's early verse and which the improvisatory structure and stylistic range of this Italian lyric genre have enabled him to make his first experiments with—Milton's masters have been Tasso; and behind Tasso, the Homer of the *Iliad*, and also, in my view, the Homer of the *Odyssey;* Dante, in the *Commedia;* and certainly also, diffused but pervasive to the poem, the Virgil of the *Aeneid.*

But with so free-ranging an eclecticism as its base—among critical theories, literary techniques, and poetic masters, ancient and modern—it is a striking fact that no one of, nor selection from among, these contributory sources enables one to "explain" *Lycidas* or to predict that from these sources Milton would have produced a poem of this kind. As a first experiment with the techniques and some of the subjects from which he expected to make his mature poems, *Lycidas* bears testimony not just to the scope and inquisitiveness of Milton's preparatory literary studies but, more significantly, to the synthesizing power of a talent that could create from this literary stuff a work so radically unlike any of its literary sources, with no real analogue in the earlier vernacular literature of either England or Italy in the Renaissance.

If I sought, however, for critical works that probably gave Milton fundamental suggestions for *Lycidas,* I would look first to Dante's pioneering analysis of the canzone in *De Vulgari Eloquentia* and then to Tasso's "La Cavaletta." It is only in Dante that Milton would have found the hint for what is the real novelty in his conception of the poem: the idea that a poem might be constructed on an imagined musical accompaniment, made up of two different melodies (or, in Milton's version, two different keys), which would not form an actual setting for the poem when it was completed, but which the poet nevertheless heard in his mind as he wrote, and whose musical suggestions he followed in the structural shaping of his verse ("that strain I heard was of a higher mood"). Milton had already touched on such a method of composing a poem in *Comus.* But in *Comus* the blending of verse with music, a conjunction inherent in the dramatic form of the masque, had been an intermittent effect, appearing only at certain important points in the drama. In *Lycidas* it is fundamental to Milton's conception of the entire poem. The innovation, however, which Milton has made in Dante's suggestion—if this was, in fact, the hint that he built on for the poem—is an attempt to "wed" the "divine sounds" of his verse and music more closely by building the two strains of music into the texture, verbal color, and rhythm of the poem, so that the music does not remain just an unheard accompaniment but is heard in the poetry itself.

The only other critical work which shows significant correspondences to what Milton has actually made of this Italian genre in
Lycidas is Tasso's outline for a new-model canzone in the dialogue
"La Cavaletta." For the new kind of canzone, yet to be written,
Tasso had suggested that the poem might recover to itself the artistic
component of a complementary musical accompaniment, which
since Dante's time it had generally lost, and through a new kind of
conjunction of the two arts produce an artistic effect that Dante had
never dreamed of. If composers could be found to set the poem to a
new music, itself still to be conceived, which would reproduce the
stern gravity of the Greek Dorian mode, the literary power of the
verse to incite virtuous action could conjoin with the ethical compul-
sion of its accompanying music to recreate that synesthetic artistic
effect which had been the *virtù* of the noble lyric genre of antiquity.

The stern Dorian mode, however, could not sound alone throughout the poem: it must be "tempered" with another strain of "sweetness." This second strain, moreover, would also require a new music,
one purged of the lasciviousness and flaccid sensuality that had corrupted many of the contemporary canzoni about the delights of
love, no less than their languishingly erotic musical settings. With
these two strains of music sounding in his ears, a music as yet only
imagined, the writer of this new musicopoetic canzone could play
now in the one style and now in the other, in this way bringing the
whole soul of man into activity, as he tempered the stern prompt-
ings of will with the purified delights of appetite. In such a
proto-epic lyric genre, by exploiting fully the different ethical com-
pulsions of its accompanying music, the poet could then, like
Tyrtaeus in ancient Sparta, arouse his countrymen to the imperatives
of that Holy War for the True Faith that constituted the master task
of contemporary history.

At almost every point Tasso's scheme for a new kind of musical
canzone shows correspondences to what Milton has actually done
with this Italian form in *Lycidas*. And the two alternating musical
strains from which Milton has built his poem seem also to correspond to that passage in *The Republic* which, I believe, Tasso is
consciously echoing in his Platonic dialogue. The two modes of
Greek music which Socrates wished to preserve for his ideal republic,

after he had banished those other harmonies expressive of unmanly
sorrow or of sensual softness and indolence, were the Dorian and the
Phrygian: "the strain of courage, and the strain of temperance."

It is, in fact, the word *temperance*—if we define that word in
Milton's sense as a term not for a fixed ethical ideal, but rather for
an active, continuing process by which the mind reorders itself to
balance and wholeness—which describes the function that the middle
style actually performs in the artistic structure of *Lycidas*. As the
lyric mood repeatedly reasserts itself, after the irruptions of the
epic-tragic style, it operates in the poem to moderate the perturbations of fear and anxiety which the two digressions have aroused,
to restore harmony of mind, and to direct the poem, finally, to the
tempered calm achieved by its conclusion. And noticing the way in
which Milton has deployed the pastoral style in his poem, one is
reminded of Tasso's characterization of the middle, lyric style as also
the "temperato," and of his view that the effect of mixing the lyric
with the magnificent style in a poem is to produce "a gentle
tempering" of emotional extremes. For Milton, furthermore, more
clearly than for Tasso, temperance—the act of tempering—is the
emotional condition which finds its most immediate analogue in the
harmony of music; it is also, in fact, a musical term, meaning
"bringing into harmony." It is because of this power to express, or
to incite, the temperate or harmonized state of mind that Milton has
made the pastoral key the tonic strain in the musical structure of
Lycidas.

It appears, then, that my earlier conclusion that Milton conceived
Lycidas as "a pastoral elegy on classical models" should be revised to
read, "a pastoral lyric on classical and Italian models."

But this answer is still not fully satisfactory, because this definition of the purely literary archetype of the poem will not account
for one conclusion which has emerged from my analysis of the
poem—that it is built from start to finish according to a controlling
design of some kind of musical form. It is not just that *Lycidas*
draws frequent analogies to effects of the music which should
properly be the accompaniment to a poem in the lyric kind, or that
the poem is often strongly lyrical in verse movement. The entire
lament for Lycidas, the two sections in contrasting keys of the dirge
for his death and the succeeding vision of his heavenly apotheosis—

everything in the poem, in fact, except the frame-structure of the
opening and closing passages which deal with Milton's writing of the
lament—seems to be permeated by the conception of a continuous
musical structure that is unfolding according to principles of musical
development and musical coherence. We need to ask, therefore, what
unifying conception Milton has of this musical structure of its design
and characteristic artistic effect; and then to inquire what artistic
analogy there may be between the effects of such a musical form
and the poetic effects proper to a lyric poem of the kind Milton is
writing.

Let us look back over what the analysis of the musical effects of
the poem has shown. We can neglect the frame of the opening and
closing sections and concentrate only on the dirge and the conclusion which follows the lament. The emotional effect Milton intends for the conclusion is clear: it is designed to purge away grief
and end the poem with emotional calm. Before this conclusion, the
two tonalities which alternate in the dirge have each a dominant
emotional effect, and Milton defines these effects explicitly at the
end of the two passages in which each tonality is given its climactic
development. At the end of St. Peter's speech, with its final vision of
the sword of the Avenging Angel, Milton writes "the dread voice is
past." The emotional effect of this tonality, then, is to be one of
"dread"—of fear or terror. As for the other key, its effect is similarly
defined: "Look homeward Angel now, and melt with ruth." The
effect of the other tonality of the dirge is to be "ruth" or pity. We
have here, then, a poem which, as it progresses, alternately arouses
the emotions of pity and fear, plays those two emotional effects in
juxtaposition as the lament reaches its emotional climax (ll. 154–64),
and then ends by purging these disturbances of mind and bringing us
to final calm.

Here finally we have a satisfactory answer to the puzzle of the
form of *Lycidas*. *Lycidas* is written on a musical design which
produces the emotional effects characteristic of tragedy as that genre
was understood by Renaissance critics who derived their ideas from
Aristotle's *Poetics*. Milton has taken the "base" form of the eclogue,
transformed it into the kind of lyric which will permit him to write
in both the middle and the lofty style, and imposed on the whole
poem a musical structure—one proper to the integral conjunction of

verse and music in lyric poems—which will make the poem achieve, as its central and unitary artistic effect, the effect that had been traditionally reserved among the major literary forms, to tragedy.

We could not appropriately say, however, that Milton conceived *Lycidas* as a "true tragedy" fully analogous to *Samson Agonistes.* In Milton's view, tragedy was a subspecies of the genre of the "dramatic poem"—his subtitle for *Samson Agonistes*—and the technique of *Lycidas,* its method of "imitation," is not dramatic. For all his aspirations toward attaining the effects of this genre, it is clear from the opening lines of *Lycidas* that Milton believes his talent has not yet developed to the point where he is capable of a full-scale attempt at tragedy. The form he devised for the poem, in fact—a form which reaches toward the high genre of tragedy but allows him to keep his feet solidly planted in the middle genre of the lyric and the low genre of the eclogue—suggests precisely this aspiring but still tentative frame of mind. As a reflection of the attitude behind the poem, this literary form shows much the same mixture of eagerness to burst out into sudden blaze with the bigger things he is training for, and a restraining doubt over whether he is yet up to it, which we have seen in the letter Milton had written to Diodati a few weeks before. The mixed form of *Lycidas,* like that letter, seems to reflect the mind of a poet who was thinking, in secret, of an immortality of fame—God help him—but who felt that his Pegasus still raised himself on very tender wings, and that he had better hold himself down, for a while, to being lowly-wise on his humbler level.

My final definition, then, of the literary form of *Lycidas* as Milton conceived it is this: *"Lycidas* is a pastoral lyric, on classical and Italian models, musically constructed in the tragic mode."

Once we have recognized tragedy as the organizing formal concept behind *Lycidas,* we can see further ways in which Milton has built some components of that literary form into the poem. It appears that Milton has made an attempt to imbue the poem not only with the pattern of emotional progression distinctive to the tragic genre but also with something like an actual tragic plot. And in doing so he would have been in accord with some Italian critical theories: those of Minturno, for instance, and also (in his analyses of the canzoni of Pigna) of Tasso, both of whom had maintained that the canzone, as the major form of the lyric poem, like the epic and the dramatic poems, might, or should, be based on a *favola* or "action."

In Aristotle's analysis of tragedy the essence of this genre was the plot. In the *Poetics* he stated unequivocally that "the first principle, and as it were the soul of tragedy, is the plot; the characters are in the second place" (50a 33). The subject of Edward King's death, however, offered neither a tragic hero who could be made into an Aristotelian protagonist for a tragic action, nor a very strong narrative element from which to construct a patterned tragic fable. If Milton wished to satisfy this basic Aristotelian prescription for a tragic poem, it might seem that he had made a sufficient obeisance to it—going about as far, in fact, as the subject of his poem permitted him—by using the speech of St. Peter, and the succeeding admonition to the Guardian Angel to "look homeward" in concern over King's death, as devices that would give to the character and death of Edward King a place and significance in the great tragic-heroic action in which England and the English church would lead God's host to eventual victory in the wars of the Reformation.

But this imaginative maneuver still did not provide *Lycidas* with a tragic plot, a coherent pattern of action that would give to the account of the event of King's death, and reflective meditation on it, the satisfying effect of a narrative progression from a beginning, through a middle, to a proper tragic end. It might seem that a poet would just have to give up attempting any such effect, and recognize that, as an argument for tragedy, the accidental drowning of Edward King simply did not afford the material for a plot structure of the sort which formed the organizing soul of genuine tragedies.

Nevertheless, it looks to me as though Milton certainly made a try. His attempt at imposing a tragic plot on the event is rather strained, but at least reveals the particular form of tragic plot which engaged his imagination as he considered plans for the genuine tragedy he might some day write. The suggestions of the schematic outline of this plot begin to appear at the start of the climactic section of the lament for Lycidas and are developed throughout the conclusion. What happens in these lines has been recognized by M. H. Abrams with an accuracy of literary perception which I can only admire and quote:

By extraordinary dramatic management, it is at this point of profoundest depression that the thought of Lycidas' body sinking to "the bottom of the monstrous world" releases the full implication of St. Peter's speech, and we make the leap from nature to revelation, in the great lyric peripety:

> Weep no more, woeful Shepherds, weep no more,
> For *Lycidas* your sorrow is not dead,
> Sunk though he be beneath the watry floar. . . .
> So Lycidas, sunk low, but mounted high,
> Through the dear might of him that walk'd the
>   waves. . . .[15]

Abrams seems to be using the Aristotelian term *peripety* here in a meaning, common in modern post-Aristotelian criticism of tragedy, which actually combines two different concepts of the basic elements of plot structure that were separate in Aristotle's thought and are sharply distinguished also in those detailed analyses of the technicalities of tragic plots which we find in most of the commentaries on the *Poetics* by the sixteenth-century Italian critics. Abrams's use of "peripety" seems to cover both the "reversal" or "change of fortune," which Aristotle had regarded as the basic ingredient of the plot of tragedy (50a 33), and the other element to which Aristotle had applied the term *peripeteia*—that is, a change in fortune in which the outcome of the action is the opposite of what had been intended or expected by the agent (52a 22). Nevertheless, since both of these meanings are implied in Milton's lines, Abrams defines exactly what Milton is suggesting as he turns the concluding section of the dirge for Lycidas toward its final tragic catharsis.

Although it involves Milton in some rather arbitrary imaginative forcing of the facts that are the subject of his poem, as well as in a somewhat literal-minded and mechanical insertion into the poem of a theoretical concept from Aristotelian criticism ("sunk low, but mounted high"), he is suggesting in these lines that the sudden death of King, and his subsequent and immediate resurrection into the life of heaven is a true tragic action, revealing the Aristotelian plot structure of a beginning, a middle, and an end. The beginning is the tragic reversal, or change of fortune—in its technical sense, the catastrophe—by which Lycidas falls from the high state which, as St.

Peter implies, had appeared to be the lot to which his earthly calling had destined him. This beginning, or fall, reaches its fully tragic plot conclusion in the outburst of lamentation of lines 154–64 ("Ay me! whilst thee the shores and sounding seas/Wash far away . . ."), a passage in which Lycidas's body, "sunk low," finally manifests the full horror of his tragic fall as his "bones" are "hurled" to "the bottom of the monstrous world."

But just at this climax of the dirge, we come on the middle or brief transition section, which it seems possible Milton may have thought of as something like a true plot turn, that begins a movement of the tragic plot through a second reversal toward an unexpected outcome. This change in fortune is first hinted at by the shift in the tonal suggestions of the lines as they describe Lycidas's body "sleeping" under the guardianship of "Bellerus old," or being finally wafted by dolphins and coming at last under the protective concern of the Guardian Angel St. Michael, who stands surveying these seas in which Lycidas met his fate. And with the succeeding surge of joy in the lines

> Weep no more, woeful shepherds, weep no more,
> For Lycidas, your sorrow is not dead . . .

we encounter the second reversal of fortune, as the tragic plot turns fully and enters on the regenerative action by which Lycidas, "sunk low," has finally "mounted high." The "great lyric peripety" at this point in the poem is, in more precisely Aristotelian terms, an example of what Aristotle had regarded as the best kind of plot, one "necessary to the structure of a tragedy of the most excellent sort," a tragic plot which is "not simple but involved" (52b 28). The distinguishing mark of an involved plot, as Aristotle defines the term, is that, unlike the simple plot, in which "the change of fortune takes place without peripety or recognition," it combines, or involves, the protagonist's reversal of fortune, which is the basic requisite of any tragic plot, with either one or both of the other two desirable components of the plot structure of a tragedy: a plot is "involved when the change of fortune is accompanied by recognition or peripety or both" (52a 11).

The reversal which takes place at line 165 of *Lycidas* accompanies Lycidas's change of fortune with both. It is involved with a peripety because Lycidas's entrance into the joy of eternal life is an outcome exactly opposite to that which had been foreseen in the catastrophe of his drowning, not only by the protagonist of that action, but also by the witnessing shepherds, who appear rather suddenly on the scene in this final section of the poem in order to function, in their reactions to the tragedy, much like the chorus of a tragic drama. The unexpectedness of this happy outcome is, in fact (Milton may wish us to notice), an unusually surprising one, since the shepherds discover that Lycidas has enjoyed that immediate resurrection into heaven which, according to *Revelation,* can be expected only by saints and martyrs, over whom "the second death" has no power.

The second plot reversal is also involved with a recognition, which Aristotle defines, in its broadest sense, as "a change from ignorance to knowledge—resulting in love or hate—by those marked out for good fortune or bad fortune" (52a 29). For both the protagonist and the witnessing shepherds, this reversal of fortune leads to a recognition that this earthly death of a man whose tragedy, they had ignorantly thought, was that he died with his promise of great achievement unfulfilled, has been subsumed in the immediate reward of eternal life and also of a "guerdon" fairer than the earthly Fame he had lost: the "Fame in heaven" which Lycidas enjoys among the "sweet societies" of saints "that sing, and singing in their glory move." As Aristotle had maintained, the very best form of that best kind of tragic plot in which the change of fortune is involved with either a recognition or a peripety is the plot in which it is accompanied by both: "the best recognition is one combined with a peripety" (52a 29).

The end of the tragic plot of *Lycidas,* which follows on this transitional middle, is the ecstatic scene described in lines 172–81. In this closing scene of the action, we see Lycidas, now mounted high through the second change of fortune that had succeeded the first reversal in his tragic fall, experiencing the consequence of a recognition which has resulted not in hate but in love, as he

> hears the unexpressive nuptial song
> In the blest kingdoms meek of joy and love;

and at last in the final line of the scene, having his tears over his tragic fall wiped forever from his eyes. After this exit of the protagonist, the last four lines of Milton's elegy shift to describing the chorus. The witnessing shepherds, like Manoah and the chorus in *Samson Agonistes*, "with new acquist of true experience from this great event," now weep no more; but finding "no time for lamentation now, nor much more cause," and having seen that

> which is best and happiest yet, all this
> With God not parted from him, as was feared,
> But favoring and assisting to the end,

are left thinking only of the example Lycidas has left to their calmed meditations, and of his continuing protective presence to them as the "Genius of the shore."

In Milton's terms, *Lycidas* is not, as I have said, a "dramatic poem." And it may be that I am overarguing my case by trying to force on *Lycidas* details of tragic plot structure that were never in Milton's mind as he wrote the poem. But Milton was fascinated with tragedy for most of his literary career; and the later tragedies he wrote in Books 9 and 10 of *Paradise Lost* and in *Samson Agonistes* both show a full concern for those technical elements in the construction of Aristotelian tragic plots which had held an equal fascination for most of Milton's critical masters among the Italian commentators on the *Poetics*. It is certainly true, at any rate, that he has managed, in his first attempt at a prototragedy, to build into *Lycidas* more of the essential literary components of an actual tragic plot, designing the latter part of the poem at least as a patterned scheme of dramatic action, than one might think possible. And even in *Samson Agonistes,* he was more interested in making his tragedy a poem than in making it a stage-play. He deliberately neglected in the writing of it, as his preface explains, some of the devices of structure that would have been needed to fit his poem to the stage, "to which this work was never intended."

It seems probable, in fact, that Milton shared Tasso's view that tragedy was not just a literary form but rather a literary mode, which could serve to pattern a wide variety of literary forms. We have seen Tasso, in "La Cavaletta," arguing that tragedy is a literary genus which is properly subordinate to the forms of the epic poem, the tragic drama, and the lyric poem. And for his conception of tragedy as independent of the stage (and thus adaptable to a lyric poem), Milton had also the warrant of Aristotle's opinion. When he conceived the tragic pattern for *Lycidas,* I suspect that he had given attention to the statement in Aristotle's *Poetics* which may also have been in his mind when he wrote the sentence I have quoted from the preface to *Samson:* "tragedy can produce its effect without performance and without actors" (50b 16).

In one important respect, however, the tragic plot of *Lycidas* breaks with Aristotle's rules for tragedy and shows a further and significant anticipation of *Samson Agonistes.* For *Lycidas,* Milton devised a plot of a sort which Aristotle had firmly disapproved of. In Aristotle's view, "the change . . . must not be to good fortune from bad fortune, but the opposite one from good fortune to bad fortune" (53a 12).

For *Lycidas* Milton wished his protagonist to experience changes in fortune of both these kinds, and his fable for the poem is a combination of these two different kinds of plot.[16] For his own version of plot, the first unit of the action was that change of the protagonist from good to bad fortune which Aristotle had thought the only pattern of events proper to tragedy. But Milton then made the first plot lead on, through a second reversal, into a subsequent pattern of action in which the protagonist rose from the depth of bad fortune to a final good fortune even richer than that which he had enjoyed before his fall from high estate.

It is clear that tragedy, in Aristotle's philosophic sense of the term, was, to Milton as it had been to Aristotle, a fundamental ingredient in his view of life. He was strongly attracted, both early and late, to poetic forms that were shaped by this literary kind; and it is the literary mode which provides the controlling design for the various poetic genres of *Lycidas, Paradise Lost,* and *Samson Agonistes.* And if he agreed with that opinion, which "hath ever been held," that the dramatic genre of tragedy, "as anciently composed" and as anciently given its theoretical definition by Aristotle, was "the gravest, moralest, and most profitable of all other poems," it must have been because, like Aristotle, he looked on the literary genre of tragedy (whose "soul" was the tragic plot) as an "imitation" of a kind of causally related sequence of events which comprise a significant actuality in any rational comprehension of human affairs.

But if Milton accepted, in some sense of the term, a tragic view of life, he did not want his tragedies to end as Aristotle had thought wisest. That he preferred a non-Aristotelian conclusion to the tragic plot was certainly, in part, a reflection of his progressivist historical view, which saw in the Christian revelation the giving of a new light that directed men to see beyond the incomplete aspirations of that noble but blinded age in which life could seek only the fair but infirm guerdon of earthly glory, and in which human limit was defined by "the blind Fury with th'abhorred shears." But it was also, just as certainly, a strong temperamental inclination on Milton's part which led him to prefer for his poems plots in which the tragic fall was only the first phase of a continuing, and finally regenerative, sequence of action. Unlike Aristotle, what Milton saw as the significant tragic pattern in human affairs—that repeated pattern in human life which the plot of tragedy accurately "imitated"—was the pattern of events, inherent in the nature of things, by which man, having first experienced a fall from high estate, which he brought on himself most commonly by some momentary trust in the complete self-sufficiency of his natural powers, comes to his own realization of his dependency on God and of God's justice: from this plot-beginning of a fall, man then progresses through a middle action in which this initial defeat and subsequent recognition initiates a new, regenerative course of action that leads him, assisted by the re-extension of God's grace, to a predestined end in which his death is swallowed up in spiritual victory and his outward defeat in the peripety and recognition of a possibility of heroic triumph greater than any he has known before.

Finally, the recognition that tragedy is a controlling literary concept for *Lycidas* enables us to arrive at satisfactory answers to two further questions about the poem: first, what Milton had in mind when (in the note he added to the Trinity Manuscript) he defined the form of the poem as a "Monody," and second, whether he was thinking of any specific kind of existing musical composition when he devised the musical structure of the poem. I began my inquiry into *Lycidas* by using, as a sighting-shot, an analogy to Stravinsky's distinction between two different concepts of musical form, represented by the symphonies of Beethoven and the compositions of Webern. But in musicalizing the form of *Lycidas*, Milton could scarcely have imagined any musical form that resembled the symphonic structures of Beethoven. With a fuller analysis of *Lycidas* as a guide, we may now be able to zero in on some musical kind that existed in the music of the late sixteenth or early seventeenth century which corresponds, in its musical means, its structural characteristics, or its designed artistic effect, to the kind of poem we have in *Lycidas.*

It is here that the term *monody* offers us an answer which will fit virtually everything we have found in an analysis of the poem. If we investigate, first, the meaning *monody* had merely as a literary term in Renaissance criticism, we find a term which is not, certainly, completely inappropriate to a poem like *Lycidas,* but which seems hardly adequate to define the complex and ambitious poetic structure of this lofty rhyme. In cinquecento criticism—for example, in the systematic works on poetics by Minturno and Scaliger—the monody is most often regarded as a minor and unpretentious literary genre, analogous to the elegy. Even though the elegy had been developed by Ovid, as Scaliger explained, into the form for a love complaint, this late usage, in his view, only reflected the origin of the genre as a poem expressing a private and personal grief: and therefore he classified the elegy and the monody together as short forms for expressing personal grief, usually over a death. In his initial classification, in the first Book of his *Poetics,* of the hierarchy of the genres, Scaliger ranks the monody below comedy in the fifth, or lowest, category, together with such minor genres as satires, elegies, songs, and epigrams.[17]

Minturno, in his Tuscan poetics, gives only brief attention to the "monodic poem," and he regards it as a lesser lyric form, written to be sung as a solo song and not to be presented on the stage.[18] From Minturno's latter conclusion, however—one that he evidently sees as the generally accepted understanding of the term—Scaliger had dissented:

> *Monody* must be understood in a quite different sense than is accepted by the learned, for it is not what they think it is. In fact, it took place as often as one man stepped forth from the Chorus to honor in mournful song the memory of the dead; he played this on the flute in the Lydian mode.

We find a further and rather individualistic interpretation of the term *monody* in Mazzoni's *Della Difesa della Commedia di Dante,* a work we know Milton admired. Mazzoni is concerned to defend Dante's work against those critics who have argued that Dante has "strayed from the right path of poetics" in the form he gave to his poem. Mazzoni's idiosyncratic conclusion about the form of the *Commedia* is that it is a "monodic comedy." While he does not think that such a genre actually existed in ancient times and regards it as Dante's own creation, he sees the form as, nevertheless, a legitimate combination of genres preexisting in classical literature, and he therefore maintains that Dante has properly derived the genre of his poem from ancient poetic law and from the use of good poets. Mazzoni's argument, in brief, is, first, that a monody, according to ancient testimony, was a sorrowful poem of lamentation for the dead: and Dante's poem speaks entirely about the dead. (In this connection he cites Origen's conclusion that the formal lyrics in *The Lamentations of Jeremiah* were "monodic.")

In addition to this conception of monody as a poetic genre, however, Mazzoni finds in antiquity a somewhat analogous use of the term to define a mode of theatrical presentation. Noting Aristotle's opinion that the presentation of tragic plots by means of actors on the stage is not essential to tragedy or to comedy, he cites ancient authority to prove that before the age of Thespis, tragedy was monodic, not performed by actors but sung solo by a single actor on stage. And he finds further evidence that monodic presentations of both tragic and comic plots, when sung or narrated by a single actor, continued on the stage in later Greek times, and in Rome at least through the time of Nero.

Dante's *Commedia* is, therefore, in the ancient and proper meaning of these two terms, a "monodic comedy": it adheres to the traditional form of monody in being a narrative poem of lamentation for the dead, which is sung, rather than dramatized on stage, by a single actor (Dante himself); but the divine intellect of Dante, "without breaking the laws of poetics, has found an invention through which he could conjoin a true and perfect monody . . . with a comic plot . . . that ends in happiness."[19]

Mazzoni's interpretations of the term *monody* is clearly specialized to fit his own argument about the *Commedia,* but that argument reflects, at any rate, a generally accepted view that, as a poetic form, a monody is a lyric poem of personal lament for the dead— and that that is about all one can say about this simple poetic genre. However, both Mazzoni's and Scaliger's interest in the historical evidence that, in the presentation of Greek tragedies on the stage, solo actors had sung either brief tragic lamentations or extended tragic fables runs parallel to a different interest in Greek theatrical monody which appears among musical theorists in the late sixteenth century, and to the meaning they gave to *monody* as a term for a new musical concept which excited some of these late Renaissance humanists.

This use of *monody* as a term for a new and historically significant development in musical form, which engaged two different groups of musical theorists and composers in the Renaissance, derives from an artistic and philosophic enterprise that D. P. Walker has accurately labeled "Musical Humanism."[20] These musical humanists were trying to achieve, through an integration of poetry with a new kind of music, in the genres of lyric and dramatic poems, a modern musico-poetic form that would reproduce the compelling emotional and ethical "effects" which, they believed, had actually been produced in antiquity by the various modes of Greek music. Their attempt to rediscover Greek music and the nature of the Greek modes, and to recapture the close conjunction of musical patterns of sound with both the meaning and the sound patterns of poetic speech (a conjunction thought to be the real cause of the "mirabili effetti" of classical music), was carried out by two groups of musicians and poets who worked independently but had similar artistic and philosophic aims.

In France the enterprise was pursued by the musicians and the Pléiade poets who were associated in Baif's Academy in the 1570s and 1580s. In Italy it was carried out by a number of musicians, of which Giovanni Bardi's Florentine Camerata, whose chief theoretical exponent was Vincenzo Galilei, was the most vigorous and articulate group. These Italian musical experiments, begun in the 1560s and continuing to the end of the century, were a contributing influence on the creation, in the early seventeenth century, of the new musical form, the opera. As some Italians conceived it, this art form, known as the *dramma per musica* or the *favola per musica*, was a synesthetic union of music, stage drama, and poetry which recreated the actual form of ancient tragedy as it had been presented on the Greek stage.

The French group of musical humanists has been investigated not only by D. P. Walker but also by Frances Yates, in *The French Academies of the Sixteenth Century*. Most of the French experiments were directed to the production of *musique mésurée*, written to the quantitative meters of *vers mésuré*, in which the poetic text was generally set to homophonic music, sung by voices in harmony. For the work of these French poets and musicians the philosophic source, as Miss Yates has shown, was Ficino and the Florentine Neoplatonism of the fifteenth century. And in Italy also the earlier Renaissance fervors of Ficino's "Academy" and his cult of "Orphic Poetry" has been an originating source for some of the Italian philosophic theories about Greek music. But for the Florentine group of musical humanists living in the changed intellectual climate of the late cinquecento, the dominant philosophic character of their musical theory was Aristotelian.

The musical form which emerged from the experiments of the Italian Camerata in producing a "Musica Nuova" was what they called "monody": musical declamation *in stilo recitativo* for a solo voice, usually with instrumental accompaniment. Monody of this kind, they believed, since it permitted the words of the text to be clearly head in direct conjunction with music precisely fitted to each word, recaptured the artistic effect that had been lost both in contemporary polyphonic vocal music and in homophonic harmonic singing by combined voices: it was the musical form by which both the philosophic content and the affective power of poetic language could be joined to the affective power of music so as to reproduce the "miraculous effects" of Greek music. In the new form of the *dramma per musica*, as it developed in the first decades of the seventeenth century, the speeches of the tragic actors were set to monody, usually in combination with solo airs, as the analogous musical form which completed the artistic effect of poetic tragedy.

The chief spokesman for the ideas of Bardi's Camerata was Vincenzo Galilei, whose *Dialogo della musica antica e della moderna*

(1581) was the manifesto for this program for recovering the affective powers of Greek music. Although some recent musicologists have tended to minimize the influence of Galilei's book and of the Camerata as generating forces for the music dramas actually produced by the Italian composers, and have preferred to seek their origin in the Italian tradition of popular solo songs rather than in humanistic theories about the arts of Greece, the recent studies of Galilei and the Camerata by Claude V. Palisca have made clear the true character of the ideas underlying both Galilei's *Dialogo* and the musical enterprise of the Camerata.[21] Palisca has placed Galilei's musical ideas in the intellectual ambience of Italian philosophic and critical thought in the late sixteenth century, and has demonstrated their affinity with contemporary artistic theories which exercised their influence not only on the Florentine theorists but also on other contemporary musical humanists, like Monteverdi, who were not connected with Bardi's Camerata.

Palisca has shown that both Galilei and Bardi were taught by the classical philologist Girolamo Mei, whom Galilei acknowledges as his mentor, together with Bardi, at the beginning of his *Dialogo*.[22] From his research on Greek music Mei had concluded that the reason why modern music was unable to produce the "effects" of Greek music was that it was based on polyphony and harmony. Polyphony and harmony confused the mind, distracting it from a rational following of the words of the text, and they also incited the senses, disturbing the passions instead of ordering them. But since polyphony and harmony (in the modern sense of the latter term) were unknown to the Greeks, Mei concluded that all Greek musical settings of poetry had been monodic.

Although some of Mei's ideas about the affective power of combining poetry with music derive, ultimately, from Ficino's Neoplatonism, he was a serious Aristotelian who founded his musical aesthetics on the *Poetics*. His chief interest was in discovering the musical form that would produce the tragic catharsis described by Aristotle. He concluded, and proved to Galilei, that monody was this musical form. And he persuaded him, further, that Greek music had been consistently monodic not only in lyric songs, but also in the performance of tragedies, in which the strophic Choral Odes had actually been sung by a solo voice.[23]

Although much of Galilei's *Dialogo* is concerned with technicalities about the Greek musical modes and the proper tuning of the
cithara and the lyre, these ideas of Mei's appear in the passages in
which Bardi, one of the interlocutors of the dialogue, attacks contemporary polyphonic and harmonic music and opposes to this
"impertinence" (p. 80) the evidence of the ethical force of the monodic music of antiquity recorded by Plato, "the divine philosopher,"
and more fully by Aristotle, who has testified to the power of such
music, in the Dorian mode, to effect "the purgation of souls by
giving vent to their feelings and assuaging them," through the faculty
possessed by "the harmonies and the melodies conforming to these
passions."[24] Galilei's view that monody was the musical form
proper to tragic poetry was also demonstrated by two musical illus-
trations of the theories in the *Dialogo* which he wrote immediately
after the publication of the book. These were settings for solo tenor,
accompanied by a consort of viols, of two different kinds of tragic
poetry: one an example of dramatic narrative, Dante's lament for
Ugolino in Canto 33 of the *Inferno;* and the other an example of
strophic lyric poetry, a portion of the *Lamentations of Jeremiah.*[25]
But Palisca makes clear that is was not in Greek music alone that
Galilei found his sources for musical monody. In addition to the
recitative-style declamation he believed characterized the Greek tragedies, Galilei saw an equally significant origin for monodic settings
of poetry in that native tradition which modern scholars regard as
the more important source for the new *dramma per musica*—the melodies of popular solo songs. Palisca has traced Galilei's interest in the
melodic Italian folk songs in his later writings, but his interest in this
parallel source for monody is also clear from the start in the *Dialogo.*
In one passage Bardi argues that monodic singing is the natural mode
of musical expression, as old as creation itself, and that folk songs of
the peasants have also served the purpose of purging the soul of its
emotional perturbations. This mode of singing "is the same as that
which the rustic farmers cultivating the fields, and the shepherds
following their flocks through the woods and hills, have made use of
to expel from their breasts the weariness brought upon them by
their continual and heavy labors. This sort of singing has always been
used by men from their creation down to our times, nor will it have
an end except together with them, and with the world itself."[26]

In summarizing Galilei's theory of monody, Palisca concludes that he sought his solution to the problems of musical composition, and of the proper musical accompaniment of words,

> in the two sources most dear to Renaissance men: nature and Greek letters. To sing a simple melodic line was first of all the way of nature: when shepherds and workers in the fields were finished with their labors, they turned for solace to popular airs, which they sang to the strumming of some instrument. Many lessons could be learned from these simple songs of the populace. A further model for modern music to emulate was provided by the odes and hymns sung to the cithara by the ancient poets. The imitation of nature, and the imitation of the classics, two principles that dominated the literary discussion of the day, thus served Galilei as the fountainheads of his musical experiments.[27]

I have discussed Galilei's *Dialogo,* not as a book I am certain Milton knew, but merely as the most renowned manifesto for the new Italian monodic music in the late sixteenth century, a book whose ideas were widely discussed in Italy at the time. As both Palisca and Walker have shown, many of Galilei's ideas derive from the common stock of that musical humanism which engaged a number of poets, musicians, and theorists in both Italy and France in the late sixteenth and early seventeenth centuries. That Milton was acquainted with, and eagerly interested in, these new musical theories is clear to any reader of his early poems. Further, he would have encountered these musical ideas not just in theoretical works, but in the new music itself. And for anyone of Milton's artistic and philosophic interests, to know this new monodic or homophonic music would also be to know the historical and philosophic ideas it expressed and exemplified.

Even before *Lycidas,* the poems written just before his residence at Horton in 1635 give clear testimony of Milton's youthful enthusiasm for the Neoplatonic theories, derived chiefly from Ficino, about the religious and literally revelatory effects produced in the mind by the "wedding" of the "divine sounds" of those two "sphere-born harmonious sisters," verse and the singing voice, a wedding he celebrated in "At a Solemn Music" and again in "Arcades" and in *Comus.* In

"L'Allegro" and "Il Penseroso," the parallel passages contrasting the opposite satisfactions to be found, on the one hand, in sensual and erotic music, probably that of vocal polyphony, and, on the other, in the grave monodic music sung to the lyre, of Orpheus (ll. 135–44; 105–08), derive from the strain in the new musical theory, characteristic of Galilei, which D. P. Walker has labeled "musical puritanism."

The same antithesis between music of these two ethically opposite kinds is fundamental to *Comus*. It appears most explicitly in Comus's speech (ll. 246–64) in which he describes the strange new effect—"divine" and literally "enchanting" to religious "rapture"—that he finds in the lady's monodic song, "Sweetest Echo" (which Milton evidently intended Lawes to conclude with an answering harmony from the voice of Echo). To Comus the effect of this new music seems completely different from that of the sensual music he had known as he had heard it sung (either, I assume, in polyphony or by voices in harmony) by Circe and her Sirens. Further, as John Demaray has shown, one of the sources on which Milton drew for *Comus* was the famous French *ballet de cour,* the *Balet Comique de la Royne,* a work that had been the public show-piece for the Neoplatonic theories of the musical humanists in Baïf's Academy, in which both the dances and the musical settings were designed as embodiments of Ficino's speculations about ancient Greek music.[28]

No attentive reader of these early poems of Milton's, moreover, will take at face value Milton's later statement that when, during his years at Horton, he went up to London to learn something new in music or mathematics, music was to him, at that time, an art in which he found only "pleasure." And though "some new discovery in music" is hardly specific, the development of Italian *Musica Nuova* in the new monodic music drama was the most striking new thing in the music of the European Renaissance, having the dramatic character of a genuine discovery of new possibilities in the art, as well as being a development which had its origin in much the same philosophic and aesthetic ideas that intensely engaged Milton's mind during his studies in these years.

There is, finally, a strong likelihood that Milton would have learned something about Italian monody, in both declamatory recitative

and melodic song, and also about the *dramma per musica*, through
his collaboration with Henry Lawes in the production of *Comus.* It
was Lawes who had first introduced the new stage monody to
England in 1617, when he collaborated with Ben Jonson in the
masque *Lovers Made Men:* in this work, according to Jonson, "the
whole Masque was sung (after the Italian manner) *stylo
recitativo.*"[29] And again, just two years before *Comus,* Lawes had
used both *stilo recitativo* and monodic song in the music he wrote
for Aurelian Townshend's masque, *Albion's Triumph,* presented at
court in 1632.

Although Milton, in writing the text for *Comus,* clearly indicated
monodic musical settings for certain parts of his masque, Lawes
added further passages of Italian monody when he set the text for its
stage performance at Ludlow Castle. In Milton's Trinity Manuscript
for *Comus,* the speech following the solo song by which the Attendant Spirit invokes Sabrina was marked, in Milton's hand, "To be
said." But in the Bridgewater Manuscript, used for the stage performance, Lawes changed this stage direction to read, "The verse to
sing or not"—allowing for a recitative to be improvised by himself as
he performed the role of the Attendant Spirit. And a part of the
Attendant Spirit's speech following Sabrina's solo song, which
Milton intended to be spoken, was set by Lawes to be sung *in stilo
recitativo.*

In summary, it seems unlikely that Milton would have given the
title "A Monody" to so ambitious a poem as *Lycidas* if he had been
thinking only of the meaning of the word in literary criticism, as a
term for a minor, unpretentious poetic genre of personal lament. If,
on the other hand, in his explorations of what was new in contemporary music during his studies at Horton, or in his collaboration
with Lawes in the writing and musical setting of *Comus,* he had
encountered the theory of monody as a modern musical form
created by the Italian humanists, he would have formed the idea of a
new art-form that would encompass almost everything he put into
the writing of *Lycidas.*

Since the poems immediately preceding *Lycidas* give certain evidence that Milton knew some of this musical theory, it seems
equally certain that when he journeyed up to London at this time
"to learn something new in music" he would have tried to acquaint

himself with some of the actual music which had emerged from the theory.[30] If he had consulted nothing more than the scores of the early Italian music dramas published in the first decade of the seventeenth century, he would have encountered not only the dry monodic declamations, pedantically illustrative of the Florentine musical theories, of Peri's *Euridice;* he would also have come to know a work as superb as Monteverdi's first, experimental opera, *La favola d'Orfeo* (1607; published 1609). This work takes the humanist theories about Greek tragic monody only as a point of departure and goes on to open up dramatic possibilities in the new style which the Florentine theorists had never dreamt of. It begins as a pastoral drama, scored for shepherds' pipes (i.e. woodwinds); but in act 3 it dramatically changes character, as Monteverdi's orchestra sounds forth the *tromboni* (big trumpets) symbolic of epic-tragedy; and it ends with the descent of Apollo to carry Orpheus to a heavenly apotheosis, concluding with a brief intrumental dance-epilogue written in the ecclesiastical Dorian mode.

Milton would probably also have discovered another of the most famous products of the new music early in the century, the "Ariadne Monody" from Monteverdi's second opera, *Arianna* (1608). Although the music for this opera was not published and has been lost, the monodic tragic aria of Ariadne in the second act, "Lasciatemi morir," became so immediately celebrated that Monteverdi rearranged it in a madrigal setting for five voices, published in 1614, a setting from which one can easily reconstruct the original solo vocal part. And in the title he gave to this madrigal setting Monteverdi merely accepted the literary name which the aria had already acquired: from the time of its first performance in 1608, it had come to be known as the "Lamento" of Ariadne, because of the analogy contemporaries saw between this brilliant example of the new musical monody and the literary meaning of *monody* as a critical term for the Greek poetic genre that was a song of grief.[31]

In the Italian musical form of monody, then, both in its generating theory and in its artistic actualization in music of striking expressive range and dramatic power, Milton would have found a new synesthetic art-form which sought, as its central artistic purpose, to realize that fusion of the "mixed power" of the "divine sounds" of poetry and music which would produce the "miraculous effects" that ancient testimony (as well as the composers of the new operas) ascribed to the songs of Orpheus. Such literally revelatory, religious effects were those Milton had read of in Plato and the Florentine Neoplatonists, had described in "At a Solemn Music," and had tried to achieve himself when he collaborated with Henry Lawes in the stage production of *Comus.*

A monody, next, would embody something of the spontaneous naturalness of the solo songs which shepherd swains, in all ages and climes, had sung to the oaks and rills in order to assuage their troubles. But this form could also rise to the poetic loftiness and force of the great lyric odes of antiquity, to the style of the "magnific odes and hymns" of Pindar and Callimachus, which the Greeks sang to the lyre, and of those divine "songs" found in the books of Jeremiah and other Hebrew prophets. Finally, it was the form in which a solo voice, singing the formal strophes of the choral odes in Greek tragedies, had wedded music to verse in an elaborate lyric so as to achieve that final catharsis of pity and fear through a reasoned tempering of the passions which was the ethical effect distinctive to tragedy.

I hope any reader who has stayed with me as I have led him over hill and over dale will not conclude that this has been just a wild-goose chase if I end my analysis of *Lycidas* by telling him that the best one-word definition of the artistic form of the poem as Milton conceived it is probably the term Milton himself used. He defined the form when he added an introductory note in his own manuscript of the complete poem and later published a headnote to its 1645 edition: *Lycidas* is, in fact, a monody.

Notes

CHAPTER 1

1   Igor Stravinsky and Robert Craft, *Themes and Episodes* (New York, 1966), pp. 117–18.

2   Northrop Frye has made much the same statement about *The Passion:* "it is the only poem of Milton's in which he is preoccupied with himself in the process of writing it. . . . It is not a coincidence that Milton's one self-conscious poem should be the one that never gets off the ground." ("Literature as Context: Milton's *Lycidas,*" reprinted in C. A. Patrides, *Milton's "Lycidas": The Tradition and the Poem* [New York, 1961], p. 208.) But *Lycidas* is a completed poem, whereas *The Passion* is a fragment, which Milton included in his 1645 volume with a note explaining that since the author found the poem "to be above the years he had, when he wrote it, and nothing satisfied with what he had done, left it unfinished." My statement about *Lycidas* stands.

3   In *At a Vacation Exercise*, written eight years before *Lycidas*, in 1629, the "graver subject" Milton was planning to undertake was a romance epic, and the structural plan for the poem is sketched in pretty clear outline. The rather vague references to his major poem in *Ad Patrem,* which was written later but before *Lycidas,* and the much more specific ones in *Mansus* and *Epitaphium Damonis,* written two or three years after *Lycidas,* are to a British epic about legendary heroes, with Arthur as the central figure. Within the next couple of years, as the sketches in the Cambridge Manuscript indicate, Milton's stronger inclination was toward a tragedy. And the literary prospectus which he introduced into *The Reason of Church Government* (1642) shows him again most interested in the epic genre, though he is considering also the genres of tragedy, pastoral drama, and the lyric.

4   Translated by W. R. Parker in *Milton: A Biography* (Oxford, 1968), 1:157. The letter is dated "September 23, 1637." However, the editors of Milton's *Complete Prose Works* (New Haven, 1953), 1:327, give reasons for thinking that this letter may

actually have been written in November 1637. They think, at any rate, that it was written before Milton wrote *Lycidas*, which he dated "November, 1637" in the Trinity Manuscript.

5 Masson presents persuasive evidence that the months just before the composition of *Lycidas* brought to Milton an awareness of the actuality of death which he had not before known. His mother died in April 1637. (It was after her death, Milton tells us in the *Second Defense*, that he began to have "the curiosity . . . to see foreign countries, and above all, Italy.") In May of the same year Horton was visited by the plague, which continued till August and caused many deaths. And August brought not only the death of King but also, a few days earlier, of Ben Jonson, who was the one living English poet to whom Milton had looked as to a master.

6 *The Italian Element in Milton's Verse* (Oxford, 1954), pp. 108, 69, 60, 71.

7 Pp. 72, 88.

8 Most of the other questions about the unity of *Lycidas* that have troubled modern critics seem to have troubled Milton no more than they trouble me. These are mostly questions about the logical rather than the artistic unity of the poem—what the "real" subject of the poem is; whether the poem is actually about Milton himself rather than King; whether it contains digressions, and, if so, what logical relations these digressions have to the subject of King's death. M. H. Abrams has surveyed these preoccupations of modern *Lycidas* criticism in his 1957 lecture, "Five Types of *Lycidas*," which is reprinted as the concluding essay in Patrides's collection, *Milton's "Lycidas": The Tradition and the Poem*. To come on Abrams's essay, which arrives at the conclusion "that *Lycidas* is really what it seems," after reading the other essays in Patrides's volume, is both entertaining and invigorating.

9 *The Burning Oracle* (London, 1939), p. 70.

CHAPTER 2

1 See Bernard Weinberg, *A History of Literary Criticism in the Italian Renaissance* (Chicago, 1961), chap. 9, "The Tradition of Aristotle's *Poetics*—I: Discovery and Exegesis," pp. 349 ff. The *Poetics* was first published in 1498, in a Latin translation by Giorgio Valla, which was followed in 1508 by the first publication of the Greek text. In the thirty years that followed this

editio princeps, according to Weinberg, Italian criticism shows "practically no activity in the tradition of Aristotle's *Poetics.*" The influence of Aristotle's literary ideas began to be significant with the publication, in 1536, of Pazzi's Greek text, accompanied by a Latin translation, which was several times reprinted. In 1541–43 Lombardi began public lectures on the *Poetics,* which were completed by Maggi and published in 1550. In 1548 Robertello published "the first of the great commentaries," based on a revised Greek text, with a Latin translation. And in 1549 Segni published an Italian translation, which was the first translation of the *Poetics* into a modern vernacular.

2   See Rosalie Colie, *The Resources of a Kind: Genre-Theory in the Renaissance,* ed. Barbara K. Lewalski (Berkeley, 1973), pp. 68–69, 103–09. This learned and delightful book is a valuable, much-needed corrective to the general view that Italian critics tended to be rigorous and legalistic in preserving the integrity of each literary genre. My only criticism is that in her enthusiasm for breaking down neoclassical legalism and her confessed personal pleasure in *genera mista,* Miss Colie overcorrects so exuberantly that one could easily conclude that most Italians of this time had no concern for the stiffening and ordering effect of genre at all. To most of them, however, a part of the pleasure in a work written in a mixed genre was that the reader was still able to discern the original qualities of the separate genres that he had combined. And Miss Colie works, toward the end of her book, to a definition of "genre" so broad and loose that it seems to me of little value for purposes of practical literary criticism.

3   See Bernard Weinberg, *A History of Literary Criticism in the Italian Renaissance,* the "Conclusions" (pp. 910 ff.) to his two chapters, "The Quarrel over Dante."

4   See above, note 2.

5   I am using the word *lyric* in a different sense from the meaning it generally has in modern criticism. In modern usage ("Elizabethan lyrics," "the lyrics from Jonson's masques"), a usage which derives from the Romantic movement, the term is most often applied to short poems with songlike prosodic effects. Milton, however, uses the term in the special meaning given to it by Italian critics of the sixteenth century, a sense both more inclusive and in some ways more precise than the modern usage (see chap. 4, pp. 53 ff.). In his usage, short

"lyrics" would be included as subspecies of the genre, but the variety of the lyric poem which most appealed to Milton—and which is most relevant to an analysis of *Lycidas*—is that loftiest species of the lyric genre represented by the Pindaric ode and Old Testament "hymns." In this sense, the term *lyric* is more closely analogous to the concept of the "ode" in the critical theory of the Romantic poets.

6 In this phrase from *Of Education,* "organic" does not, of course, have its modern, biological meaning. The fact that Milton parallels poetry with logic and rhetoric, as other kinds of the "organic arts," indicates that he is using the word in a sense that derives from Aristotle's use of *Organon*—"serving as an organ; instrumental." (See N.E.D.: "organic" (1), which cites this sentence from *Of Education.*) His phrase implies that poetry is a particular mode of using language ("discoursing") which is instrumental for a specific end, and that, like the different arts of logic and rhetoric, it is controlled by principles which give it an internal coherence and discipline that direct this mode of discourse to achieve the distinctive purpose of this art.

CHAPTER 3

1 For this generalization I have depended on the comprehensive survey of Italian critical writings of the sixteenth century made by Bernard Weinberg in his *History of Literary Criticism in the Italian Renaissance.* In his study of the large number of short treatises on particular genres (the madrigal, the elegy, the sonnet, the comedy, the verse romance) which were produced in the 1580s and 1590s by the last generation of critics who were working "in the Horatian mode" (pp. 201 ff.), Weinberg does not mention any treatises on the eclogue; and none are listed in his bibliography, which includes both published works and many still in manuscript.

   The only discussion of pastorals that I know of in Tasso's criticism is in a work I have not seen and which Weinberg summarizes, the *Risposta al Discorso del Sig. Oratio Lombardelli* (1586). From his summary it appears that this is a piece, like some of the other letters Tasso exchanged with Lombardelli, in which Tasso's real concern is with the defense of *Gerusalemme Liberata.* He discusses pastoral literary genres only as the lower grades in a hierarchy of genres that culminates in epic and tragedy, which are the most excellent of genres because they are based wholly on truth. In this hierarchy, eclogues, like "woodland fables," represent the lowest of all genres, since they have no foundation in truth; and Tasso regards pastoral drama and comedy, which deal with true settings but represent actions that are not true, as only slightly above them (Weinberg, *Literary Criticism in the Italian Renaissance*, pp. 628–30, 1029–31).

2 Edmond Faral, *Les Arts Poétiques du XIIe et du XIIIe Siècle* (Paris, 1958), pp. 86–88. According to Faral, this scheme, which analyzed each of Virgil's three masterworks as a model for one of the three styles—*"le simple, le tempéré, le sublime"*—was *"adapté communément au moyen âge."*

3 M. H. Abrams, in "Five Types of *Lycidas*," p. 227, quotes the passage from Puttenham's *The Arte of English Poesie* and points out that this phrase of Puttenham's derives from the first line of Virgil's Fourth Eclogue:

> *Musae Sicilidae, paulo maiora canamus,*
> *non omnes arbusta iuvant humilisque myricae;*
> *si canamus silvae, silvae sint consule dignae.*

4 See, for example, Scaliger's *Poetice*, bk. 5, chap. 6: *"Comparatur cum Theocrito Virgilius."* He finds that Virgil surpasses Theocritus in almost all respects, and as a final refutation of those grammarians who have had the temerity to set Theocritus above Virgil, points out that at no point do Theocritus's eclogues aspire to the elevation of the first, fourth, sixth, and tenth of Virgil's. Scaliger does express, however, some doubts (bk. 3, chap. 99) about the propriety of Virgil's use of the pastoral form for the subject of his Sixth Eclogue ("Silenus"), since, on the basis of Plato's *Symposium*, he interprets Silenus as an allegory of the Divine Wisdom. *Iulii Caesaris Scaligeri, Poetices Libri Septem* (Lyon, 1561), pp. 249–51, 150.

5 Minturno not only disapproves strongly of Virgil's attempts to lift the eclogue above the lowly station to which it belongs: he seems to have a low opinion of the literary form itself. In his earlier work, *De Poeta*, he classifies bucolic poetry as one of the forms of "epic" poetry (i.e. poetry which "imitates" solely by means of words, as distinguished from the two other categories of "melic" poetry, which makes use also of musical harmony, and "scenic" poetry, which uses both music and the rhythms of

choric dance). His second Book, on "epic" poetry, concludes with a discussion of the bucolic genre. After observing that Theocritus and Virgil are the most eminent luminaries in this form, Minturno explains that, as everyone knows, the eclogue is content with a rustic simplicity, preserving a humble manner, avoiding grave subjects, and treating only such matters as are appropriate to country folk. These truths being self-evident, Minturno finds it extraordinary that Virgil would allow characters who should be of the most countrified simplicity to speak of Augustus and the Consul Pollio, or to lament the death of Julius Caesar. And he questions whether three of Virgil's Eclogues (4, 6, 10) can properly be regarded as bucolics at all, since they dispense with shepherd speakers and deal with matters, like the return of the Golden Age, which are beyond the mentality of country people. Virgil's Fourth Eclogue, in fact, seems to irritate Minturno particularly. He quotes the three opening lines (cited above, in n. 3), and remarks that it is "quasi absurdum" to introduce things like this into a rustic song, which is a kind of poem that is not worthy of a consul's ear.

After this discussion of the classical models for the eclogue, Minturno does not follow his normal pattern of going on to discuss the works of Italian writers in the genre. Instead, he announces that this will suffice for the subject of bucolic and other forms of "epic" poetry, and he bows out of the discourse with plans to resume on the following day with a discussion of "melic" poetry. This Book of *De Poeta* then ends with a brief conversation among Minturno's auditors, who include Sannazaro *("Syncerus")*, Summonte, and others. They decide that, now that the serious business has been finished for the day, they will relax and have dinner. Sannazaro is complimented on his adaptation of both the simplicity of Theocritus and the elegance of Virgil to the Latin eclogues of his *Piscatoriae,* and the company suggests that he could discourse to them on the principles of the modern eclogue on classical models. Agreeing that eclogues are an appropriate subject for adolescent youth to discuss over dinner and wine, the company adjourns. What Sannazaro had to say is not recorded. *De Poeta* (Venice, 1559), pp. 162–69.

Minturno gives the eclogue even shorter shrift in his later work on vernacular poetry, *L'Arte Poetica.* In the first Book he sets up the same scheme as that of *De Poeta,* dividing poetry into the categories of "epic," "melic," and "scenic." He lists "heroic and bucolic poems" among the chief categories of "epic" poetry, and explains that the varieties of bucolic poetry include "those pastoral discussions [*ragionamenti pastorali*] which are called eclogues" and works which mix prose and verse, like Sannazaro's *Arcadia,* Boccaccio's *Ameto,* and his own *Amore Innamorato* (pp. 3–4). But in the dialogue on "epic" poetry which comprises the remainder of Book 1, Minturno discusses only the genres of the heroic poem and the romance, and evidently decides just to ignore bucolic poetry. In his second dialogue, on "melic" poetry, one of the interlocutors is Bernadino Rota, author of the *Ecloghe Pescatorie,* but though Bernadino enters into the discussion of even the most minor genres of vernacular verse, he never puts in a word for the eclogue. Minturno frequently quotes passages from the verse eclogues of Sannazaro's *Arcadia* to illustrate devices of style or prosody, and on occasion quotes also from one of his own eclogues, "such as it is" (p. 372); but in this work Minturno seems to have decided that, so far as the genres of pastoral literature are concerned, the less said about them the better. *L'Arte Poetica* (Venice, 1564).

6 I am quoting here from the preface to *Samson Agonistes* because of the close parallel it shows with the ideas expressed in the passage from *Of Education.* From the late 1630s to the end of his career, Milton shows a complete consistency in his estimate of which one of the foreign literatures provides the authoritative models for an English poet when he finds himself dissatisfied with "what among us passes for best."

7 F. T. Prince points to the derivation of this stanza from the canzone and describes it as "one of Spenser's most original and elaborate experiments" (*The Italian Element in Milton's Verse,* p. 163).

8 For my knowledge of the sources which Sannazaro has incorporated in the *Arcadia,* and for the backgrounds of the book in contemporary Italian literature and humanistic scholarship, I have depended chiefly on the introduction and annotations in Michele Scharillo's thoroughly scholarly edition of the book, *Arcadia di Jacobo Sannazaro . . . con note ed introduzione* (Turin, 1888). But for a summary of more recent scholarship I have relied on the introduction by Ralph Nash to his translation

of *Arcadia and Piscatorial Eclogues* (Detroit, 1966). My quotations from the *Arcadia* are from Nash's translation.

9   James Holly Hanford, "The Pastoral Elegy and *Lycidas*," reprinted in his *John Milton, Poet and Humanist* (Cleveland, 1966), pp. 147–48.

10 The name *Sincero*, first used, apparently, in the *Arcadia*, was evidently the basis for the academy-name *Actius Syncerus* which Pontano gave to Sannazaro on his admission to the Neapolitan Academy, and which Sannazaro used as a literary pseudonym throughout his life.

11 See, for example, the moody passage on p. 72 in which Sincero speaks of his unhappiness

> when in this feverish period of my youth I call to mind the pleasures of my delicious homeland, among these Arcadian solitudes in which—by your leave I will say it—I can hardly believe that the beasts of the woodlands can dwell with any pleasure, to say nothing of young men nurtured in noble cities. [Nash]

12 Scherillo, pp lxxvii–ix. The first published edition of any of Theocritus's work (including only Idyls 1–18, together with the orations of Isocrates and Hesiod's *Works and Days*) appeared in Milan about 1480. The Aldine edition of 1495 included the first twenty-nine idyls, together with poems by Bion and Moschus. And further poems by Theocritus were added in the Rome edition of 1515. Scherillo gives evidence, however, that Theocritus's works were beginning to be known through manuscripts in the 1470s.

13 Thomas G. Rosenberger, *The Green Cabinet: Theocritus and the European Pastoral Lyric* (Berkeley, 1969), pp. 4–5.

14 Nash, pp. 103–05.

15 Ibid., p. 109.

16 Ibid., pp. 74–75.

17 Ibid., p. 153.

18 *Second Defense,* trans. Helen North, *Complete Prose Works,* vol. 4, pt. 1 (New Haven, 1966), p. 609.

19 For the specific echoes of the *Iliad* in lines 70–76 of *Lycidas*, see chap. 5, p. 134.

20 *Italian Element,* p. 108.

21 In "The Youth of Milton" (reprinted in *John Milton: Poet and Humanist,* pp. 51–57), J. H. Hanford has carefully delineated

the important change in Milton's thought which followed his study of Plato during the Horton period; and he has shown that at the same time Milton's earlier pleasant companionship with Diodati, as a sort of alter ego, underwent a striking change into a friendship of very high resonance. I think Hanford is certainly correct in his identification of the source for this new and ardent Platonic idealism, which found expression also in *Comus*. He argues that it does not derive purely from the works of Plato, and that it is different in character from the Neo-platonism characteristic of the sixteenth and seventeenth centuries, which idealized the love of women. Its true source is the more heroic strain of Neoplatonism developed by Ficino, Pico della Mirandola, and the other Neoplatonists of the Florentine "Academy" of the late fifteenth century. This earlier Renaissance Platonism found its ideal in male friendship, which it exalted into an impassioned love of that Beauty which is Virtue, through which one might gain insight into the Divine Wisdom; and I think it is probably what Milton regarded as "Platonic or Socratic love" (a phrase coined by Ficino). There is much of this Florentine Platonism also in the thought of Tasso, where it coexists rather uneasily with the Aristotelianism prevailing in the intellectual climate of the Christianity of the Late Renaissance and the Counter-Reformation.

22 Milton's statement, which Dryden recorded in his "Preface to the Fables," was that Spenser was his "original." I think F. T. Prince is right in taking the word to mean "father" (*Italian Element*, pp. xii-xv) and in regarding Milton's sense of Spenser's fatherhood to him as a psychologically complex bond that needs to be taken more seriously than J. H. Hanford took it in "The Youth of Milton" (p. 54).

23 See C. P. Brand, *Torquato Tasso: A Study of the Poet and of his Contribution to English Literature* (Cambridge, 1965), p. 63.

24 See Ernest Grillo's essay, "Renaissance Pastoral Drama," in his edition and translation of *Aminta, A Pastoral Drama* (London, 1924), pp. 17–19; and W. L. Grant, *Neo-Latin Literature and the Pastoral* (Chapel Hill, N.C., 1965), p. 118.

25 II, ii, 302–12. Translations are mine unless otherwise indicated. None of the critical writings I am working with has been translated except *De Vulgari Eloquentia* and Tasso's *Discourses on the Heroic Poem*, trans. Mariella Cavalchini and Irene Samuel (Oxford, 1973).

26 For the range and variety of Tasso's sources for *Aminta,* see
    Grillo's essay, pp. 17–18, 29, and Brand, *Torquato Tasso,* pp.
    39–40. In addition to his indebtedness to earlier Italian verse
    eclogues and pastoral plays, and to the eclogues of Theocritus,
    Moschus, and Virgil, Tasso drew on Euripides (for his prologue),
    and on Anacreon, Ovid and the Latin elegists, the Italian *favola
    boschereccia,* Sannazaro's *Arcadia,* and the Greek romances.

27 The Choruses, which seemed a striking novelty to one contem-
    porary observer, were apparently added for the second perfor-
    mance of the play. See Brand, pp. 38–39.

28 P. 74.

29 See Milton's account of this period of his youth in *An Apology
    for Smectymnuus* (*Works,* Columbia Edition [New York, 1931],
    vol. 3, pt. 1, pp. 302–03), and Hanford's commentary on this
    passage in relation to the poems of this period in "The Youth of
    Milton," pp. 21–32.

30 Brand, p. 48.

31 *De Vulgari Eloquentia,* Bk. 2, chap. 12.

32 Tasso uses Dante's analysis of the canzone in *De Vulgari
    Eloquentia* as the basis for his own analysis of this poetic form
    in the dialogue, *"La Cavaletta, o Vero de la Poesia Toscana"*
    (see chap. 4, pp. 110 ff.).

33 P. 81.

CHAPTER 4

1 *Complete Prose Works,* 1:815–16. I have corrected here what
   seems a clear misprint in Milton's published text, which has
   been preserved in modern editions. The text reads, "in their
   matter most an end faulty." Douglas Bush annotates "most an
   end" as meaning "for the most part." But that usage is an odd
   one, which I have not seen anywhere else in Milton's work, or in
   Renaissance literature. And the distinction between the
   "matter," or subject, of a work, and its "end," or purpose, is
   standard in the analysis of rhetoricians.

2 See Frances Yates, *The French Academies of the Sixteenth
   Century* (London, 1947).

3 For a modern critic who wishes to cite this text of Aristotle's in
   a form close to the one read by men of the Renaissance, the
   Poetics presents a problem rather like that of the Bible. The
   most recent translations of the work have profited not only

from improved Greek scholarship but also from the discovery of
another manuscript unknown to the editors of Milton's time.
But my citations from the *Poetics* do not require minute textual
precision; and I have quoted from an English translation which
seems reasonably equivalent to the form of the text of the
Poetics as it was quoted by Italian critics and by Milton (who,
judging from the epigraph to *Samson Agonistes,* read the work
in a Latin translation). My quotations are from Allan H.
Gilbert's translation of Alfred Gudeman's version of the *Poetics,*
printed in his *Literary Criticism: Plato to Dryden* (Detroit,
1962). But having been warned of inaccuracies in Gilbert's translation, I have modified it at a few points from the more
scrupulous translation by Gerald F. Else, *Aristotle's Poetics*
(Ann Arbor, 1967).

4 Translated by Edward Henry Blakeney.
5 See Bernard Weinberg, *A History of Literary Criticism in the
Italian Renaissance,* p. 96. In Italy the work was widely read in
Trissino's Italian translation. Dante's original Latin text was not
published until 1577, in Paris.
6 My quotations from *De Vulgari Eloquentia* are from the translation by A. G. Ferrers Howell, in *A Translation of the Latin
Works of Dante Alighieri,* Temple Classics (London, 1904). Unless otherwise indicated, all the passages cited are from the
second Book.
7 As *De Vulgari Eloquentia* indicates, this is the meaning of
"parlar materno" in *Purgatorio,* XXVI. 117.
8 See Patrick Boyde's "Note on Dante's Metric and Versifica-
tion," in K. Foster and P. Boyde, *Dante's Lyric Poetry* (Oxford,
1967), 1:xlv. This introduction presents a brief and lucid explanation of Dante's complicated analysis of canzone structure
in Book 2 of *De Vulgari Eloquentia.* Boyde explains further that
the same musical convention which dictated the structure of the
canzone stanza also determined the structure of the regular
Italian, or "Petrarchan," sonnet, which can be regarded as a
standardized form of a single canzone stanza (pp. l–li). The
structural division between the *ottavo* and the *sestetto* of the
sonetto derives from the shaping of the verse structure to the
two contrasting sequential melodies which were "sounded" by
the instrumental accompaniment. In Dante's technical terminology for the parts of a canzone stanza, the octave of the
sonnet consists of two four-line *pedes,* set to the first melody

and to the repeat of it, and the sestet, of two three-line
voltae, which are set to the second melody and to its repeat.

9 Ibid., pp. xliv–v.
10 *Prose Diverse,* ed. Caesare Guasti (Florence, 1875), pp. 11, 120.
11 *L'Arte Poetica* (Venice, 1564). My references and quotations in
this and the following paragraphs are drawn from Book 3, pp.
182–86 and 195.
12 P. 182.
13 Ibid.
14 P. 170.
15 P. 167.
16 Minturno, in this passage, pretty clearly implies his belief–
derived from the *Timaeus,* which was the only Platonic Dialogue
generally known to the Middle Ages– in one Platonic doctrine
which the church had long and firmly rejected as heretical. In
referring to Plato's doctrine of prenatal recollection, he describes this concept, with due theological propriety, as an
"opinion" of Plato's; but he nevertheless accepts it as sound,
since he makes it the logical premise for his argument about the
celestial origin of man's impulse to lyric poetry. This opinion of
Plato's had appealed to some theologians of the early Christian
centuries; but it was finally condemned as heretical in the year
540 by the Council of Constantinople, which rejected Plato's
view that the soul came, at birth, from its created abode in one
of the celestial spheres and returned to that sphere at death,
and instead established as orthodox the doctrine that God
created each human soul individually at the moment of the
birth of its body. Later Aquinas, who had been underwritten by
the Council of Trent as the most authoritative theologian and
given the title of "Doctor of the Church," demonstrated again
the heretical nature of this doctrine of Plato's (*Summa
Theologica,* III, Suppl., Qu. xcvii, Art. 5). Dante, however, discussed Plato's idea at some length in Canto 4 of *Paradiso,* suggesting that he had found it appealing and on some grounds
rationally plausible. He concluded, nevertheless, that it could
not be reconciled with the tenets of the Christian faith.

Plato's opinion, however, seems to have taken on new life in
the pervasive Neoplatonism of the Renaissance. Milton discusses
one aspect of the doctrine–the view that the soul, after the death'
of the body, lives out its immortal life not in the Empyrean but,
rather, within the world of Nature, in the celestial spheres–in

"Il Penseroso," ll. 88–91, where he seems to think this belief of Plato's at least plausible; and he appears to me actually to accept it in both *Comus* and *Paradise Lost*. And exactly the same conception of the whereabouts of the soul's life after death is clearly implied in the final stanza of Spenser's "Epithalamium."

17 Minturno's phrase is *primi Theologi*, which directly translates the Latin *prisci theologi* of Ficino and Pico. There is no good equivalent in English, except for some such barbarism as "primal theologues." "Theologians" is unsatisfactory because the word suggest teachers, like the Scholastics, of logically systematic religious doctrine, and one distinguishing characteristic of the *primi Theologi*, in Ficino's view, was that they had done their religious teaching not through abstract concepts or by logical disputation but rather through the more powerful, and more philosophically comprehensive, theological vocabulary of religious myth and poetic fiction.

18 *L'Arte Poetica,* 3:169.

19 P. 175.

20 P. 176.

21 P. 173.

22 Weinberg quotes a lecture on the sonnet, delivered in 1592 to the Academy of Perugia by Cesare Crespi, in which Crespi bases his exposition of the different decorums for the sonnet and the canzone on Minturno's analysis in *L'Arte Poetica* (pp. 263–67). And in his *Defense* of Dante's *Commedia* (1587), Mazzoni interrupts his argument about Dante's work for a long "digression" on the verse forms of the Tuscan poets, in the course of which he comes on the "bellissima speculatione" over whether "the stanzas of the ballate and canzoni should be called 'strophes' or 'antistrophes' in conformity with the custom of the Greeks, or else all 'strophes' as was customary with the Latins." Deciding that, in our fuller knowledge of ancient literature, we can see that it was really toward these classical verse forms that the Tuscan poets, in their spontaneous prosodic enterprise, were actually reaching, Mazzoni concludes that "for the future it is incumbent upon every fine wit who takes delight in the compositions in this language to wish to bring into use this correspondence of the verses" to the strophic stanza forms of antiquity, at least "in the syllabic character of the verses" and in their placing in the stanza, as those ancient forms "have now become

clear to us." *Della Difesa della Commedia di Dante* (Cesena, 1688), 2:511–17.

23 Pp. 184–86.

24 P. 169.

25 P. 242. In the lecture on the sonnet cited in note 22, above, Cesare Crespi follows Minturno in making this fact the essential difference between the sonnet and the canzone: though both forms share the essential subject matter of lyric poetry—gods, heroes, and loves—the sonnet is distinguished from the canzone by lacking the digressions and ornaments which give the canzone an epic "majesty." And it is precisely because of this requirement of clarity and discipline of structure that Crespi prefers the sonnet to the canzone, because "in long compositions the poets, no matter how mediocre they may be, usually put many things which, with their beauty and their grace, compensate for other things which are less beautiful and less grave" (quoted and translated by Weinberg, p. 237).

26 P. 183.

27 P. 177.

28 P. 184.

29 *Paradise Lost*, 1. 549–59.

30 See, for example, the Florentine critic Benedetto Varchi, whose work antedates Minturno's two treatises. In 1553 he delivered to the Academy of Florence the first five "Lectures" of his projected Poetics, which were later published, uncompleted, in his collected *Lezzioni*. Varchi shares Minturno's view that the "Hymns" of Pindar are "nothing other than *canzoni* in our fashion" (*Opere* [Trieste, 1859], 1:717). And in his first lecture, in which he defines the categories by which the Tuscan poetic forms can be assimilated to the genres and poetic practices of Greece, he categorizes the major genres on the same Aristotelian principle (imitation by words alone, by words joined to rhythm, and by words joined to "harmony or music") that forms the basis of Minturno's three categories. For his third category, however, Varchi wishes to specify as generic properties of a poem in this musical kind the Italian equivalents of the Greek musical instruments that had accompanied the different forms of lyric poetry in antiquity. Pointing out that the Greeks had subdivided this genre into the "Auletic" poem, which was accompanied by wind instruments, and the more noble form of the "Citharistic" poem, accompanied by the string instrument

of the lyre, under which the form of the lyric was included, Varchi finds the true analogy to this ancient genre in the modern Italian lyric poems sung to the accompaniment of lyres, lutes, *gravicembali,* and other stringed instruments (1:689).

Varchi did not complete the subsequent lecture he had planned on lyric poetry, so we do not have his prescriptions for the exact way in which the Italian canzone should accord with its natural forebear, the Pindaric hymn. But there is a suggestive passage in his later work *L'Ercolano* (1570) which indicates that in the 1560s some Florentines were attempting to make their lyric poems fully Greek, and presumably Pindaric, not only in critical theory but in musical fact. Varchi describes an entertainment given in honor of the visit to Florence by Don Alfonso d'Este, Tasso's patron, whose court at Ferrara was the center of highest Italian musical culture of his time. On this occasion a striking effect had been produced when Messer Silvio Antonio performed for Alfonso a poem which he sang over the accompaniment of a lyre played "all'improviso." Varchi found in this Italian actualization of the ancient lyric poem a powerfully expressive effect which suggested possibilities that Italian poets might well explore (1:151–52).

31 "Lezione sopra il sonnetto di Monsignor della Casa," *Prose Diverse,* 2:121.

32 "Delle differenze poetiche," quoted and translated by Weinberg, p. 631.

33 *Prose Diverse,* 1:73.

34 This and other quotations on the following pages, unless otherwise indicated, are taken either from Book 5 of the *Discorsi del Poema Eroico* or from the earlier version of that discourse in the third Book of the *Discorsi dell'Arte Poetica.*

35 The phrase "un non so chè" (literally, "an I-don't-know-what") will appear several times in passages quoted in the following pages. Tasso uses the phrase so idiosyncratically that it seems best to leave it untranslated. As a critical term, this phrase of Tasso's did not arrive in English literature until more than a century later, when it appears in the guise of the "je ne sais quoi" of early Augustan criticism. But by that time Tasso's term, radically modified by its passage through the strongly legalistic mentality of the French critics of the mid- seventeenth century, has been given a new twist by French criticism, so that, as the *je ne sais quoi,* his original concept was finally translated

into Pope's "grace beyond the reach of art," the critical escape-clause which gave remission to the legalism of the "rules" and "laws" of French neoclassical literary theory.

36 My quotations are from the section "The School of Giorgione."

37 In *The Italian Element in Milton's Verse;* and for *Paradise Lost,* in Steadman's article, "Demetrius, Tasso, and Stylistic Variation in *Paradise Lost," English Studies* 47 (1966):329–41.

38 I have used John Steadman's translation of Demetrius's terms, as both more faithful to the Greek original and closer to the sense in which Tasso interpreted these words than the translation by W. Rhys Roberts in the Loeb Library edition of *De Elocutione.* In Roberts's translation Demetrius's four types are: the "plain," the "elegant," the "forcible," and the "elevated."

39 *Prose Diversi,* 1:205–07.

40 Ibid., p. 64. Here and on the following pages I am drawing on either Book 3 of the *Discorsi dell'Arte Poetica* or the considerably revised and expanded version of that early discussion of the poetic styles in Book 5 and the early part of Book 6 of the *Discorsi del Poema Eroico.*

41 *De Elocutione,* p. 385.

42 In the original the final clause is, "ma questa asprezza sente un non so chè di magnifico e di grande."

43 *Prose Diverse,* 1:56.

44 My quotations from *"La Cavaletta"* are from *I Dialoghi di Torquato Tasso,* ed. Cesare Guasti (Florence, 1859).

45 *The Republic* (trans. Jowett), 3. 398–99.

CHAPTER 5

1 Barker's analysis appears in his article, "The Pattern of Milton's *Nativity Ode," University of Toronto Quarterly* 10 (1941):171–72. In the most recent revision of J. H. Hanford's *A Milton Handbook* (1970, with James G. Taaffe) this analysis of *Lycidas* is cited, with the remark that "Arthur Barker's comments on the three-part structure have come to be regarded as standard" (p. 139).

2 Musical analogies have long been used by critics of *Lycidas* as metaphoric formulations of how the poem seems to be constructed, for example, by George Saintsbury, by J. H. Hanford ("two musical keys"), and by M. H. Abrams in "Five Types of *Lycidas.*"

3 *A Second Defense,* in *Complete Prose Works* (Yale, pp. 613–14).

4 Compare the reference to the Dorian musical mode in the passage from *Paradise Lost* cited on p. 93, in which Milton's text spells this musical term *mod.*

5 I recognize that the terms *mode* and *key* (or *tonality*) represent quite different musical concepts, and that the system of ancient Greek music was based on modes, and that of modern music, for the most part, on keys, since modern Western music properly uses only two modes, major and minor. But I am inclined to think that the musical metaphor on which Milton has built the two contrasting styles of *Lycidas* was that of style rather than mode and that the references to "mood" in the text have the value of a conjoining pun rather than a reference to this musical effect. I have therefore sometimes used the terms as though they were interchangeable. But I find when I think of certain passages in *Lycidas* as analogues to musical keys, I find something that corresponds to what I hear in the poem, whereas when I try to analogize them to modes (major or minor) it doesn't work. My conclusion, then, is that Milton thought of *Lycidas* as like a structure of musical keys, rather than of alternating modes, ancient or modern.

6 Milton's description of the pastoral style as like "smooth-sliding Mincius; crown'd with vocal reeds" seems, however, to echo not Tasso or Demetrius but rather the description of the middle style by Quintilian, an authority whom Tasso cited on occasion but whom Milton, to judge from his eleventh Sonnet, held in rather more esteem. In his *Institutes of Oratory,* Quintilian defines the "florid style," which "some call a mean" between the other two styles (the "plain," and the "grand or energetic") as follows:

> The middle sort will abound more with metaphors and be rendered more attractive by figures of speech; it will seek to please by digressions; it will be elegant in phraseology; with perfectly natural thoughts, but flowing gently, like a clear stream overshadowed on either side by banks of green wood. [Book 12, chap. 10, sec. 60; translated by J. S. Watson]

7 See Milton's analogous use of *deep* in "At a Vacation Exercise" (ll. 33–35) in the sense of "high," with a secondary meaning of "profound":

where the deep transported mind may soar
Above the wheeling poles, and at Heav'n's door
Look in. . . .

8 Modern English-speaking readers have virtually lost a sound effect important to Renaissance poetry by the change of the pronunciation of the letter *r* into a liquid, phonologically analogous
to *l*. In sixteenth- and seventeenth-century English (and on into
the early eighteenth century) *r* was a strikingly harsh sound, a
guttural or, at times, nearly a dental stop, and it was generally
trilled, as in Italian and Spanish. As the Nurse told the young
Romeo, "*r* is the dog's letter." (She was illiterate, remembering
her hornbook, which had translated the grammarians' term for
this letter "littera canina.") In the lines demonstrating the use
of significant sound effects in both Dryden's "To Oldham" and
Pope's "An Essay on Criticism," the letter *r* is used as one of the
technical tricks to produce harshness of sound and roughness of
movement in a verse line:

Dryden: "Through [dissyllabic, from the trilled *r*] the
harsh cadence of a rugged line."
Pope: ("harsh surges lash the sounding shore" in this way:)
"The hoarse rough verse should like the torrent roar."

The loss of the sound of this roughly guttural or percussive *r* is
serious for the reader of Milton's verse. We are told by John
Aubrey, in his "Notes for the Life of Mr. John Milton," that
"He pronounced the letter R very hard. *litera canina.* A certain
sign of satirical wit. [From Jo. Dryden.]"

9 *The Reason of Church Government* (1642), in *Works*, vol. 3, pt.
1, p. 238. Milton expresses the same view of *The Apocalypse* as
a poem in the form of tragedy in his preface to *Samson
Agonistes*.

10 In view of the controversy over this matter in Italian criticism, it
may be questioned whether Milton would have regarded Dante's
Commedia as a poem in the epic form. We know from *On
Education* that Milton admired (for widely understandable
reasons) Mazzoni's *Difesa* of Dante's poem, but I doubt that
Milton would have accepted Mazzoni's conclusion that the form
of the work is that of a Monodic Comedy. "Monodic Comedy,"
as a description of a poetic genre, is really an academic abstrac-
tion, and I think Milton would have known that no practicing

poet from the beginning of the world had ever actually conceived a poem as written in such a poetic form. It seems to me
very likely that Milton would have taken the more practical
view of Tasso, who, in the conclusion of the final Book of his
Discorsi del Poema Eroico, simply ignored all the critical hair-
splitting over the genre of the *Commedia,* and placed Dante's
work alongside the Homeric epics and the *Aeneid* as the only
modern poem which merited comparison with these ancient examples of the heroic poem.

11 See the article "Ritornel" in *Die Musik in Geschichte und
Gegenwart;* and W. S. Rockstro's article "Ritornello" in *Grove's
Dictionary of Music and Musicians.*

12 See the article "Intermedio" in *Die Musik in Geschichte und
Gegenwart;* and J. W. Dent's article "Intermezzo" in *Grove's
Dictionary.* For further discussion of the form of the *dramma
per musica* see below, pp. 163 ff.

13 Rockstro, "Ritornello," 7:183. Peri's work was performed in
1600 and the score was published in 1601. *Orfeo* was performed
in 1607 and published (text and music) in 1609.

14 I am seriously suggesting that *Lycidas* reflects a deliberate
secrecy and reticence on Milton's part about fully revealing his
private artistic intentions in composing the poem; and I am
basing this conclusion on more evidence than the mere use of
the phrase "but in secret" in Milton's letter to Diodati. J. H.
Hanford (in "The Youth of Milton," pp. 40–42, 55–59) has
shrewdly noticed a new, hermetic attitude about the secret
mysteries of his poetic intents which first appears, rather suddenly, in Milton's thinking during the Horton period. As
Hanford points out, Milton was ready to speak freely and publicly about his poetic plans and ambitions throughout the poems
of his undergraduate years, and he did so most publicly in *At A
Vacation Exercise* in 1629. But Hanford also notes the surprising fact that in Milton's "Letter to a Friend," which accompanied the sonnet "On his having arrived at the age of
twenty-three," and which was written as a formal apologia for
his preparation and dedication to a high career, neither the letter nor the sonnet gives any hint that this career will be a poetic
one. The letter, in fact, allows the friend to believe that Milton
is still planning a career as a churchman. From this point on, in
his Horton years, Hanford shows, Milton reveals his poetic plans
only to Diodati, and often with some suggestion, like that in the

letter I have quoted, that he is letting Diodati in on secrets about his poetic ambitions which no one else must know, and which, it may be, he intends not to reveal publicly until he bursts into sudden blaze in his projected major poem.

Milton's study of the Italian poets in the latter years at Cambridge reflects the same psychological pattern of a long-maturing literary plan kept under wraps for years before he allowed it to show in his own poetry. The date in Milton's copy of della Casa's *Rime* (which has been preserved) indicates that his study of della Casa's stylistic innovations (and of Tasso's) must have begun by 1629. But, as Prince has shown, it is not until *Lycidas,* eight years later, that Milton first reveals in his own poetry his intention of taking della Casa's and Tasso's adaptations of Virgilian diction and syntax as a stylistic model for his English verse.

15 "Five Types of *Lycidas,*" in Patrides, *Milton's "Lycidas": The Tradition and the Poem*.

16 In Milton's typical scheme for a tragic action, two different plots are combined sequentially in the life of a single protagonist, who experiences first a fall from high estate, and then, in the second plot, a subsequent rise back to good fortune. Milton's tragic plots (whatever term we apply to them) thus fall under Aristotle's condemnation of the use of the double plot in tragedy, since Aristotle had objected to the change from bad to good fortune on the ground that it "does not furnish the pleasure properly derived from tragedy but rather that suitable to comedy" (53a 30).

17 *Poetice,* p. 6. The other passage of Scaliger cited below is quoted, as translated by Rita Carey Guerlac, in Scott Elledge, *Milton's "Lycidas"* (New York, 1966), pp. 108–09.

18 Vol. 2, chap. 28.

19 Jacopo Mazzoni, *Della Difesa della Commedia di Dante, distinta in sei Libri* (Cesena, 1688), 2:379–88. The complete work was not published until 1688. The first three Books, from which my quotations are taken, were published in 1587.

20 D. P. Walker, "Musical Humanism in the Sixteenth and Early Seventeenth Centuries," *The Music Review* 2 (1941):1–13, 111–21, 220–27, 288–308; 3 (1943): 55–71.

21 Claude V. Palisca, "Girolamo Mei: Mento to the Florentine Camerata," *Musical Quarterly* 40 (1954); 1–20. In addition to this article, see Palisca's "Vincenzo Galilei and Some Links

between 'Pseudo-Monody' and Monody," *Musical Quarterly* 46 (1960): 344–60; and his book *Baroque Music* (Englewood Cliffs, N.J., 1968).

22 Vincenzo Galilei, *Dialogo . . . della musica antica e della moderna* (Florence, 1581), p. 1.

23 Mei's first work on the Greek modes was published in 1576. At this time he also undertook the instruction of Galilei in a series of letters, parts of which Galilei incorporated in his *Dialogo*. The first of these letters was published in 1602, after Mei's death, as his *Discorso sopra la musica antica e moderna*.

24 Galilei, *Dialogo*, pp. 83, 80.

25 Nino Pirotta, "Temperaments and Tendencies in the Florentine Camerata," *Musical Quarterly* 40 (1954):173.

26 Galilei, *Dialogo*, p. 36.

27 *Musical Quarterly*, 46 (1960):347.

28 John G. Demaray, *Milton and the Masque Tradition* (Cambridge, Mass., 1968). This famous production of the French musical humanists has been analyzed in detail by Frances Yates, in *The French Academies in the Sixteenth Century*, and also in a further article, *"Poésie et Musique dans les 'Magnificences' au Mariage du Duc de Joyeuse*, Paris, 1581," in *Musique et Poésie au XVIe Siècle* (Paris, 1954), pp. 241–56.

29 *The Works of Ben Jonson*, ed. C. H. Herford and P. Simson (Oxford, 1941), 7:449.

30 Gretchen Finney, in *Musical Backgrounds for English Literature, 1580–1650* (New Brunswick, 1963), has the distinction of being the first scholar to recognize the significance of music in Milton's early poems, and to explore some of the parallels between those works and Italian music and music theory. But though I share her view that one of the contributing sources for *Comus* is the form of the *dramma per musica*, I am not convinced by the specific musical model she postulates for this work. And I think her argument (chap. 10) that *Lycidas* is modeled on an Italian oratorio made up of solo air, recitative, and chorus (as well as her argument that it shows specific debts to Striggio's libretto for the *Orfeo* of Monteverdi) is disproved by the evidence in the text of *Lycidas* that Milton conceives of the poem as analogous to a solo song, "a monody." Although I believe that the musical form of monody, and perhaps some impressive works of monodic music, gave Milton suggestions for attempting in *Lycidas* a poetic form which would be analogous

to a musical monody, I believe that his debt to this art form in Italian music is general and suggestive rather than specific. I think when he wrote *Lycidas* it is unlikely that, in evolving the structure of his poem, he tried to follow, as a model, any particular piece of monodic music, by Monteverdi or any other composer.

31 Hans Heinrich Eggebrecht, "Monodie," in *Musik in Geschichte und Gegenwart,* 9:476.

Index

Abrams, M. H., 153–54
Aeneid (Virgil), 4, 30
Ameto (Boccaccio), 29
Aminta (Tasso): erotic license of,
44–45; influence on Milton,
39–40, 47; as pastoral drama, 21,
43, 64; style of, 48–49; verse
structure of, 46–47
Antistrophe, 71, 89
Apocalypse of St. John, The, 137
Arcadia (Sannazaro): digressions,
31–32; influence on Milton, 39;
influence on Virgil, 35–36; lofty
style of, 38–39; model for Spenser,
29; use of countryside in, 30, 31
Aracdia (Virgil), 30–31
Arianna (Monteverdi), 169
Aristotle: influence on Italian critics,
18–19, 25, 94–95, 164, 172–73n;
influence on Minturno, 78–79;
Poetics, 18, 56–57, 78; tragedy
and, 153, 155, 156, 158
Ars Poetica (Horace), 19, 23, 57, 96
Arte Poetica, L' (Minturno):
Aristotle's influence on, 78–79;
and *canzone*, 70–71, 85–87; Dante's
influence on, 84–85; divinity of
poetic creation and, 81; epic digression in, 89–90; *favola* and, 83;
musical poetry and, 90–93; Pindar
and, 88–89; Plato's influence on,
78–79; religious nature of lyric in,
72–73, 84; *volta* and, 69–70
Asprezza, 105–08, 135, 136

Baif's Academy, 56, 162
Balet Comique de la Royne, 167
Ballate, 19

Barker, Arthur, analysis of *Lycidas*,
126–27
Beccari, Agostino, *Il Sacrificio*, 41
Bembo, Pietro: encouragement of
vernacular, 19; *Prose della Volgar
Lingua*, 19
Boccaccio, Giovanni: *Ameto*, 29;
imitation of Virgil, 30–31
Bucolics (Virgil), 12, 44

Camerata, Florentine, 162–64
Camillo, Giulio, 117
Canzone, 19–20, 70–74, 84–87,
117, 122, 181–82n; metrics of,
63–66; Petrarch and, 37, 54, 84;
Pindaric, 87, 92–93; Tasso and,
46–49
Catullus, Gaius Valerius, Latin
epigrams, 20
Cavaletta, La (Tasso): art and judg-
ment in poetry and, 112–13;
canzone and, 117, 122; Dante's
poetry rules and, 112–14;
hermeticism and, 116; music and,
117–21, 122–23; *ottava rima* and,
119; Plato's influence on, 121;
tragedy and, 157
Cavaletta, Orsina, 111
Cavaletto, Ercole, 111
Cicero, Marcus Tullius, poetic classification of, 101, 102
Commiato, 144–45
Comus (Milton), 2–3, 148, 167
Concetti, 98
Congedo, 144–45
Crespi, Cesare, 183n, 184n

193